W9-DCL-687

THE SCIENCE OF THE CROSS

THE SCIENCE OF THE CROSS

A Study of
St John of the Cross

By
EDITH STEIN
(Teresa Benedicta of the Cross, O.C.D.)

Edited by
Dr L. GELBER and Fr ROMAEUS LEUVEN, O.C.D.

Translated by
HILDA GRAEF

Copy 2

The Library of Living Catholic Thought

CHICAGO
HENRY REGNERY COMPANY
1960

NIHIL OBSTAT: HUBERTUS RICHARDS, S.T.L., L.S.S.
CENSOR DEPUTATUS
IMPRIMATUR: E. MORROGH BERNARD
VICARIUS GENERALIS
WESTMONASTERII: DIE XXXI OCTOBRIS MCMLIX

Made and printed in Great Britain by
William Clowes and Sons, Limited, London and Beccles
for Henry Regnery Company
14 E. Jackson Boulevard, Chicago 4, Illinois

First published in the United States of America 1960

CONTENTS

v

THIS book is a translation of Dr Edith Stein's
Kreuzeswissenschaft, which forms Volume I of her
complete works edited by the Very Reverend
Father Romaeus Leuven, Provincial of the Dis-
calced Carmelites of Holland, and Dr L. Gelber,
Archivist of the Husserl Archives, and published by
Éditions Nauwelaerts in Louvain, Belgium.

TRANSLATOR'S PREFACE

THE present study by Edith Stein, the first of her principal works to appear in English, was written shortly before her death. She called this presentation of the great Carmelite doctor, St John of the Cross, *Science of the Cross (Kreuzeswissenschaft)*, a title that seems almost prophetic, seeing that she herself was soon to be perfected in this painful science in the gas chambers of Auschwitz. This connexion between her last work and the consummation of her own vocation—her name in Carmel was Benedicta of the Cross—makes its study a very poignant experience. The reader feels that what she says about suffering and the Cross are not mere words, no detached analysis of St John's mystical doctrine, but part of her own life; for while she was writing this book she had frequently to present herself before the Nazi authorities in occupied Holland and suffered all the humiliations that were inflicted by them on the members of her race. Nevertheless, she preserved her calm even in this time of fear and anguish, so much so that just in these years she could write the present work, which reflects her own feelings—she suffered to the very roots of her being for her persecuted people—as it were in a clear mirror, whose serenity is unclouded by self-pity or nervous excitement.

The *Science of the Cross* is remarkable also for another reason. The interpreters of St John of the Cross are generally professional theologians and spiritual authors, whose approach is, on the whole, theological and mystical. Edith Stein, on the other hand, was a professional philosopher, more exactly a phenomenologist, a disciple of Edmund Husserl. Though after her conversion she also studied Catholic theologians, especially St Thomas Aquinas, her approach remained that of a phenomenologist. This is true also for the present work— we need only refer the reader to her exquisite phenomenological study of the concept of the Night. This quite different approach gives the work a freshness and a direct appeal frequently absent from more conservative presentations.

A word must be said about the translation. The citations from St John of the Cross are not taken from the standard English edition of his works by the late Professor Allison Peers for two reasons. One is

that Allison Peers translated in a deliberately archaic style, which
Edith Stein, in her rendering of St John of the Cross, does not; so
that the difference of style between Edith Stein's own text and that
of the citations from St John of the Cross would be far more marked
in the English translation than it is in the German original. The
second is that Edith Stein's translation differs in many places from
that of Allison Peers. Where these differences are very marked we have
indicated them in the footnotes. The chapter division, however, which
is different from that of Edith Stein, who used an earlier Spanish
edition, follows Allison Peers throughout.

HILDA GRAEF

Oxford,
Feast of St John of the Cross, 1957

EDITORS' PREFACE

THE tree of the Cross blossoms eternally, bearing ever new fruit. For the Cross of Christ is more than a symbol, it is an effective sign. It symbolizes "the bridal union of the soul with God" which "is the end for which the soul was created, bought by the Cross, accomplished on the Cross, and sealed with the Cross for all eternity" (p. 207).

Thus we should understand *The Science of the Cross*, which Edith Stein, the disciple and assistant of Edmund Husserl, the founder of phenomenology, left us as her last testament. Following the example of St John of the Cross, she, too, took up this cross in which she recognized the deep faith and sublime destiny of her own life. Studying the works of the Doctor of the Church she arrived at the concept of the science of the Cross in the twofold meaning of a theology of the Cross and a school of the Cross, that is to say, life under the sign of the Cross.

The whole work is devoted to the development of this idea; hence it appears as a penetrating interpretation of the doctrine of the Cross, as a personal confession and also as a modern presentation of the Father of the Carmelite Friars.

This interpretation is all the more profound since the author, obeying the powerful religious aspiration of her soul, herself took the road described by the saint; because as a Carmelite she became familiar with his language and because she herself was a remarkable thinker with great psychological and educational experience.

Her work is also a personal confession, because this work does not express the tradition of the Order but is the attempt of a daughter of Carmel to explain the life and teaching of her spiritual Father from her own point of view. Sister Benedicta herself adds in a passage of the work: "We must therefore examine whether it agrees with his teaching and may even serve to throw a yet clearer light on it" (p. 121).

It is, finally, a modern presentation, because Edith Stein outlined the personality of St John of the Cross in a contemporary form when she herself had reached the height of her phenomenological studies.

As to the meaning of the doctrine and the contribution it constitutes, we must recognize in Edith Stein's interpretation of the life and work of St John of the Cross a further confirmation of the teaching of the Order despite its deviations from the classical commentaries. This interpretation reflects purely and convincingly the basis of the Carmelite idea that the doctrine of the Cross is a reality.

Love and total surrender of the soul to God is the door to the mystical life; the vanity of the world must ever and again be emphasized for us creatures tied to our senses as we are. Faith not only prepares us to receive the message of the Cross, it is itself a participation in the Way of the Cross and the Crucifixion; it achieves its perfection in the perfect union with God through love.

May the word of the Cross, as Sister Benedicta of the Cross uttered it, become for us all the seed that bears fruit a hundredfold.

P. Fr Romaeus Leuven, o.c.d.,
Dutch Provincial.

The title *Works of Edith Stein* designates the authentic edition of her writings, who as a Carmelite was called Sister Benedicta of the Cross. The present volume is part of an English translation of the new critical edition of her works which has appeared after her death.

The volumes of this collection, corresponding to the problems and the professional tasks in which the author was interested, deal with subjects taken from three spheres: philosophical studies, religious meditations and educational essays. The collection of volumes is organized according to the distribution of these matters without taking into account the chronological order of the works. Thus the first volume of Edith Stein's works is devoted to her most important religious work, which happens also to be that which she wrote shortly before her death. The second volume offers us under the title *Finite and Eternal Being* the most complete philosophical work of Edith Stein. In the third volume the readers will find a series of educational studies and articles. The composition of the following volumes will be inspired by the same order.

The English edition of the works of Edith Stein is based on the German original and will only present those works the contents of which are of interest to a non-German public. It omits the scientific appendices which deal with the state of the manuscripts, the method employed for their editing and textual criticism. The English reader who specializes in the subject will have recourse for all the questions of interest to him to the indispensable entirety of the original edition.

Biographical note

Edith Stein was born at Breslau on 12 October 1891. After her school years she studied from October 1911 to Easter 1913 at the university of her home town. She then pursued her studies of philosophy, psychology, history and German philology at the University of Goettingen. In January 1915 she passed her state examination at Goettingen *pro facultate docendi* in philosophy, history and German. After a brief period of teaching at schools in Breslau she received in the summer of 1916 the doctorate of philosophy at the University of Freiburg in Breisgau, where she became the assistant of her master E. Husserl. From 1922 to 1932 she taught at the girls' school of the Dominican nuns of the convent of St Magdalena at Speyer. In 1932 she became a lecturer at the Educational Institute at Munster, a post which she lost on account of her Jewish origin when the National Socialists came to power in 1933. From 1928 to 1933 she also gave numerous lectures both in her own country and abroad on the occasion of conferences and days of study. From this period date her publications in the *Jahrbuch für Philosophie und Phänomenologische Forschung* and her translations of St Thomas Aquinas and Newman, which made her known to a large public.

The profound meaning of the existence of Edith Stein, such as it has so far unfolded and will develop still further, springs wholly from her religious evolution. Born of Jewish parents and educated in the spirit of the Mosaic faith, she was thirty years old when Divine Providence led her to the Catholic Church. As a convert she received at her baptism on 1 January 1922 the name Teresa. And on 15 April 1934, when she had arrived at the summit of her research and her teaching, she renounced the world in order to enter the Carmelite Convent of Lindenthal at Cologne, thus realizing a desire she had nourished for a long time.

Because of the National Socialist persecution which threatened Edith Stein, the religious authorities transferred her to the Carmelite Convent of Echt in Holland, where she arrived on 31 December 1938. There she lived and worked until she was arrested by the Gestapo on 2 August 1942. After a brief internment at the concentration camp of Westerborck in Holland she was deported to Auschwitz on 7 August 1942, where she was killed in the gas chamber about 10 August.[1]

[1] See the documents of the Dutch Red Cross, dated 1947, in the possession of the Archivum Carmelitanum Edith Stein.

Origin and aim of the Work

As we have said before, the present study of St John of the Cross is the last work written by Edith Stein. She began it in August 1941 and continued to work on it until she was arrested. Hence it seems that its composition took scarcely eleven months. This remarkably short time can be explained only by the intensity of continuous work devoted to a book that had long matured in her mind; for if the study of the sources of St John of the Cross represented indubitably a new task for Edith Stein, the spirit of his doctrine had long been at work in her heart. Thus she writes about this subject in a correspondence dating from 1941 that has so far remained unedited [1]:

"The work with which I am occupied makes me live almost continually in the thought of St John of the Cross. That is a great grace. May I ask you, Reverend Mother, to pray that I may do something good for his Jubilee?"

The same correspondence tells us that the preparatory studies for this work date back to 1940. Edith Stein writes thus in September of that year:

"I am at the moment busy assembling the material for a new work. Our dear Mother desires that I begin again as much intellectual work as is possible according to our way of life."

In August 1941, after innumerable efforts, she had at last got all the principal materials necessary for her work. She mentions this in the correspondence quoted above. We would here quote several passages which will throw light on the author's evaluation of her sources:

"I know quite well that Baruzi is an unbeliever. But in my opinion it is impossible to disregard him when writing on our Father John of the Cross." (13 October 1941.)

"I now possess the work of Baruzi . . . a book of over 700 pages printed in very small type with all the scholarly apparatus. I could already see from the preface of the second edition what are the weak points. But he writes with great devotion and one cannot replace him by anyone else if one wants to write a more detailed study." (21 October 1941.)

"I have just received the large work of P. Bruno. I am very pleased, because there are great gaps in Baruzi which must be filled." (11 November 1941.)

---

[1] A gift of the Carmel of Echt, Holland, to the Archivum Carmelitanum Edith Stein.

The different indications given by the religious development and the intellectual activity of the author show us that with this last work she offers us the ripe fruit of her deepest personality.

The first indication comes from the spiritual evolution of Edith Stein. Indeed, if the reading of the writings of St Teresa of Avila led her to the Catholic Church, the meditation on the doctrine of the Cross won her for the Carmelite life. That this evolution was nourished by the sustained study of mystical literature must necessarily be assumed if we consider the autonomy and power of this thought. Edith Stein's habit of using letters she had received for making notes gives us a striking proof of this. Among her extracts from St Augustine [1] there is a page, dated Heidelberg, 27 November 1930, with the following words:

"I am sending you herewith a small work of the Catholic poetess Ruth Schaumann. If she should be unknown to you I hope to have introduced you to a very interior woman who is akin to us in more than one respect. I like to remember, for example, our conversation about the cross with . . . at Ludwigshafen, which showed your inclination towards mysticism."

The philosophical evolution of Edith Stein gives us another indication pointing in the same direction. Having first been interested in depth psychology, the author then turns towards modern philosophy where the phenomenological tendency receives her particular attention. This is followed by a period of intensive work marked by a growing religious emphasis in the domains of sociology and education. The author's interest is soon directed towards scholastic philosophy which she tries to reconcile with modern philosophical conceptions. Finally, after a period of study, translation and interpretation of the most eminent Catholic philosophers the central questions of religious philosophy come to the fore. And if we want to establish an organic link between the evolution which we have just described and the present work, we must situate the latter both at the end of this evolution and at the beginning of a new religious and philosophical departure.

We are given a last indication by Edith Stein's own writings. It is possible to go ten years back and find the stages of this interior preparation which resulted in the study of St John of the Cross. We would mention the following articles and studies among others:

"The mystical passion of penitence"; "Feast of St John of the

[1] In the possession of the Archivum Carmelitanum Edith Stein.

Cross", written probably in 1934; "The Exaltation of the Cross"; "Ave Crux Spes Unica", dating from 1939; "The Erection of the Cross", dating from 1941.[1]

Treatises in direct relation to *The Science of the Cross*, on inwardness and the meaning of the human being: *On the Problem of Empathy* (1917)[2]; *Contributions to the Philosophical foundations of Psychology and the Arts*[2]; *Finite and Eternal Being, Attempt of an Ascent to the Meaning of Being* (1936).[3]

The aim of her work is twofold. Its immediate occasion was the fourth centenary of the saint, for which Edith Stein was given the task to contribute the literary part of the celebration. That this corresponded to her deepest desire is evident from the work itself which Edith Stein gave to her Order and to the world, as well as from the correspondence that has been quoted above. In September 1940 she wrote thus:

"I am most grateful to be able once more to produce something, before my brain gets altogether rusty."

For Edith Stein this task meant that she would show, through the meditation of the writings, the life and the spiritual evolution of St John of the Cross, that this work and this life melt into the most complete unity under the sign of Redemption.

Nevertheless, the indirect end Edith Stein had in mind when writing her work was to interpret in her own personal way the laws which govern spiritual being and life. She sums up these laws in the expression *Science of the Cross*, which she has coined herself; and, without losing sight of the immediate purpose of her work, she derives the fundamental principles of her own doctrine from the life of the saint as from their source.[4] On the other hand, in order that her presentation should in every point remain in accordance with the truth, she always carefully distinguishes between what comes from her own mind and what belongs to the authentic thought of the saint. And here a characteristic trait of Edith Stein's personality undoubtedly manifests itself. Whilst studying the thought of another intent on following its development, she finds herself irresistibly drawn to

---

[1] The manuscripts belong to the Archivum Carmelitanum Edith Stein. They will be published as part of the *Works of Edith Stein*.

[2] Studies previously published (Dissertation; *Jahrbuch für Philosophie und Phänomenologische Forschung*). They will be re-edited in the *Works of Edith Stein*.

[3] See *Works of Edith Stein*, Vol. II.

[4] For a more exact study of this question see pp. 1, 19ff, 23f, 121f, 131ff, 208. The reading of these extracts will afford a general view of the purpose which the analyses of Edith Stein pursue as well as their result.

furnishing a personal work.[1] Moved by the creative force of her spirit
and by the joy she feels in it, this daughter of St John of the Cross
enlarges her working method. This is why, instead of giving a commentary of the texts of the saint, she extends his teaching on the Cross
into a philosophy of the person. In her discussion of the fundamental
laws of spiritual being her attention is given especially to the questions
which concern the essence and the destiny of the human person: the
ego, the person and liberty on the one hand; spirit, faith and contemplation on the other.[2]

The personality of Edith Stein in the light of the Science of the Cross.

To conclude, we would sketch the spiritual physiognomy of the
author such as it is reflected in this work. These traits take shape in
it according to the authenticity of their tragic nobility and offer us
an unequalled picture of her strong personality.

In the light of the circumstances which presided over the birth of
the work, and taking into account the ideological climate—that of
the National Socialist dictatorship—which influenced the psychological attitude of Edith Stein, the choice of the theme and the conception of the work appear as the supreme expression of a profound
attachment to the Carmelite ideal. They represent at the same time a
sublimation of human suffering, an act of definite detachment and the
passing beyond the finite world. According to the progress of her
spiritual evolution Edith Stein thus transcends her attachment to her
own life and transfers the centre of gravity beyond earthly power and
activity. Hence the last chapters of her work reveal the serenity of a
soul certain of eternity, and on which the world has no longer any
hold.

At the same time it becomes clear that this renunciation, as distinct
from what would only be resignation or disgust with life, is animated
by the most profound religious faith and nourished by a vitality that
has arrived at its maturity. The soul of Edith Stein, the centre of the
mystic union, tends to establish itself in God, the supreme principle
and goal of all existence.

The consideration of the developments to follow will permit us to
form an idea of this religious ascent.

In fact, in the work of Edith Stein problems are raised which lead
to an enlargement of the original design; while treating them, the
author develops and completes the intellectual edifice raised by her

[1] See the French edition, *Œuvres d'Edith Stein*, Vol. II, Preface.   [2] See p. xxi.

spiritual father, St John of the Cross. The analysis of the Night, the Ascent, the union with God, etc., progresses not in a logical and deductive manner, but rather in an intuitive and inductive way.

The life of Edith Stein, especially during her last ten years, had been lived under the sign of the Cross, and as such furnishes us an example of that unity of doctrine and life which remains the fundamental idea of her interpretation. This presupposes a twofold perfect mastership: the intellectual mastership as regards the manner in which the author dominates the whole complex of the problems, and the spiritual mastership of the interior itinerary that leads to the goal. The authentic filiation which links Edith Stein to her blessed father marks this mastership, hence it is possible to attribute to the author what she herself writes on the subject of St John of the Cross:

"Thus the poet found abundant inspiration in the glowing, colourful pictures of the Old Testament singer; the theologian had another rich source at his disposal. The soul is one with Christ, living by his life, though only if it has surrendered itself to the crucified Saviour and has made the whole way of the Cross with him. This is nowhere more clearly and poignantly expressed than in the message of St Paul. His Letters contain already a fully formed science of the Cross, a theology of the Cross drawn from his own intimate experience."

"Thus we, too, can approach these divine secrets of a chosen soul with holy fear and reverence. But once the veil has been lifted we are no longer allowed to be silent about it. For here we have what is lacking in the *Ascent* and the *Night* in the form in which they have come down to us, that is to say, a description of the soul at the end of its long way of the Cross, in the blessed state of union.

"It has been said before that even the first works were evidently written by someone who had already arrived at the goal." [1]

As regards the religious and philosophical orientation of Edith Stein it is permitted to ask oneself which directive ideas, emanating from the personality and the teaching of the mystical Doctor, influence her so much that she makes them the themes of her own reflexion.

At this period of her life her interest is centred in the first place in the central themes which constitute the Science of the Cross. These are mainly the Ascent of the soul to God through the crucifixion of the active and passive Nights and the virginal union of the soul with its God.

[1] See pp. 9, 141.

In close dependence of this doctrine personal ideas lead her to the elaboration of a philosophy of the person, the *leitmotiv* of the research and creative work of Edith Stein. Beyond the duality of the human person—expressed in the incarnation of the spirit and free will—her penetrating glance tends towards the exigencies of metaphysical truth; it aims at harmonizing philosophical knowledge and a conception of the world on one hand, and life and doctrine on the other, that is to say at engaging life in the same sense as doctrine.

Edith Stein undertook the present work in the service of the Lord and in order to glorify her father in the Order of Carmel. Before she could put the last touch to it, she was called to become, through her actions and as a victim of men, the complete model that shows forth the doctrine of the Cross. Her work, itself incomplete, remains to us as her last testament.

For this reason, by publishing the work of Edith Stein, we propose to bring her task to completion, adding the complement of the word to the action which was the life of Sister Teresa Benedicta of the Cross.

DR LUCY GELBER.

FOREWORD

IN the following pages the attempt has been made to understand
John of the Cross in and through the unity of his being as it is
expressed in his life and works, considering him from a point of
view that enables us to envisage this unity. Hence we do not give a
description of his life nor an exhaustive evaluation and presentation
of his teaching. But the facts of his life and the contents of his writings
must be utilized if we would penetrate to this unity. The documents
are cited extensively, but after they have been presented the author
attempts an interpretation, offering what she believes a lifetime of
effort to have taught her about the laws of intellectual and spiritual
being and life. This applies particularly to her theories on spirit,
faith and contemplation which have been inserted in various places,
especially in the section "The Soul in the Realm of Spirit and the
Spirits". What is there said on ego, freedom and person is not derived
from the writings of our holy Father John. Though certain points
of contact may be found, such theories were remote not only from
his leading intention but from his mode of thought. For only modern
philosophy has set itself the task of working out a philosophy of the
person such as is suggested in the passages just mentioned.

We have utilized the books of the Carmelite Bruno de Jesu Maria,
Saint Jean de la Croix, Paris 1929, and *Vie d'Amour de Saint Jean de la
Croix*, Paris 1936, as well as that of Jean Baruzi, *Saint Jean de la Croix
et le problème de l'expérience mystique*, Paris 1931. The latter has fur-
nished many suggestions but has relatively rarely been cited, because
it is impossible to rely on his presentation without a critical discussion,
which would not have been within the scope of our work. Those who
know Baruzi will discover the traces of his influence as well as the
points that are criticized. It is one of his indisputable merits that he
was tireless in discovering and utilizing the sources; among the
questionable points is his view that of the two manuscript versions
of the *Spiritual Canticle* and the *Living Flame of Love* the later ones
should be considered apocryphal—in the case of the latter work
possibly, in that of the former most probably—and that we have
probably only an apocryphal or mutilated version of the *Ascent* and

the *Dark Night*, where the manuscript tradition is uniform. (Cf. Book
I: "Les Textes", pp. 3ff, and the introductions to the individual works
in the latest Spanish edition of the works: *Obras de San Juan de la
Cruz Doctor de la Iglesia*, editadas y anotadas por el P. Silverio de
Santa Teresa C.D., Burgos 1929 ff.)

INTRODUCTION: MEANING AND BASIS OF THE SCIENCE OF THE CROSS

IN September or October 1568 the young Carmelite John de Yepes, whose religious name had until then been John of St Matthias, moved into the poor little house of Duruelo where he was to lay the foundations of the Teresian reform. On 28 November he vowed himself with two companions to the observance of the primitive Rule, taking the name "of the Cross". This symbolized the ideal he sought when he left the monastery he had originally entered, thus publicly renouncing the mitigated Rule. Indeed, he had already desired this for some years, when he had obtained the personal permission to follow the primitive Rule. His new name expressed at the same time an essential characteristic of the Reform: the life of the Discalced Carmelites was to be the following of Christ in the way of the Cross, indeed a share in the Cross of Christ.

As has just been observed, John was no longer a novice in the science of the Cross. In the Carmelite Order the "title of nobility" indicates that God wants to unite the soul to himself through a special mystery. By changing his name, John showed that henceforth his life was to be lived under the sign of the Cross. If we speak of a *Science of the Cross* this is not to be understood in the ordinary meaning of science: it is no mere theory, i.e. no combination of—really or supposedly—true axioms, no ideal structure of thought. It is, indeed, known truth, a theology of the Cross, but it is living, actual and active truth: it is placed in the soul like a seed, strikes root and grows, giving the soul a certain character and forming it in all it does or leaves undone, so that its own being shines forth and is recognized in it. In this sense we speak of a science of sanctity, and this is how we understand the science of the Cross. This form and force living in the depth of the soul nourish the philosophy of this man and the way in which God and the world present themselves to him, and thus they can be expressed in a theory. In the doctrine of St John of the Cross we have such an expression. Hence we would search his writings and his life for what constitutes their unity and character. But first we must ask how a science in this sense can be established.

1

There are naturally recognizable signs indicating that human nature as it actually exists is in a state of depravation. This includes the inability to assimilate and react to facts according to their true value. This inability may either be due to an innate dullness or to a general blunting of the sensibility that has developed in the course of life, or, finally, to an indifference to certain frequently recurring impressions. What we have often heard is quite well known to us and therefore "leaves us cold". To this may often be added an excessive preoccupation with one's own individual interests which makes us indifferent to other things. We know that this inner rigidity is wrong and suffer from it. But the fact that it corresponds to a psychological law does not help us to overcome it. On the other hand, we are happy if we find by experience that we are still capable of deep and genuine joy; and deep, genuine sorrow, too, is like a grace compared with the rigid inability to feel anything. This lack of sensibility is particularly painful in the religious sphere. Many Christians feel depressed because the events of the Gospel do not—or do no longer—impress them as they ought and fail to affect and shape their lives. The example of the saints shows how it ought to be: where there is truly living faith there Christian doctrine and the mighty deeds of God are the content of life which shape everything and before which everything else must give way. This is "holy objectivity" (*heilige Sachlichkeit*), i.e. the original receptivity of a soul re-born by the Holy Spirit. Such a soul reacts to all events in the proper way and at the right depth; it has in itself a living, moving power joyfully ready to let itself be formed, unhampered by false inhibitions and rigidity. If a saintly soul thus assimilates the truths of faith they become the science of the saints. If the mystery of the Cross becomes its inner form it grows into the science of the Cross.

Holy objectivity is in some way related to the objectivity of the child which still receives and reacts to impressions with unabated energy free from inhibitions. It is true, this natural reaction will not always be reasonable, since the understanding is still immature. Besides, as soon as the intellect is involved there are many inner as well as outer sources of error and deception leading it into wrong ways. Suitable surroundings, however, may prevent this, for the soul of a child is easily formed, and what penetrates it may well shape its whole life. If the soul of a child is nourished on the Gospel, suitably presented at an early age, this may easily become the foundation of a saintly life. Sometimes grace also gives an early extraordinary vocation, so that the objectivity of the child is joined to that of the saints. Thus St Bridget is reported to have first heard of the suffering and death of Jesus when she was ten years old; in the following night the Saviour appeared to her on the Cross, and from that time she could never contemplate the Passion of our Lord without shedding tears.

In the case of St John of the Cross we must further consider that he was an artist. Among the various arts and handicrafts he practised as a boy were carving and painting. We still possess drawings of his dating from a later period of his life; his sketch of the ascent of mount Carmel is well known. As Prior at Granada he constructed a model of a contemplative monastery. He was also a poet who felt the need to express his interior experiences in verse. His mystical treatises are but later explanations of the poems he had been inspired to write. Thus in his case the peculiar objectivity of the artist must also be taken into account. In the unbroken power of his impressionable nature the artist is akin to the child and to the saint. But, different from holy objectivity, this impressionability leads the artist to see the world in the light of certain values, and this may easily be to the detriment of others. This corresponds to the specially responsive attitude of the artist. What touches him within is formed into an image demanding also external expression.

In this context the term image is not restricted to the sphere of painting and sculpture but includes also those of literature and music. This image expresses something while being at the same time fashioned into a small self-contained world of its own. Moreover, every genuine work of art is also a sign, no matter whether this has been actually in the intention of the artist or whether he is a realist or a symbolist. By calling it a sign we mean that it signifies and expresses something of the infinite plenitude of meaning which all human knowledge seeks to penetrate; further, that it does so in a way to suggest this fullness of meaning which yet can never be exhausted by human knowledge. Thus understood, all genuine art is revelation, and all creative activity is a sacred ministry. Nevertheless, it remains true that the artistic temperament has its dangers, and not only if the artist fails to understand the sanctity of his calling. The danger is that the artist may rest satisfied with the creation of the image, as if no other demands were made on him. Our meaning will become especially clear in the case of the image of the Cross. There is scarcely a believing artist who will never have felt the urge to represent Christ crucified or carrying his Cross. But from the artist, too, the Crucified Lord demands more than such an image. He asks of him as from every other man that he should follow him: that he should form himself, and let himself be formed, into the image of him who bore the Cross and died on it. The artistic formation may be a hindrance for the forming of the self, but not necessarily so; it may even serve the latter, because the interior image will be fully shaped and assimilated only with the assistance of the external image. Thus, if nothing else prevents it, this will become the inner form which desires to be actively expressed through the imitation of Christ. Even the externally created picture may become a spur constantly urging the artist to form himself in its image. We have every reason to assume that this happened in the case of John: in him childlike, artistic and holy objectivity combined, preparing the most fertile soil for the message of the Cross which then developed into the science of the Cross. We have mentioned above that his artist's nature showed itself already in childhood. There are also many witnesses to his early election to sanctity. His mother later told the Discalced Carmelites of Medina del Campo that her son had behaved like an angel when he was still a child. This pious mother impressed on him a tender love for the Mother of God, and we know from reliable sources that our Lady intervened twice to save the boy from drowning. All other information about his childhood and youth indicates that he was a child of grace from his earliest years.

I. THE MESSAGE OF THE CROSS

§1. EARLY ENCOUNTERS WITH THE CROSS

IT must now be considered how the seed of the message of the Cross was sown in this fertile soil. There is no evidence to tell us when and how John first met the image of Christ crucified. Most probably his devout mother would take her small son to the parish church in his native city of Fontiveros. There he would see the Saviour on the Cross, his face disfigured by pain, real hair hanging down to the shoulders covered with wales.[1] And when the young widow who had to bear so much distress and sorrow spoke to her children of the heavenly Mother, she surely took them also to the Sorrowful Mother under the Cross. We may even reverently assume that Mary herself instructed her young servant in the mysteries of the science of the Cross; for who would know its worth better than the wisest of virgins?

John certainly met the image of the Cross also in the workshops where he was employed. Perhaps he attempted even then to carve crosses, as he liked to do later. True, we can only offer conjectures; but our view that he must have met the Cross at an early age is supported by the certain fact of his precocious love of penance and mortification. When he was only a boy of nine he abandoned his bed and made himself a couch of twigs. Several years later he allowed himself only a few hours' rest on this hard bed, because he devoted part of the night to his studies. As a young pupil he would beg alms for his school mates who were even poorer than he and later for the poor in hospital. After many failures in other occupations he began to nurse the sick and selflessly persevered in this hard work. According to the testimony of his brother Francis he had to nurse in a smallpox hospital (*al hospital de las bubas*).[2] It has also been suggested that this accommodated patients suffering from syphilis.[3] Whether this was so or not, the boy is certain to have seen among his patients not only physical disease but psychological and moral misery, and he would

---

[1] Cf. P. Bruno de Jesu Maria, O.C.D., *St. Jean de la Croix*, Paris 1929, p. 4f.
[2] Bruno, *loc. cit.*, pp. 10, 377.
[3] Cf. J. Baruzi, *op. cit.*, p. 77f.

often have to struggle against his pure and tender nature to carry out his duties faithfully. Only the love of Christ crucified could give him strength to do this, as he was determined to follow him in the steep and narrow way. It was probably the desire to know Christ better and to model himself on him that led John to take up his studies at the Jesuit College to prepare himself for the priesthood, while continuing his nursing at the same time. Later he refused a well-paid post as chaplain at his hospital so as to embrace the poverty of an Order,[1] animated no doubt by the desire to be better able to listen to the message of the Cross. The same wish prevented him from finding peace in the mitigated Observance of the Carmelites of his time and led him to the Reform.

§2. The Message of Scripture

Perhaps John was introduced to the study of Scripture in the College of the Jesuits. Even before this time he must have met the words of our Lord, and among them the word of the Cross, in sermons, instructions and in the liturgy. In the Carmelite Order Scriptural instruction is part of the daily routine, and when, as a young religious, he was later sent to study at Salamanca, the interpretation of the Sacred Text under the guidance of trained exegetes was an essential part of his training. We know from his later years that he lived wholly in and with the Bible, one of the few books he always kept in his cell, and his works abound in Scriptural quotations. The words of the Bible became the natural expression of his inner experience and came spontaneously to his pen. The secretary and confidant of his last year, Father John the Evangelist, tells us that John of the Cross hardly needed to open the Bible because he knew it almost by heart.[2] Thus we may be sure that the Scriptural message of the Cross continued to penetrate his heart throughout his life. It is, however, quite impossible to treat exhaustively this source of his science of the Cross, perhaps the most important of all. For we must presuppose that the whole Bible, the Old as well as the New Testament, was his daily bread. The Scriptural citations in his works are so numerous that it is impossible to discuss them all. On the other hand, it would be wrong to limit ourselves to these and to suppose that words not cited by him had no influence on him. We can only show by various groups of examples how the message of the Cross penetrated the consciousness of the saint.

[1] *Ibid.*, p. 91.   [2] Bruno, *loc. cit.*, p. 269.

Our Lord himself has spoken of the Cross on several occasions and in various senses. When he prophesied his suffering and death[1] he envisaged the shameful wood on which he was to end his life in a literal sense. But when he said: ". . . He that taketh not up his cross and followeth me is not worthy of me" [2] or "If any man will come after me, let him deny himself and take up his cross and follow me" [3] the Cross symbolized all that is so oppressive and contrary to nature that it seems as hard as death. And the disciple of Jesus is to bear this burden daily.[4] The prophecy of his death confronted the apostles with the image of Christ crucified and still confronts everyone today who reads or hears the Gospel. It contains a silent demand for an adequate answer. The invitations to follow Christ on life's way of the Cross suggest this answer, at the same time elucidating the meaning of the death of the Cross; for they are followed immediately by the warning: "Whosoever will save his life shall lose it; but he who shall lose his life for my sake, shall save it".[5] Christ gives his life to give men access to eternal life. But they themselves must surrender their earthly life; to rise with Christ they must also die with him, certainly the lifelong death of suffering and daily self-denial, if necessary also the death of martyrdom for the message of Christ.

The Passion narratives of the Gospels present a detailed picture of the crucified Sufferer that had been anticipated in the words of our Lord himself. These images must have made an indelible impression on the pure, receptive heart of St John and on his artist's imagination. We must also assume that he assisted at the great services of Holy Week, even taking an active part in them as a server. For in the liturgy of Palm Sunday, Maundy Thursday and Good Friday, the last days of Jesus, his death and repose in the grave are dramatically re-enacted before the faithful in poignant words and tunes urging them to take part in the events. If even cold-hearted, worldly men and unbelievers cannot remain indifferent at these ceremonies, what an effect must they not have had on the youthful saint who later could hardly speak of spiritual things without falling into ecstasy, and who was ravished out of his senses when listening to a song.

When he began his Scriptural studies the Gospel accounts were supplemented by the prophecies of the Old Testament, probably above all by Isaias' presentation of the Suffering Servant to which his

---

[1] Matt. 20. 19; 26. 2.   [2] Matt. 10.38
[3] Matt. 16. 24; cf. Mark 8. 34; Luke 9. 23; 14. 27.   [4] Luke 9. 23.
[5] Luke 9. 24; cf. Matt. 10. 39; Luke 17. 33; John 12. 25.

attention must have been directed by the Breviary Lessons for Holy
Week. In them he not only found ruthlessly realistic descriptions of
the Passion but also the great historical background of the drama of
Golgotha: God, the almighty Creator and Ruler of the world who
crushes the nations like potter's clay, and who is yet also the Father
who surrounds his chosen People with his loving care, the tender and
jealous lover who woos Israel his bride through the centuries, yet is
always rejected, as John has hymned it in his *Shepherd's Song*.[1]
Prophets and Evangelists vie with each other to draw the picture of
the Messias who comes, obedient to his Father, to win back the
bride, who takes her yoke upon himself to deliver her from it, who
even does not shun death to win life for her. This is echoed in the
"Romances".[2] These extend the bridal relationship from Israel to all
mankind, in accordance with the announcement of the Kingdom of
God in the prophets as well as in the Gospels.

Something else must have impressed John when reading the
prophetical books, that is the relation between the prophet and his
Lord and God, the vocation and election of a man on whom the
Almighty has laid his hand. In such a relationship God makes a man
his familiar friend who knows and announces his eternal counsels; in
return God demands of him complete surrender and boundless
devotion, taking him out of the community of natural-minded men
and setting him up as a sign of contradiction. This is indicated not
only by Holy Scripture itself but also by its interpretation in the
tradition of the Carmelite Order. The memory of the prophet Elias,
the "guide and father of the Carmelites",[3] survived even under the
mitigated Carmelite Rule. The *Institutio primorum monachorum*[4]
presented him to the young religious as the model of the contemplative
life. The prophet is told by God to go into the desert and hide in the
brook Carith opposite the Jordan, to drink of the brook and to live
on the food which God will send him.[5] Thus he becomes the pattern
of all those who withdraw into solitude, renounce sin, sensual delights,

[1] N. 7 in Campbell and Allison Peers. The *Shepherd's Song* is the complaint of the
scorned love of the Saviour. We would not assert that John means by the bride the people
of Israel. The reference to the individual soul is equally possible.

[2] N. 9ff, *op. cit.*

[3] *S. Propheta Dei Elias Ord. Carmelitarum Dux et Pater*, inscription on the statue of the
prophet in the Vatican basilica.

[4] According to the chroniclers of the Carmelite Order the original was written in Greek.
The Latin translation of the Patriarch Aymeric of Antioch (ed. Salamanca 1599) is still
extant. A French translation was published by *La Voix de Notre Dame du Mont Carmel*,
vols. I, II, 1932–3.

[5] 3 Kings 17. 2–4.

indeed all earthly things (this is meant by "opposite the Jordan") and hide in the love of God (*Carith* being interpreted as *caritas*). The stream of divine grace will quench their thirst with delight, and the doctrine of the Fathers will offer them solid food for their souls: the bread of contrition and penance, the meat of true humility. Here John may have found the key to what God was doing in his own soul. Certainly, God's plan of salvation envisages all men, and for their sake the chosen People. But salvation concerns each individual soul. God woos every one of them with tender love as his bride and cares for it like a father. This divine wooing can sting the soul, as it were, so that it cannot find rest. This, too, is perfectly expressed in Scripture in the *Canticle*, which John echoes in his own *Spiritual Canticle*. We shall discuss later how the motif of the Cross is sounded throughout this work.

Thus the poet found abundant inspiration in the glowing, colourful pictures of the Old Testament singer; the theologian had another rich source at his disposal. The soul is one with Christ, living by his life, though only if it has surrendered itself to the crucified Saviour and has made the whole way of the Cross with him. This is nowhere more clearly and poignantly expressed than in the message of St Paul. His Letters contain already a fully formed science of the Cross, a theology of the Cross drawn from his own intimate experience.

"Christ sent me . . . to preach the gospel; not in the wisdom of speech, lest the cross of Christ should be made void. For the word of the cross, to them indeed that perish is foolishness; to them that are saved, that is, to us, it is the power of God." ". . . The Jews require signs, and the Greeks seek after wisdom. But we preach Christ crucified: unto the Jews indeed a stumbling block, and unto the Gentiles foolishness: But unto them that are called, both Jews and Greeks, Christ, the power of God and the wisdom of God. For the foolishness of God is wiser than men: and the weakness of God is stronger than men." [1]

The Word of the Cross is the gospel St Paul preaches to Jews and Gentiles. He presents it as a simple testimony, without oratorical adornments and without attempting to convince his hearers by rational proofs. He draws all his strength from his subject. This is the Cross of Christ, i.e. Christ's death on the Cross and the crucified Christ himself. Christ is the strength of God and the wisdom of God,

[1] 1 Cor. 1. 17f. and 22–25.

not only because he is sent by God, being the Son of God and himself God, but because he has been crucified. For his death on the Cross is the means which God's unfathomable wisdom has devised to redeem us. In order to show that the strength and wisdom of men cannot accomplish their redemption God gives his redemptive power to him who appears weak and foolish by human standards; who desires to be nothing of himself but lets only God's power act in him, who has "emptied" himself and "become obedient" "even unto the death of the cross".[1] The redemptive power raises to life those in whom the divine life had died through sin. This power has entered into the Word of the Cross, through which it penetrates to all who accept it without demanding signs or rational proof. In them it becomes that formative, life-giving power which we have called the Science of the Cross. Paul himself became its adept: "I, through the law, am dead to the law, that I may live to God: with Christ I am nailed to the cross. And I live, now not I: but Christ liveth in me. And that I live now in the flesh: I live in the faith of the Son of God, who loved me and delivered himself for me."[2] In those days when it was night around him but light in his soul, the zealous defender of the Law realized that the Law was only a tutor preparing men for Christ. It could make them ready to receive life, but it could not itself give life. Christ took upon himself the yoke of the Law by fulfilling it and by dying for and through the Law. Thus he freed from the Law those who want to receive life from him. But they can receive it only by surrendering their own life. For those who have been baptized into Christ have been baptized into his death.[3] They are submerged in his life so as to become members of his Body; as such they suffer and die with him, but also rise with him to eternal and divine life. Its fullness will be given us only in the state of glory. But even now, "in the flesh", we have a share in it, because we have faith. We believe that Christ has died for us to give us life. This faith unites us to him as the members are united to their Head, opening our souls to receive his life. Thus living faith in Christ crucified and surrender to him give us life and are the beginning of future glory. Hence our only glory is the Cross: "God forbid that I should glory, save in the cross of our Lord Jesus Christ: by whom the world is crucified to me, and I to the world."[4] If a man has decided to follow Christ he is dead to the world and the world is dead to him. He bears the marks of the Lord in his body,[5] is weak and despised by men, but for this very

[1] Phil. 2. 7f.   [2] Gal. 2. 19f.   [3] Rom. 6. 3ff.   [4] Gal. 6. 14.   [5] Gal. 6. 17.

reason he is strong, because God's power is strong in the weak.[1]
Knowing this, the disciple of Jesus not only accepts the Cross that
has been laid on him but crucifies himself: "They that are Christ's
have crucified their flesh, with the vices and concupiscences."[2] They
have fought an unrelenting battle against their nature so that the
life of sin should die in them and make room for the life of the spirit.
This is the point. The Cross is not an end in itself. It is raised up and
points above itself. Nevertheless, it is not only a sign, it is the strong
weapon of Christ, the shepherd's staff with which the divine David
fights against the infernal Goliath, with which he knocks at the gate
of heaven and opens it. Then the divine light streams out, embracing
all those who follow the crucified Lord.

§3. THE SACRIFICE OF THE MASS

To die with Christ on the Cross and to rise with him becomes a
reality for every believer and especially for every priest in the sacrifice
of the Mass. According to Catholic doctrine this is the renewal of the
sacrifice of the Cross. If a man offers, or shares in it with a living faith
the event of Golgotha will happen also for and in him. John used to
serve Mass as a child and no doubt also in the Order until he himself
was ordained priest. We know from the accounts of his life that the
mere sight of an image of the Cross could throw him into ecstasy.
How deeply must he not have been affected by the actual sacrifice,
especially later, when he offered it himself. We have an account of his
first Mass. He celebrated it in the monastery of St Anne at Medina
del Campo in September 1567, perhaps within the Octave of the
Nativity of our Lady, in the presence of his mother, his eldest brother
Francis and the latter's family. Reverent fear had urged him to refuse
the priesthood and had been overcome only by obedience to the
orders of his superiors. Now, at the beginning of the holy sacrifice,
he was filled with the thought of his unworthiness. He ardently desired
to be perfectly pure in order to touch the sacred Host with undefiled
hands. He therefore asked God to prevent him from ever mortally
offending him and to give him contrition for all the faults he might
commit if God refused his help, but to keep him from falling into
them. At the consecration he heard the words: "I grant your request."
From that moment he was confirmed in grace and had the purity of a

[1] 2 Cor. 12. 9.   [2] Gal. 5. 24.

two-year-old child.[1] To be pure of guilt yet to feel the pain due to it —is not this the true union with the Immaculate Lamb who took upon himself the sins of the world, is not this Gethsemani and Golgotha?

John certainly always remained very conscious of the greatness of the holy Sacrifice. We know that at Baëza he once left the altar in ecstasy without finishing the Mass. A woman present exclaimed that angels ought to come to finish this Mass, since the saintly Father did not remember that he had not finished it. At Caravaca he was seen surrounded by rays emanating from the Host. He himself owned in a confidential conversation that he sometimes abstained from saying Mass for several days because his nature was too weak to endure the overwhelming consolations.[2] He loved especially to say the Mass of the Holy Trinity. For this sublime mystery is closely linked to the sacrifice of the Mass which was instituted according to the decision of the Three Divine Persons, is celebrated in their honour and communicates their eternal life. We do not know how many illuminations the saint may not have received at the altar during his priestly life. But his growth in the science of the Cross and his progressive mysterious transformation into Christ crucified have certainly been largely accomplished in the service of the altar.

§4. VISIONS OF THE CROSS

The heart of every person living in the Christian civilization, but especially the heart of the priest receives the message of the Cross in word, image and liturgical celebration. Yet not everyone is able and prepared to accept and respond to it as fully as John of the Cross. Moreover, apart from special graces during Mass, it came to him in an extraordinary form. He had repeated visions of Christ crucified; about two of them we have detailed information. In his teaching John has treated visions, locutions and revelations as inessential accessories of the mystical life. He has always warned against them, because there is the danger of deception, and if a man sets store by such things he will be delayed on his way to union. Moreover, John was very reserved as regards both his outer and his inner life. If he spoke of

[1] Cf Bruno, *loc. cit.*, p. 54f, and the *Vida* of Gerardo de San Juan de la Cruz in *Ed. Crit.*, I, 36f.
[2] Bruno, *loc. cit.*, p. 225

these visions, this means that they must have had a special significance. Both were followed by a storm of sufferings and persecutions. Hence they may well be considered to have been prophetic.

The first vision came to him at Avila, at the Convent of the Incarnation, where St Teresa of Jesus had called him to act as the nuns' confessor. There one day, as he was contemplating the Passion, Christ crucified appeared before his bodily eyes, bleeding and covered with wounds. The apparition was so clear that he could make a drawing of it as soon as he had returned to himself. The small, yellowed piece of paper is still preserved in the Convent of the Incarnation.[1] The drawing makes a very modern impression. The Cross and the Body are strikingly foreshortened, as if seen from the side; the Body is far removed from the Cross, hanging by the hands (these, pierced by large, extraordinarily protruding nails, are particularly expressive). The head has fallen forward so that the features cannot be distinguished; but the neck and the upper part of the back, covered with wales, are visible. The saint gave the picture to Sister Ann Mary of Jesus and told her his secret. This is very understandable, because our Lord himself had told this nun something of his most intimate secrets (for example, the grace he had received at his first Mass). We do not know whether the Saviour spoke any words when he bent so low from the Cross. But an intimate exchange must surely have taken place. This happened before the Reform was attacked by the Calced Carmelites, from whose animosity John suffered more than any others.

The second apparition took place towards the end of his life at Segovia, where he had called his beloved brother Francis, to whom we owe the following account: ". . . When I had been there for two or three days I asked him to let me depart. He said I should stay a few more days, because he did not know when we would see each other again. This was the last time I saw him. One evening after supper he took my hand and led me into the garden; when we were alone he said to me: 'I will tell you something that happened to me with our Lord. We had a crucifix[2] in the monastery, and one day, when I was standing before it, it seemed to me that it would be more

---

[1] A good reproduction can be found in the book of Fr Bruno, p. 136; there the sources for the accounts are also noted. (This drawing inspired Salvador Dali's well-known painting 'Christ of St John of the Cross.'—Translator.)

[2] Fr Bruno writes that this was Christ carrying his Cross, painted on leather (*Vie d'amour de Saint Jean de la Croix*, p. 238). He published this picture in his book *Saint Jean de la Croix*, p. 236. But would the saint really have called such an image *crucifijo*?

suitably placed in the church. I wanted it to be venerated not only by the friars but also by those outside. And I carried out this intention. When I had placed it in the church as suitably as I could I once stood before it in prayer. Then he said to me: Brother John, ask me for what you want me to give you for the service you have done me. Then I said to him: Lord, I want from you sufferings which I might bear for you, and that I should be despised and accounted for nothing.'"[1]

When John uttered this desire it could easily be fulfilled through natural circumstances. At this time Nicholas Doria was Provincial of the Reformed Carmel. He was a fanatic who wanted to change Teresa's work according to his own ideas. John vigorously defended the inheritance of the Holy Mother and the victims of Doria's fanaticism, Father Jerome Gratian and the Carmelite nuns. The Chapter of the Discalced Carmelites opened in Madrid on 30 May 1591. Before going there the saint said goodbye to the Carmelites of Segovia. The Prioress, Mary of the Incarnation, exclaimed excitedly: "Who knows, Father, whether Your Reverence may not come back as our Provincial!" He replied: "I shall be cast away like an old kitchen rag." And so it happened. He was not given another office but sent into the solitude of La Peñuela where he received the news of the sufferings of the Carmelite nuns. They were severely questioned in order to obtain material against John, whom Doria wanted to expel from the Order. Shortly afterwards his last illness forced him to leave la Peñuela where no medical attention was available. Thus he arrived at the last station of his way of the Cross: Ubeda, where the Prior, Francis Chrysostom, was his bitter enemy. Covered with festering wounds, John found there all the insulting treatment he could desire. The summit of Golgotha had been reached.

[1] Thomas Perez de Molina wrote down the account of Francis, who could not write. According to him the words were: "Lord, that all may attack my honour and think nothing of me for love of you" (cf. *Vie d'Amour*, p. 239). We have reproduced the account as literally as possible to preserve its touching simplicity and to show the tender relationship between the two brothers, who were intimately united to each other throughout their life. At the beginning of the Reform John had called his mother and his brother with his wife to Duruelo to look after the household. The mother did the cooking, the sister-in-law the washing, the brother swept the cells. This may at first seem surprising in a saint who demanded such strict detachment from all creatures. But there is no contradiction here. If John acted in this way he could well afford to do so; the company of his loved ones was for him no hindrance in the contemplative life. Their relations had probably been so strongly supernaturalized even from his childhood that they were no snare to him. If the nearest blood relations are also the nearest in the spiritual sphere, there results an understanding that is, as it were, a foretaste of eternal bliss. This also explains these confidential communications.

§5. THE MESSAGE OF THE CROSS

There is a third witness to the fact that John had unusual experiences before images of the Cross,[1] and probably these occurred even more often than we know. In our view they were meant to prepare and encourage him to bear the Cross. Now the message of the Cross must include all that is symbolized by the term Cross, all the burdens and sufferings of this life, because only they can give a man the true science of the Cross. The saint became familiar with sorrow and trouble in his early childhood. His father died early, his mother had to struggle hard for their daily bread, and John's own efforts to contribute something to the support of the family failed time and again. All this must have made a deep impression on him, though we have no written evidence for it. Nor do we know anything about the psychological effects of the crises during his first years in the Order.

We are better informed on his inner life in his later years. One night after hearing confessions John left the conventual church after the ringing of the Angelus and went back to his small house where he lived with his companion, Father Germanus. Suddenly a man attacked him and beat him with a stick till he collapsed. It was the revenge of a lover whose girl he had converted.

When John recounted this event he added that he had never felt such sweet consolation in all his life: he had been treated like the Saviour himself and tasted the sweetness of the Cross.

When he was a prisoner at Toledo he had ample opportunity for this. He had begun the reform of the Order at Duruelo, had moved to Mancera with his growing community and after teaching in the Noviciate at Pastrana he had been superior of the first college of the Order at Alcala. In 1572 St Teresa called him to Avila, where she had gone as Prioress of the Convent of the Incarnation, which she had left some years before to begin her Reform. There she was to eradicate the abuses that were rife and to lead the large community to a genuinely spiritual life, though retaining the Mitigated Rule. To accomplish this difficult task she needed good confessors. She could find none more suitable than John, whose profound experience in the inner life was well known to her. At Avila he worked quietly from 1572 to 1577, and his labours bore rich fruit. At the same time the Reform outside made good progress. St Teresa founded one convent after another, and there were also many new houses of the Reformed

[1] Cf. Bruno, *Saint Jean*, p. 329.

Friars. Brilliant men had entered the Order and undertaken its external direction, above all Father Jerome Gratian and Father Ambrose Marianus. This success of the Teresian Reform diminished the influence of the Calced Carmelites professing the Mitigated Rule, who consequently organized a violent resistance. We cannot here investigate why John, too, was persecuted, and with particular vehemence, though his activities were exclusively spiritual. In the night from the third to the fourth of December some Calced Fathers and their accomplices invaded the house of the two confessors of the convent of the Incarnation and kidnapped them. John's whereabouts remained a mystery. St Teresa learned that he had been abducted by the Prior Maldonado, but where he had been taken did not become known till after his liberation nine months later. He had been blindfolded and taken through a lonely suburb to the Monastery of Our Lady of Toledo, the most important house of the Carmelites of the mitigated Observance in Castile. There he was interrogated, and when he refused to abandon the Reform he was treated as a rebel. He was imprisoned in a tiny room, about ten feet by six, in which, as Teresa wrote later,[1] "though he is so small he could hardly stand upright". This cell had neither a window nor an opening for air except a slit high up in the wall. When he wanted to say his Breviary the prisoner "had to climb on the little stool and wait till the sun fell on the wall".[2] The door was secured with a padlock. When in March 1578 news was received that Father Germanus had escaped, the hall before the prison cell was also locked. In the beginning the prisoner was led into the refectory every night to take his meal of bread and water sitting on the floor. Later this was done only three times a week, and finally only sometimes, on a Friday. In the refectory John was also given the discipline. Stripped to the waist, he would kneel with bowed head, while all went past him striking him with the scourge. Since he bore all this with patience and love he was called a hypocrite. Yet he was "immovable as a rock" when asked to give up the Reform. They even tried to bribe him, offering to make him Prior if he would change his mind. Then he broke his silence and told them he would not return to the Mitigated Rule even if it should cost his life. The young novices who witnessed these insults and sufferings wept with pity and, seeing his quiet

---

[1] N. 246 in Allison Peers's edition. Letter of August 1587 to Jerome Gratian.
[2] Jerome of St Joseph, *Historia del V. P. Juan de la Cruz*, Madrid 1641, lib. III, cap. VII. (One of the sources quoted must have exaggerated with regard to the height of the room.—Translator.)

patience, said, Here is a saint.[1] When he was scourged his tunic was soaked in blood, yet he was not allowed to change it throughout the nine months of his imprisonment. It is easy to imagine how much he suffered from this especially during the hot summer months. The food he was given caused him such pain that he thought they wanted to kill him with it. At each mouthful he would make an act of love to overcome temptations against charity.

We know how closely united he was to his nearest relatives. He was also wholeheartedly devoted to the work of the Reform, to St Teresa and the others associated with him in this great enterprise, who had, like him, and for the most part under his personal direction, devoted their lives to the ideal of the primitive Carmel. Later, when his duties detained him in Andalusia, he openly expressed his longing for Castile and his circle of friends there: "Since I was swallowed up by that whale and cast up in this strange harbour, I have never had the joy of seeing you again nor the saints who live there."[2] Now he was so completely separated from them that he could not even send them any message all these months. "Sometimes I was saddened by the thought that it would be said of me that I had turned my back on the work I had begun, and I felt the sorrow of the holy Mother."[3]

But there were even more painful privations. On 14 August 1578 the Prior Maldonado came into John's dungeon with two other religious. The prisoner was so weak that he could scarcely move. He did not look up, thinking his warder had entered. The Prior kicked him with his foot and asked why he did not rise in his presence. When John asked his pardon, assuring him he had not realized who had entered, Maldonado asked him: "Of what did you think, that you should have been so absorbed?" "I thought that tomorrow will be the feast of our Lady, and that it would be a great consolation to me if I could say Mass."[4] How much he must have missed saying Mass during those long months. Even the feast of Corpus Christi, on which he would kneel before the Blessed Sacrament for hours, he had to spend without Mass or Holy Communion.

Could there be a harder school of the Cross than to be helplessly delivered to the fury of enraged enemies, tortured in body and soul, cut off not only from all human consolation but also from the sources

[1] Cf. the Sources given by Bruno, *St. Jean*, p. 407ff.

[2] Letter to Catherine of Jesus from Baëza, of 6 July 1581. St Teresa also wrote on his behalf to Fr Gratian to obtain his recall to Castile (Letter 362 from Palencia).

[3] This he later told the Ven. Anne of St Albert. Cf. Bruno, *St. Jean*, p. 174.

[4] This request was flatly refused, but immediately afterwards our Lady herself came to his assistance; cf. *loc. cit.*, p. 183ff.

of the sacramental life of the Church? Yet even this was not yet the deepest suffering. For all this could not separate him from the Triune source of power that he knew by faith.[1] His spirit was not imprisoned, he could raise himself up to that ever-flowing fountain, sink into its unfathomable depth, into the fullness that nourishes every created thing, even the human heart itself. No earthly power could separate him from his God—but God himself could withdraw. In his prison cell John experienced this darkest of nights.

| A donde te escondiste, | Where can your hiding be, |
| Amado, y me dejaste con gemido? | Beloved, that you left me thus to moan? |

This cry of the soul's pain was uttered in the dungeon of Toledo.[2] We do not know when John first felt the sweetness of God's nearness. But everything points to the fact that he was initiated into the mystical life of prayer at a very early age. To be free for God he had separated from his loved ones, had then abandoned his studies and left his first monastery. His office at Avila, indeed his whole activity in the Order was devoted to freeing other souls for God and leading them into the way of union. For this ideal of the Reform he endured the sufferings of gaol. For the sake of his beloved Master he gladly endured all insults and brutalities. And now this sweet light seemed to fade from his heart. God left him to himself. This was the keenest pain with which no earthly suffering could be compared. Yet it was proof that God's love had elected him. It seemed to lead to death, but it was the way of life.

No human heart has ever entered into such a dark night as the God-man in Gethsemani and Golgotha. No human mind can penetrate the unfathomable mystery of the dereliction of the dying Christ. But Jesus can give chosen souls some taste of this utmost bitterness; it is the ultimate proof of their love for him. If they do not shrink from it but willingly let themselves be drawn into the dark night, then this very night will become their guide:

> Oh night that was my guide!
> Oh darkness dearer than the morning's pride,
> Oh night that joined the lover
> To the beloved bride
> Transfiguring them each into the other.[3]

[1] Cf. the poem, 'How well I know that fountain . . ." (Que bien sé yo la fonte . . .). Fr Gerardo thinks that, except for a few lines added later, this poem was written in prison.

[2] Cf. the Introduction to the *Spiritual Canticle* in *Ed. Crit.*, II, 137ff, the verses of the Canticle in the present work, part II, §3, 2a. (N.2 in Allison Peers and Roy Campbell. All the poems are cited from the latter translation unless otherwise stated.—Translator.)

[3] "Song of the Dark Night", stanza 5.

This was John's great experience of the Cross at Toledo: extreme abandonment, and in just this abandonment union with Christ crucified. This may perhaps explain the contradictory accounts[1] of the time of his imprisonment: for we are told on the one hand that he rarely or never received consolations and that his soul suffered as much as his body; and on the other, that a single one of the graces which God bestowed on him there could not be repaid by many years in gaol. We shall explain later how the soul arrives at the true knowledge of itself and of God's infinite greatness and holiness precisely by experiencing its own nothingness and weakness in the dark night that purifies it, adorns it with virtues and prepares it for union. These are certainly precious graces for which no price is too high. They alone would have been sufficient to make him speak of his tormentors as of great benefactors when he was staying with the Carmelite nuns at Toledo after his escape from prison. But as he also said on this occasion that he had never enjoyed such fullness of supernatural light and consolation as during his imprisonment, we must assume that he there transcended the graces of suffering. The verses of the *Dark Night* and of the *Spiritual Canticle* which were written at that time bear witness to his blissful union with God. The Cross and the night are the way to the heavenly light: this is the good tidings of the Cross.

§6. Content of the Message of the Cross

We have considered the ways by which the message of the Cross may have reached John. In the following sections we would show the effects of this message on the doctrine and life of the saint. But first we must give a provisional outline of this message to become familiar with its contents. We will here present it in the words of the Master of the Science of the Cross himself:

"'How strait is the gate and how narrow the way that leads to life, and few there be that find it' (Mt. 7. 14). In this passage it should on no account be overlooked what weight and emphasis is given to the small word *how*. It is probably meant to tell us: truly, it is very narrow, narrower than you believe. . . . This way to the high mountain of perfection can be ascended only by those travellers that bear no burden that might pull them down. . . . And as God alone is the

---

[1] Bruno, *St. Jean*, p. 179.

2*

goal that should be sought and gained he alone must be sought and gained. . . . Now the Lord wanted to show us this way, hence he gave us this marvellous teaching which is, incredible though it be, the less practised by spiritual souls the more necessary it is for them. 'If any man will follow me, let him deny himself and take up his cross and follow me. For whosoever will save his life shall lose it and whosoever shall lose his life for my sake . . . shall save it' (Mk. 8. 34f). O if only one could truly explain, try and taste . . . the content of this sublime teaching. . . . Loss of all sweetness in God . . . aridity, disgust and pain . . . is the purely spiritual Cross, the nakedness of poverty in the spirit of Christ. . . . True spirituality seeks in God the tasteless rather than the pleasant; it is more inclined to suffering than to consolation and rather renounces all good things for God's sake than possesses them. It prefers aridity and sorrow to sweet communications, since it knows that in the former consists the imitation of Christ and the denial of self, while the other is nothing but to seek oneself in God. . . . To seek God in God means . . . to be prepared for Christ's sake to choose what is distasteful, both on the part of God and of the world." According to the will of Christ renunciation "must be a mortification and destruction of all the will esteems in the temporal, natural and spiritual spheres". If a man carries the Cross in such a way he will realize that it is a "sweet yoke" and "a light burden" (Mt. 11. 30), for he will "find in all things great relief and sweetness". "Spiritual union with God is achieved only when the soul has been almost annihilated in most profound abasement. . . . This union consists . . . only in a death on the Cross while living in the body, in the sensual as well as in the spiritual sphere, outwardly as much as inwardly." [1] This cannot be otherwise, because in God's marvellous plan of salvation, Christ "redeems and unites the soul to himself by the same means by which human nature was spoiled and ruined. For as in paradise human nature had been destroyed and delivered to ruin through eating the forbidden fruit, so it has been redeemed and restored by him under the tree of the Cross." [2] If the soul wants to share in his life it must pass with him through the death of the Cross; like him it must crucify its own nature by a life of mortification and self-denial and surrender itself to be crucified by suffering and death, as God gives or permits it. The more perfect this active and passive Crucifixion, the more intimate will be the union

---

[1] *Ascent of Mount Carmel*, 2.7.
[2] *Spiritual Canticle*, explanation of stanza 23.

with Christ crucified and the more abundant will be man's share in the divine life.

With this the principal motifs of the science of the Cross have been stated. We shall meet them again and again when listening to the teaching of the saint and re-tracing his life. For they are the deepest influences by which his life and work have been shaped.

II. THE DOCTRINE OF THE CROSS

INTRODUCTION: ST JOHN OF THE CROSS AS A WRITER

IN order fully to understand the doctrine of St John of the Cross and its psychological background we must give an account of the characteristics, indeed the uniqueness, of his writings, their origin and their fate.

Since the Church has proclaimed the saint one of its Doctors, everyone wanting to inform himself on questions of Catholic mysticism must seek guidance from him. And even for those outside the Catholic Church he is one of the leading minds, a reliable adviser who cannot be by-passed by those anxious to penetrate into the mysterious realm of the interior life. Yet St John of the Cross did not give a systematic presentation of mysticism. His aim was not to develop his subject theoretically, though he was theoretician enough sometimes to become involved in objective discussions more than was compatible with his original intention. What he really wanted to do was to "lead men by the hand" (as the Areopagite said of himself[1]) and to support his work as a director of souls by his writings. Not all of these have survived. Everything he composed before his imprisonment was destroyed either by himself or by others. The second persecution (within the Reform) has also deprived us of many of his writings, including valuable notes the Carmelite nuns had taken of his oral instructions. Of his letters, too, only a small portion has come down to us. And of the four great treatises still extant, the *Ascent of Mount Carmel, Dark Night, Spiritual Canticle* and *Living Flame of Love*, the *Ascent* and the *Night* are unfinished.[2] Despite these gaps and certain problems raised by them enough has been preserved of the saint's literary remains to supply us with material sufficient to answer our question.

His extant writings are based on St John's own most personal experiences during his imprisonment at Toledo. The bliss and torment of a heart visited and wounded by God are first expressed in

---

[1] *De divinis nominibus*, 2. 2; Migne, *PG*, 3. 640.
[2] We will not here discuss whether they remained unfinished or were mutilated later.

22

lyrical form in the thirty stanzas of the *Spiritual Canticle* which were written in prison. The poem on the *Dark Night*, commented on in the treatise bearing its name as well as in the *Ascent*, probably also owes its origin to his sufferings there. There are conflicting reports as to whether John *wrote* these canticles in prison or only *memorized* them; in any case, he communicated them to his friends after he had regained his freedom. He later wrote his commentaries on them at the request of his spiritual sons and daughters. In these expositions the experience of the poet is translated into the language of the philosopher and theologian, yet technical scholastic terms are used sparingly, and the work contains a wealth of living imagery. Moreover, the basis of experience is broadened: his own experience is supplemented by the knowledge he had gained in his work as director of souls. This prevents a one-sided presentation and too sweeping generalizations; St John always takes account of the great variety of spiritual experience and of the suppleness of grace guiding individual souls according to their special conditions. Finally, Holy Scripture is to him a constant source of instruction in the laws of the interior life, in which he finds his inspirations authoritatively confirmed. On the other hand, his own experience opens his eyes for the mystic significance of the sacred Books. The bold imagery of the Psalms, the parables of our Lord, even the historical narratives of the Old Testament—everything becomes transparent to him, giving him an ever richer and deeper insight into the one essential thing: the soul's way to God and God's workings in the soul.

God has created human souls for himself. He wants to unite them to himself and to give them even on earth the immeasurable fullness and ineffable bliss of his own divine life. This is the goal to which he directs them and to which they are meant to tend with all their might. But the road is narrow, the ascent steep and laborious, and most men fall by the way. Few pass beyond the first beginnings, a very small number reach the goal. This is due to the dangers of the road —dangers from the world, the devil and one's own nature—but also to ignorance and lack of suitable direction. Souls do not understand what is happening in them, and they rarely find someone capable of opening their eyes. John offers himself to them as an experienced guide. He has pity with those who go astray and it grieves him that God's work should fail before such obstacles. He is both willing and able to help, for he knows all the most hidden paths in the mysterious realm of the interior life. Indeed, he cannot say all he knows about it;

he must constantly restrain himself so as not to say more than his subject requires.

The saint certainly did not write for everybody. It is true, he would not exclude anyone. But he knows that he can be understood only by a special circle of readers who have already some experience in the inner life. He thinks in the first place of the Carmelite friars and nuns, whose special vocation is interior prayer. But he knows that God's grace is not confined by convent walls and the religious habit. In fact, we owe the *Living Flame of Love* to one of his spiritual daughters in the world. Hence he writes for contemplatives whom he wants to take by the hand at a definite point of their way: at the cross-roads where most of them are perplexed and know not what to do, because in the way they have so far pursued they are suddenly confronted by insuperable obstacles. On the other hand, the new way that opens before them leads through impenetrable darkness—who would be brave enough to enter on it? The two roads in question are those of meditation and contemplation. So far the hour of meditation has been devoted to exercising the powers of the soul, perhaps according to the Ignatian method: we have used our senses, our imagination, memory, understanding and will. But now these refuse to work; all efforts are in vain. The spiritual exercises, until then a source of interior joy, now become a torment, unbearably arid and ineffective. On the other hand, there is no inclination either to take interest in worldly things. The soul would like best to be quite still without moving, letting all its powers rest. But this seems sloth and waste of time. This, roughly, is the state of the soul which God wants to introduce into the "dark night". In ordinary Christian language such a state would be called a cross. It has been noted before that the "Cross" and the "Night" are related to each other. But the vague statement that there is a certain connexion between the two will not help us. In some passages of St John's writings the importance of the Cross is stated so emphatically that our conception of his life and doctrine as a science of the Cross would certainly be justified. But these passages are comparatively few. The leading symbol in his poems as well as in his treatises is not the Cross but the Night: it is certainly central in the *Ascent* and the *Night*; in the *Canticle* and the *Living Flame* (which mostly treat of the state beyond the night) it is still faintly present. Hence to understand the importance of the Cross for St John we must carefully investigate the relation between Cross and Night in his works.

§1. CROSS AND NIGHT (NIGHT OF THE SENSES)

1. DIFFERENCE IN THE CHARACTER OF THE SYMBOLS:
SIGN AND COSMIC EXPRESSION

The first question to be examined is whether Cross and Night are symbols in the same sense. The term symbol is used with several different meanings. Sometimes it is taken in a very wide sense, expressing anything perceived by the senses that signifies something spiritual, or anything known from natural experience that points to something unknown, perhaps even to something inaccessible to natural knowledge. In this wider sense Cross as well as Night can be called symbols. But if we pay attention to the difference between *sign* and *image* we shall become aware of a contrast. The image points to what is imaged because it is intrinsically similar to that; whoever sees the image is at once referred to the original which he either recognizes or comes to know through this image. On the other hand, there is no need for the sign and what it signifies to be related in this way; their relation is established by arbitrary agreement, which must be known if the sign is to be understood. Evidently the Cross is not an image in the real sense. (If it is called an image this means not much more than symbol in the sense just described.) There is no immediately obvious similarity between the Cross and suffering, and there is no arbitrarily established sign-relationship either. The Cross has acquired its meaning through an historical event. It is not a mere object of nature but an instrument, made and used by men for a certain purpose. As an instrument it has played an immensely important part in history. Everyone living within the Christian orbit knows something of this. Hence the visible shape of the Cross points directly to the wealth of meaning embodied in it. Thus it is a sign, but one whose meaning has not been arbitrarily fixed but truly belongs to it because of its efficacy and its history. Its visible shape points to the fullness of its meaning, hence it is truly a sign.

The Night, on the other hand, is a natural phenomenon; the opposite of light, it envelops us and all things. It is not an object in the true sense of the word: it does not stand over against us, nor does it stand upon itself. It is no image either, in so far as this implies a visible form. For the Night is invisible and formless. Yet we perceive it; indeed it is much nearer to us than all objects and forms, it is much more closely related to our being. Just as the light makes the things and their visible qualities stand out, so the night swallows them up and threatens to swallow us up, too. What is drowned in it is not just nothing: it continues to exist, but indistinctly, invisible and without form, as the night itself, or like a shadow or a ghost, hence it is threatening. At the same time our own being is not only outwardly imperilled by the dangers hidden in the night, it is also inwardly affected by it. The night deprives us of the use of our senses, it impedes our movements, paralyses our faculties; it condemns us to solitude and makes our own selves shadowy and ghostlike. It is a foretaste of death. And this has not only a natural, but also a psychological and spiritual significance. The cosmic night affects us in a similar way as what is called Night in a metaphorical sense. Or, conversely, what produces similar effects in us as the cosmic night is called Night metaphorically. Before trying to grasp what this is we must realize that even the cosmic night has a double aspect. The contrast of the dark and uncanny night is the gentle, magic night, flooded by the soft light of the moon. This night does not swallow up things, but lights up their nocturnal aspect. All that is hard, sharp and crude is now softened and smoothed; features which in the clear daylight never appear are now revealed; voices, too, are heard which the noise of the day tends to drown. And not only the luminous night, the dark night, too, has values of its own. It ends the noise and bustle of the day; it brings quiet and peace. All this has its effects also in the psychological and spiritual spheres. There is a nocturnal, gentle transparence of the spirit freed from the busy-ness of the day, relaxed but also collected, so that it can be drawn into the profound relationships of its own being and life, in the natural and the supernatural worlds. And there is a deep and grateful repose in the peace of the night. Of all this we should be aware if we would understand the night symbolism of St John of the Cross. We know from the testimonies of his life and from his poems that he was extremely sensitive to the cosmic night and all its nuances. He spent whole nights by the window or out of doors, looking out on the vast scenery. And he finds words to describe the beauty of the night unsurpassed by any of its poets (*Spiritual Canticle*, stanza 15).[1] The soul compares the Beloved with the Night:

La noche sosegada	Before the dawn comes round
En par de los levantes de la aurora,	Here is the night, dead-hushed with all its glamours,
La música callada,	The music without sound,
La soledad sonora,	The solitude that clamours,
La cena, que recrea y enamora.	The supper that revives us and enamours.

[1] Campbell, n. 2, p. 19.

When, in his treatises, John speaks of the night in the role of the thinker his words reflect the fullness of what it means to him as the poet and the man. We have tried to interpret the symbolic expression in a few words without thereby exhausting its meaning. Now we would attempt to grasp the content of the symbol which John has treated extensively and which we shall have to discuss in greater detail later on. For the moment a preliminary insight into the peculiar symbolic relationship must suffice. The mystic night must not be given a cosmic meaning. It does not invade us from without but arises in the interior of the soul and assails only the particular soul in which it appears. Nevertheless, the effects it produces in this soul are similar to those of the cosmic night: it effaces the outside world, even though this may be flooded with daylight. It makes the soul solitary, arid and empty, renders its powers incapable of acting and frightens it by the threatening terrors it conceals. Yet here, too, there is a nocturnal light opening up a new world in the interior and illuminating, as it were, the outside world from within, so that it is given back to us completely changed.

We would now elucidate the relation between the cosmic and the mystic night as much as possible from what has so far been said. Here we have evidently not to do with an externally established sign, nor with an historical relationship as in the case of the sign of the Cross. There is, on the contrary, a far-reaching agreement in the contents of both "nights" allowing us to call the natural and the spiritual phenomenon by the same name. Speaking of the *image* of the night, this means that the term belongs in the first place to the cosmic night, from which it is transferred to the mystic night in order to explain something unknown and difficult by something similar, but familiar. There is, however, no image-relationship, for one is not modelled on the other. We may rather think of a symbolic relationship such as exists between sensible and spiritual realities, just as facial expression reflects character, and nature may reveal spiritual and even divine things. There is an original communication and an objective relationship between the two, enabling the sense world to lead to the knowledge of spiritual things. All that remains of the image-relationship is the similarity, though what is "equal" in both cannot properly be grasped but only hinted at by certain analogical features. What distinguishes this from the image-relation is not only the lack of an image properly so called, but also the fact that we are not here concerned with definitely circumscribed shapes and forms. Hence there is also a contrast to mimic expression, meaning that a certain psychological change corresponds to a change in the expression of the face which an artist can reproduce. On the other hand, the night, whether the cosmic or the mystic one, is something formless and comprehensive, the fullness of whose meaning can only be hinted at, but not exhausted. It includes a whole view of the world and a state of existence, and this is the factor that is common to both. In both the natural and the mystical night there is something that cannot be grasped; yet one can be compared with the other and used to make the other accessible, not by an arbitrarily chosen comparison but in a symbolic experience that penetrates to primeval relationships and is thus capable of expressing the ineffable in an adequate image.

So we are now able to summarize the difference in the symbolic character of Cross and Night: the Cross is a sign of all that is causally and historically related to the Cross of Christ; the Night is the necessary cosmic expression of the mystic world-view of St John of the Cross. The prevalence of the Night-symbol in his works is a sign that he speaks pre-eminently as a poet and mystic, not as a theologian, though the theologian carefully supervises thought and expression.

2. THE SONG OF THE DARK NIGHT

We will now examine the mystic Night to show how it echoes the message of the Cross. Our point of departure will be the *Canticle of the Dark Night*, since the two great treatises on the mystic Night are based on that.[1]

NOCHE OSCURA	DARK NIGHT
I	I
En una noche oscura,	Upon a gloomy night,
Con ansias en amores inflamada,	With all my cares to loving ardours flushed,
Oh dichosa ventura!	(O venture of delight!)
Salí sin ser notada,	With nobody in sight
Estando ya mi casa sosegada.	I went abroad when all my house was hushed.
II	II
A escuras, y segura,	In safety, in disguise,
Por la secreta escala disfrazada	In darkness up the secret stair I crept,
Oh dichosa ventura!	(O happy enterprise)
A escuras, y en celada,	Concealed from other eyes
Estando ya mi casa sosegada.	When all my house at length in silence slept.

[1] Campbell, n. 1.

III

En la noche dichosa
En secreto, que nadie me veía,
Ni yo miraba cosa,
Sin otra luz, ni guia,
Sino la que en el corazón ardía.

III

Upon that lucky night
In secrecy, inscrutable to sight,
I went without discerning
And with no other light
Except for that which in my heart
    was burning.

IV

Aquesta me guiaba
Más cierto que la luz del mediodía,
A donde me esperaba
Quien yo bien me sabía,
En parte donde nadie parecía.

IV

It lit and led me through
More certain than the light of noon-
    day clear
To where One waited near
Whose presence well I knew,
There where no other presence
    might appear.

V

Oh noche, que guiaste,
Oh noche amable más que el
    alborada,
Oh noche, que juntaste
Amado con amada,
Amada en el Amado trasformada!

V

Oh night that was my guide!
Oh darkness dearer than the morn-
    ing's pride,
Oh night that joined the lover
To the beloved bride
Transfiguring them each into the
    other.

VI

En mi pecho florido,
Que entero para él sólo se guardaba,
Allí quedó dormido,
Y yo le regalaba,
Y el ventalle de cedros aire daba.

VI

Within my flowering breast
Which only for himself entire I save
He sank into his rest
And all my gifts I gave
Lulled by the airs with which the
    cedars wave.

VII

El aire del almena,
Cuando ya sus cabellos esparcía,
Con su mano serena
En mi cuello hería,
Y todos mis sentidos suspendía.

VII

Over the ramparts fanned
While the fresh wind was fluttering
    his tresses,
With his serenest hand
My neck he wounded, and
Suspended every sense with its
    caresses.

VIII

Quedéme, y olvidéme,
El rostro recliné sobre el Amado,
Cesó todo, y dejéme,
Dejando mi cuidado
Entre las azucenas olvidado.

VIII

Lost to myself I stayed
My face upon my lover having laid
From all endeavour ceasing:
And all my cares releasing
Threw them amongst the lilies there
to fade.

3. THE DARK NIGHT OF THE SENSES

(a) Introduction to the Meaning of the Night

The poetic metaphor is sustained throughout, uninterrupted by any didactic explanation. But the two explanatory treatises, the *Ascent* and the *Dark Night*, give the clue to its meaning.

The soul that sings the Canticle has passed through the night and reached the goal of union with its divine Spouse; hence it praises the night that has become the way to its happiness. The joyous exclamation "O venture of delight" is reiterated. Yet darkness and fear are not forgotten; they can still be revived by the memory.

The house the bride has left is the sensual part of the soul.[1] It is at rest, because all its desires have been silenced. The soul could leave them behind only because God himself freed it from them, it could not have done so by its own power. This brief explanation indicates the difference between active and passive night and their mutual relationship, which will later be treated in greater detail. The soul must indeed strive with all its energy to be delivered from the fetters of its own sensual nature, but God must help it—more, "prevent" it with his own action: his initiative inspires and perfects the action of the soul.

Detachment is described as a night through which the soul must pass. It is such as regards the point of departure as well as the way and the goal. At the start the soul must renounce its desire for the things of this world. Since this renunciation places it as it were in darkness and nothingness it is called night. The world we perceive with our senses is naturally the firm ground that carries us, the house where we feel at home, where we are fed and provided with all we need; it is the source of our joys and pleasures. If it is taken away from us, or if we are compelled to leave it, it is truly as if the ground were cut away from under our feet, as if we were immersed in night and ourselves about to drown and vanish. But this is not really so. We are actually led in a safe way, though it is dark and shrouded in night.

---

[1] *Ascent,* I. I.

This is the way of faith, which is a way because it leads to the goal of union, but a way through the night, because compared with the clear insight of natural reason the knowledge of faith is dark: it makes us acquainted with something, but we cannot see this. Hence the goal we attain by the way of faith is also night: as long as we are on earth God remains hidden from us even in the most blissful union. Because our spiritual eye is not adapted to his too radiant light it seems to look into the darkness of night. But just as the cosmic night is not equally dark throughout, so the mystical night, too, has its periods with their corresponding degrees of darkness. When first the world of sense is drowned this is like the beginning of the night, dusk after daylight. Faith, on the other hand, is midnight darkness, because it takes away not only the activity of the senses, but also the natural knowledge of reason. But when the soul finds God, it is as if the dawn of the new day of eternity were already breaking into its night.

Even this brief survey might to a certain extent elucidate the relationship between Night and Cross; but this will become even clearer if we now consider the phases of the Night in detail.

(b) The Active Night as the Imitation of the Cross

St John of the Cross calls the beginning or the first part the *Dark Night of the Senses*.[1] At this stage it is most important to mortify the joy in desiring anything whatsoever. This, of course, does not mean that we should no longer perceive things with our senses; for they are the windows through which the light of knowledge penetrates the prison darkness of our bodily life. Hence they cannot be discarded as long as this life lasts. But we must learn to see, hear and so forth as if we did not see and hear; that is to say our fundamental attitude to the world of sense must change. For the natural man this attitude is normally not merely intellectual: he lives in the world as a man of action, desiring many things. He is tied to the world by a thousand bonds, because it offers him the satisfaction of his desires, urges him to action and itself provides scope for this. Man's activities are generally determined by his desires, which concern food and clothing, work and rest, play and recreation or intercourse with others. He is happy and contented as long as he does not meet inordinate obstacles. We stress the qualification "inordinate", because he will normally be aware from his youth that a life quite without

---

[1] It is treated in the First Book of the *Ascent of Mount Carmel*, being the first part of the Dark Night.

restrictions is impossible in this world. He knows by education and experience that unbridled indulgence of all his instincts is bad for his own nature, so that even common sense prescribes some voluntary restraint and orderliness in his life. Regard for others points in the same direction, for without restrictions life in community would be impossible; moreover, they are also enjoined by natural and moral law. This self-control does not interfere with the natural rights of the instincts except that they are harmonized with other rights. With the beginning of the Dark Night, however, something quite new enters a man's life. He had been comfortably at home in the world, relished its enjoyments, desired them and indulged this desire. Now all this, which to the natural man means living in the bright light of day, is darkness[1] in the eye of God and incompatible with the divine Light. If the soul is to have room for God all these dark desires must be pulled up by the roots. To meet this demand means to fight one's own nature along the whole line, to take up the Cross and let oneself be crucified. In this connexion St John mentions our Lord's words: "He who does not renounce all he possesses (by desire) cannot be my disciple" (Lk. 14. 33). He proves in detail that when the soul is dominated by its desires it is truly in darkness, for it is fatigued and tormented, darkened, defiled and weakened by them. The desires deprive the soul of the Spirit of God from whom it turns away when it surrenders to the animal spirit. To engage in battle with one's desires or to take up one's Cross means actively to enter into the Dark Night. The saint gives some brief instructions for this of which he says himself: "One who sincerely desires to train himself in these will need no others, since he will have all in these." They are:

"(1) Always desire to imitate Christ in all things and to model your life on His. Therefore you must meditate on it, so that you will be able to imitate it and to behave in all things as He would behave.

"(2) In order to accomplish this well you must renounce every enjoyment offered to your senses and cast it from you, unless it be solely for the honour and glory of God.

"And this you are to do for love of Jesus, who knew no other joy and desire in His life than to accomplish the will of His Father. This He called His meat and food. If, for example, you are offered a pleasure by listening to things that do not contribute to the service of God,

---

[1] This darkness, which is caused by sin, is quite different from the darkness that has its origin in God and causes the other darkness to vanish.

you ought to have neither pleasure in it nor want to hear them. . . .
In the same way practise renunciation with regard to all your senses
if you can easily reject their impressions. For if this is not possible
it suffices for you not to have any pleasure if these things approach
you. Be also careful to mortify your senses and preserve them
untouched by this pleasure. Then they will be, as it were, in darkness
and you will make great progress in a short time.

"The following maxims may serve as effective means for mortifying
and harmoniously ordering the four natural passions of joy, hope,
fear and grief. For where these passions are calmed and well ordered,
the good things mentioned above will thrive greatly as well as many
others. Hence these maxims are very valuable and the root of great
virtues. Strive always to direct your inclination:
—Not to what is easier, but to what is more difficult,
—not to what is more pleasant, but to what is unpleasant,
—not to what gives you more joy, but to what gives you less,
—not to what brings you consolation, but to what makes you dis-
consolate,
—not unto rest, but unto weariness,
—not to the more, but to the less,
—not to what is brighter and more precious, but to the lowly and
unnoticed,
—not to what wants to be something, but to what wants to be nothing,
—Do not seek the better in things but the worse. Desire for Christ's
sake to enter into complete detachment and freedom and poverty of
all there is in the world. These works you shall embrace with all your
heart and strive to subject your will to them. . . . If what we have
said be truly practised it will suffice to introduce a man into the Night
of the Senses. . . ." [1]

We need not explain any further that the Dark Night of the Senses
is identified with the willing carrying of the Cross. But this does not
cause death, and to traverse the night completely a man must die to
sin. He can surrender himself to crucifixion, but he cannot crucify
himself. Hence what has been begun in the active Night must be perfected by the passive Night, that is, by God himself. "However much
the soul may try, it cannot purify itself by its own effort so effectively
as to be in the least prepared for the perfect union of love with God,
unless He takes it into His hand and purifies it in that dark fire. . . ." [2]

---

[1] *Ascent*, I. 13.   [2] *Dark Night*, Night of Sense, 3. 3.

(c) *The Passive Night as a Crucifixion*

It has been mentioned above that the soul can actively enter into the Dark Night only because God's grace prevents, draws and supports it throughout. But in the case of beginners this preventing and assisting grace has not yet the character of the Dark Night. On the contrary, God treats them as a tender mother treats her small children whom she carries in her arms and feeds with sweet milk: in all their spiritual practices, in prayer, meditation and mortifications they receive much joy and consolation, this joy becomes their motive for devoting themselves to these spiritual practices. They do not realize how imperfect this is and how many faults they commit in their virtuous exercises. The saint shows by vivid examples that beginners commit all the seven capital sins transposed into the spiritual sphere: spiritual pride that delights in its own graces and virtues, despises others and instructs rather than accepts instruction; spiritual avarice can never have enough books, crucifixes, rosaries, etc.[1] To be freed from all these defects we must be weaned from the milk of consolations and be nourished on solid food. "When they have exercised themselves for some time in the way of virtue, been faithful to meditation and prayer and freed themselves, through the sweetness and enjoyment they have found in this, from attachment and love for the things of this world, they have at last gained some spiritual strength in God by which they are able to hold in check the desire for creatures and endure some hardships and aridities without longing for that better time when they felt more taste and enjoyment in spiritual practices. . . . Then God turns all this light into darkness, shuts the door and blocks up the source of the sweet waters of the spirit from which they had till then drunk whenever they wanted. . . . Now . . . He places them in darkness, so that they do not know where to turn with their imagination and their thoughts."[2] All pious exercises seem tasteless, even repulsive. Three signs show that this is not due to sins and imperfections but to the purifying dryness of the Dark Night:

(1) The soul no longer has any joy in creatures;

(2) it "thinks of God with painful anxiety and care and believes it does not serve Him properly and that it goes back, because it does not find any pleasure in divine things".[3] For it would not worry about this if its dryness were due to tepidity. In the purgative aridity, however, a man always desires to serve God. And the spirit grows

---

[1] *Ibid.*, ch. 2.   [2] *Ibid.*, ch. 8.   [3] *Ibid.*, 9. 3.

strong, while the sensual part feels limp and weak for lack of enjoyment. "God is transferring the good things and powers of the sensual part to the spirit, and since sensuality and natural power cannot receive them they suffer privation, remaining dry and empty. For man's sensual part is not capable of receiving the things of the spirit. Hence, when the spirit is finding enjoyment, the flesh feels disgust and is slow to act. The spirit that is being fed at the same time becomes far stronger, more vigilant and circumspect than before so as not to be remiss in the service of God."[1] But, as it is not yet used to purely spiritual sweetness it feels at first nothing of this but only aridity and displeasure;

(3) The purifying aridity is recognized by this, that "the soul can no longer meditate and reflect nor use the interior sense of the imagination despite all its efforts. . . . In this state God no longer communicates Himself through the senses, as He had done before by means of inquiring reflexion . . . but He has now begun to communicate Himself by means of pure spirit, where there is no longer a sequence of thoughts, in an act of simple contemplation for which neither the inner nor the outer senses of the natural man have any capacity." This dark contemplation that is arid for the sensual man is "something hidden and mysterious even for him who possesses it. . . ."[2] It usually communicates to the soul "an inclination and longing for solitude and repose, without its being either capable or even desirous of thinking of anything definite".[3] If souls were now to be quiet "they would soon find that most delightful interior refreshment in this repose and forgetfulness of all things. For this refreshment is so delicate that the soul normally does not feel it if it desires it inordinately or is particularly anxious to enjoy it. . . . It is like the air which disappears as soon as one tries to catch it with one's hands. . . . In this state God treats the soul in such a wise and leads it in such a peculiar way that if it would attempt to do the work of God by its own strength and power it would hinder rather than further it." The peace God wants to give to the soul through the aridity of the sensual man is "spiritual and exceedingly delightful", and "its action is tranquil, delicate, still, satisfying and peaceful, quite different from the earlier enjoyments which were more strongly felt by the senses".[4] Thus it is understandable that only the dying of the sensual man is felt, but not the beginning of a new life hidden in this death.

It is no exaggeration to call the sufferings of souls in this state a

---

[1] *Ibid.*, 9. 4.   [2] *Ibid.*, 9. 8.   [3] *Ibid.*, 9. 6.   [4] *Ibid.*, 9. 7.

crucifixion. In their inability to use their faculties they feel as if held by nails. The aridity is aggravated by the fear of being on the wrong track. "They live in the belief of having lost all spiritual good things and being abandoned by God." They strive to be active as formerly but can do nothing in this way and only disturb the peace God wants to produce in them. They should now do nothing else but "keep patience and persevere in prayer without any activity; here they are only asked to preserve their soul free and unhindered by any knowledge or thought, but in peace, without worrying what they should think and consider. It is enough for them to remain in a quiet and loving attention to God and to discard all anxiety, activity and any undue desire to sense and taste God." Instead of which, left without expert guidance, they labour in vain and perhaps even torture themselves with the idea that they should rather give up prayer because they are wasting their time. If they would quietly surrender themselves to this dark contemplation they would soon realize the "loving ardours" expressed in the second line of the *Canticle of the Dark Night*. "For contemplation is nothing else but a secret, peaceful and loving infusion of God which, if it be not hindered, inflames the soul with the spirit of love." [1] In the beginning this kindling of love is normally not perceived at all. The soul, rather, feels only aridity and emptiness, painful anxiety and fear. And if it should feel something of love, this is a painful longing for God, an aching wound of love. Only later will it realize that God wanted to purify it by the night of the senses and to subject them to the spirit. Then it will exclaim: "O venture of delight!" and it will recognize that this unobserved escape was actually a great gain: it freed the soul from the slavery in which it was held by the senses, gradually detached its inclination from the creatures and turned it towards eternal things. The "Night of Sense" was the "narrow gate" (Matt. 7. 14) leading to life. Now the soul is to walk in the narrow way of the "Night of the Spirit". Few, however, advance so far, but even the advantages of the first Night are very great: the soul gains in self-knowledge, it realizes its own misery, finds nothing good in itself and thus learns to approach God with greater reverence. Only now does it become aware of the greatness and majesty of God. The freedom from all sensual supports enables it to receive illuminations and to become receptive to truth. Therefore it says in the Psalm "In the desert land, waterless, dry and pathless, I appeared before thee, that I might see thy glory" (Ps. 62. 3). The

---

[1] *Ibid.*, 10. 6.

singer means to convey "that not the many spiritual joys and pleasures
. . . were the preparation and means to the knowledge of the glory of
God but the dryness and detachment of the sensual man".[1] By
"desert land" John understands the inability to form a concept of
God by discursive thought or to make progress by considerations
supported by the imagination.

In dryness and emptiness the soul also grows humble. Pride must
needs disappear if a man finds nothing in himself that might cause him
to look down on others; on the contrary, the others will now seem
much more perfect to him, and he will begin to love and esteem them.
At this time a man is also too much concerned with his own misery
to take much notice of others. Because the soul is helpless it becomes
submissive and obedient; it desires to be instructed in order to gain
the right road. It is thoroughly cured of spiritual avarice; if a man no
longer enjoys any spiritual practices he grows very temperate, doing
everything purely for God without seeking his own satisfaction. It is
the same with all other imperfections. They disappear, and with them
all trouble and unrest. Instead, there will be profound peace and the
constant remembrance of God. The only care left is not to displease
him. The dark night becomes the school of all virtues. To remain
faithful to the spiritual life without finding consolation and refreshment in it is a training in resignation and patience. Thus the soul
attains to a pure love of God, acting solely for his sake. It gains fortitude by persevering in all adversities, and the perfect purification from
all sensual inclinations and desires leads it to the freedom of the spirit
in which the Twelve Fruits of the Holy Spirit are brought to maturity.
This purification protects the soul from its three enemies, the world, the
flesh and the devil, which are powerless against the Spirit. The soul has
gone forth "with nobody in sight". And now, as the passions are calmed
and sensuality has been put to sleep by aridity, all its house is hushed.

The soul has escaped and reached the way of the spirit, which is
also called the way of proficients or illuminative way, where God
wants to instruct it himself without its own activity. Now the soul is
in a state of transition; contemplation gives it purely spiritual joys
in which the purified senses also begin to share. But sometimes it still
returns to meditation. Joy, too, alternates with painful trials. Before
the Night of the Spirit begins, aridity and emptiness are aggravated
by distressing trials and agonizing temptations: the imagination is
seized by the spirit of impurity and blasphemy; a spirit of vertigo

[1] *Ibid.*, 12. 6.

attacks the soul, casting it into a welter of scruples and perplexity. In these storms the soul is to be tried and hardened. But not all men are tried with equal severity; many never pass beyond this transition state at all. Those, however, who are destined to reach the goal must suffer much. The higher the degree of union to which God wants to lead them, the more thorough and lengthy will be the purification. For even the proficients are still full of many habitual imperfections from which they must be freed in the Night of the Spirit. The senses, too, are perfectly purged only together with the spirit, for there are the roots of their imperfections.[1]

The description of the purgative way clearly shows that this night is not without light, even though the eyes of the soul cannot see it, because they are not yet adapted to it. In his comparatively short discussion of the Night of the Senses St John of the Cross strongly emphasizes its precious fruits. But this manner of treatment is not opposed to the message of the Cross. As has been mentioned before, when our Lord foretold his suffering and death on the Cross he added to it the joyful prophecy of his Resurrection. According to the Liturgy of the Church the way leads *per passionem et crucem ad resurrectionis gloriam*. The sensual man dies as the spiritual man develops. But this marvellous new birth has so far only been hinted at. St John described the Night of the Senses only briefly, because he was anxious to come to his main subject, the Night of the Spirit. Hence the relation between death and resurrection will be treated only after the Dark Night of the Spirit.

§2. SPIRIT AND FAITH. DEATH AND RESURRECTION (NIGHT OF THE SPIRIT)

INTRODUCTION: DEVELOPMENT OF THE QUESTIONS

St John of the Cross has described the Night of the Spirit as the narrow way. Now he had earlier written that faith is the way, and its darkness that of midnight. Hence faith must play a dominant part in the Night of the Spirit, and this necessitates a discussion of what the saint means by spirit and by faith. This is no easy task, for though all his works presuppose an ontology of the spirit, he has written no treatise on this; perhaps he may not even have attempted to form a theory of his habitual knowledge of the subject, which determined his occasional utterances. He is even less likely to have examined the

---

[1] Cf. *Night of the Spirit*, ch. 3.

sources of this knowledge. This was irrelevant to the object he had in view. For us, too, it would be too much of a digression to pursue this important question. But we cannot by-pass the objective questions as to what John meant by spirit and by faith. These must be answered on the basis of what he says about the Night of the Spirit, despite a certain difficulty arising from the fact that the Dark Night has been treated twice, in the *Ascent* and in the *Night*, and that both parts are incomplete.

I. THE STRIPPING OF THE FACULTIES IN THE ACTIVE NIGHT

(a) *The Night of Faith as the Way to Union*

The second Night is darker than the first, because the latter only affects the lower, sensual part of man and is therefore more external. The night of faith, on the other hand, touches the higher, rational part, hence it is interior, depriving the soul of the light of reason and blinding it.

"The theologians call faith a certain, but obscure, lasting habit of the soul"; obscure, because "it invites the soul to believe the truths revealed by God Himself, which are above all natural light and exceed human reason beyond all proportion. Hence it is that this excessively bright light which the soul receives in faith becomes deep darkness for it, since the greater deprives and conquers the lesser." "Thus the light of faith devours and conquers by its excessive strength the light of our reason, which by itself extends only to natural knowledge." [1] It can, however, be rendered receptive to supernatural things if God wants to raise it to supernatural knowledge. Left to itself reason can gain only natural knowledge by the means that are natural to it; that is, through the senses that present it with an object. "Then it must retain the conceptions and impressions of objects, either as they are or in similes." [2] If one speaks to a man of something he has never seen, and if he knows nothing similar that could help him, he will indeed be able to grasp the name but will never form an idea of the thing, as a man born blind does not know what colour is. We are in a similar condition with regard to faith. It tells us of things we have never heard or seen; nor do we know anything resembling them. We can accept what we are told only by eliminating the light of our natural knowledge. We must consent to what we hear without its being introduced

[1] *Ascent*, 2. 3. 1.   [2] *Ibid.*, 2. 3. 2.

to us by one of our senses. Hence faith is a completely dark night to the soul. But for this very reason it gives it light: a knowledge of absolute certainty surpassing every other knowledge and science, so that only perfect contemplation will produce the right conception of faith. Hence it is said: *Si non credideritis, non intelligetis* (If ye believe not, ye shall not understand. Is. 7. 9).[1]

So faith is not only a dark night but also a way to the goal the soul desires, that is, union with God. For faith alone gives us knowledge of God. And how could we be united to God without knowing him? But if faith is to lead it to its goal the soul must conduct itself in the proper way. It must enter the night of faith willingly and with full consent. Having renounced all desire for creatures in the Night of the Senses, it must now die to its natural powers and senses and even to its reason in order to reach God. To attain to the supernatural transformation it must leave behind all natural activities; more, it must renounce even the supernatural good things if God grants them. It must detach itself from everything within the sphere of its natural powers. "It must remain in darkness like a blind man, leaning upon dark faith and choosing it as its light and guide, leaning on nothing it understands or enjoys or feels or imagines. For all this is darkness leading it astray or holding it up. Faith, however, is above all such understanding, enjoyment, feeling and imagining." [2] If the soul would attain to what faith teaches it must become and remain completely blind to all these things. For if a man is not yet quite blind he will not willingly let himself be led by a guide, but will still trust in what he sees himself. "Thus it is also with the soul. If it relies on what itself knows, enjoys or feels of God . . . it may easily stray or stand still on this way, because it does not surrender blindly to faith, which is its true guide." In order to reach union with God we must "simply believe in the Being of God, which is not a matter of reason or will or imagination nor of any other sense; for in this life one cannot grasp what God is. Even if we may here have the most exalted impressions of God or know or enjoy Him, this is yet infinitely far from what God really is and from the pure possession of God." If the soul desires to "be completely united in this life by grace to Him with whom it is to be united through glory in the next, as, according to St Paul, 'eye hath not seen nor ear heard neither hath it entered into the heart of man'" (1 Cor. 2. 9; Is. 64. 4), then it must "become, as far as possible, completely insensible to all that can enter by the eye,

<hr>

[1] *Ibid.*, 2. 3. 4.   [2] *Ibid.*, 2. 4. 2.

be perceived by the ear, conceived by the imagination and grasped by the heart; the heart here meaning the soul".[1] If it still relies on its own powers it will only place obstacles in its way. Its goal can be reached only by leaving its own and entering the true way. Indeed, "to strive for the goal and to leave one's own way is to arrive at that goal which has no way, that is God. For the soul that has reached this state no longer knows ways and modes, nor does it cling to them. Indeed, it cannot even cling to them", to any special way of understanding, tasting or feeling: "It now possesses all modes at the same time, as one possessing nothing yet possessing all things." By leaving its natural limits both interiorly and exteriorly, the soul "enters without limits into the supernatural which knows neither kind nor mode, because it possesses all kinds in its essence". The soul must rise above everything intellectual and spiritual that can be known and understood naturally, also above that which can be tasted and felt by the senses in this life. The more highly the soul still esteems this the farther it is from the highest good. But if it despises all this in comparison with the highest good, then "the soul in darkness mightily approaches union through faith".[2]

For a better understanding the saint here inserts a brief explanation of what he means by union: this is not the substantial union of God with all things, by which they are kept in being, but a "union and transformation of the soul in God through love". Unlike the former, this union is not permanent but is established only "when the will of the soul and the will of God are merged into one, so that there is nothing in the one that would resist the other. Hence, if the soul "is so completely stripped of all that is opposed to the divine will and is conformed to it, it is transformed into God by love. By this we not only understand every single action that is opposed to the divine will, but also every habit contrary to Him. . . . And because no creature and nothing a creature can achieve reaches the essence of God or corresponds to Him, the soul must rid itself of every creature and of all its works and faculties. . . . Only in this way does the transformation in God come to pass." It is true, the divine light already dwells in the soul in a natural manner; but only if for the sake of God it rids itself of all that is not God—and love means just this—can it be enlightened and transformed into God. "Then God communicates to it His own supernatural Being so that itself seems to be God and calls

---

[1] *Ibid.*, 2. 4. 4.   [2] *Ibid.*, 2. 4. 5f.

its own what is God's." The union goes so far "that in this communication and transformation all that belongs to God and the soul becomes one. Thus the soul seems to be God rather than the soul." It is God by participation, but despite the transformation it retains "its natural being that is so totally different from the divine Being".[1]

(b) The Stripping of the Faculties as the Way of the Cross and Death on the Cross

The stripping needed for this transforming union is effected in the understanding by faith, in the memory by hope, and in the will by love. As has been seen, faith gives the understanding a certain but obscure knowledge. It presents God as inaccessible light, as incomprehensible and infinite, before whom all natural powers fail. Thus reason is reduced to its own nothingness: it realizes its own impotence and God's greatness. Hope empties the memory, since through it the latter is occupied with something not yet possessed. "For how can a man hope for what he already sees fulfilled?" (Rom. 8. 24). It teaches us to hope all things from God and nothing from ourselves and other creatures; to expect unending beatitude from him and for this end to renounce all enjoyment and possession in this life. Finally, love frees the will from all things, since it is our duty to love God above all. This, however, we can do only when we have given up the desire for any creature. This way of total renunciation had already been interpreted as the narrow way found only by the few (Matt. 7. 14). This is the way that leads to the high mountain of perfection in which a man can walk only if he be not dragged down by any burden. It is the way of the Cross our Lord showed to his disciples: "If any man will follow me, let him deny himself and take up his Cross and follow me. For whosoever will save his life shall lose it; and whosoever shall lose his life for my sake . . . shall save it" (Mark 8. 34f). In these words Christ demands not only some retirement and improvement here and there; a little more prayer and some mortification combined with enjoyment or consolations and spiritual sweetness. Those who are content with this flee "as from death itself" "as soon as they meet some solid perfection that consists in being deprived of all sweetness in God, in aridity, distaste and labour. This is the purely spiritual Cross, the detachment of poverty in the spirit of Christ." The other

[1] *Ibid.*, 2. 5.

attitude is "nothing else but seeking oneself in God . . . the direct opposite of love. To seek oneself in God means to seek only gifts and enjoyments in God. . . . To seek God in Himself does not mean only to give up both for love of God, but to be joyfully prepared for Christ's sake to choose just that which is tasteless both as to God and to the world: this is love of God."[1] To hate his soul, and thus to save it, means for Christ's sake to renounce "whatever the will may desire and enjoy, and to retain only what tastes of the Cross. . . ." To drink the chalice with the Lord (Matt. 20. 22) means to die to nature, in matters of sense as well as spiritually. Only thus can one ascend by the narrow way. "For here there is only renunciation . . . and the Cross. This is the staff on which one leans and which makes progress much easier. Hence the Lord says in St Matthew: 'My yoke is sweet and my burden light' (11. 30). Now this burden is the Cross. For as soon as a man resolves to take upon himself the Cross, that is in all things only to seek and joyfully to accept trials, he will actually find in all things great relief and sweetness and will walk in this complete detachment from all things without wanting anything. But as soon as he is selfishly attached to anything, whether it be divine or earthly, he is no longer detached from all things. Hence he will not be able to walk and progress along this narrow path." Spiritual souls should realize "that this way to God does not consist in many meditations or in particular exercises nor in delightful feelings . . . but in the one thing necessary . . . seriously to deny oneself both interiorly and exteriorly, to be ready to suffer for the sake of Christ and to die to oneself in all things. If a man trains himself in this . . . he will achieve and find in it all and more than all. If, on the other hand, one is remiss in this practice . . . all other virtuous exercises are nothing but wandering about in a maze that does not help towards any progress, even though such souls may make the most exalted meditations and have angelic communications with God." Christ is our way. All depends on understanding how we should walk after his example. "In the first place: there is no doubt that He died to sense spiritually throughout His life and naturally at His death. For, as He said himself, He had nowhere in life to lay His head (Matt. 8. 20). In death He had even less. Secondly, it is certain that at the moment of His death He was interiorly wholly abandoned, indeed, as it were, annihilated, since His Father left Him without any consolation and relief, hence in the utmost aridity. Therefore He cried out on the Cross: 'My

[1] *Ibid.*, 2. 7.

God, my God, why hast thou forsaken me?' (Matt. 27. 46). This was probably the greatest desolation He had to endure in His life as to sense. But just then He accomplished also a greater work than throughout His whole life with all its signs and miracles . . . the reconciliation and union of mankind with God through grace. And this happened at the moment when the Lord was most annihilated in all things . . . in the esteem of men, for when they saw Him dying on the Cross they mocked Him; according to nature, for it was completely annihilated through death; in the help and comfort from His Father, for at that moment He left Him without any help, so that He should pay the debt and unite man with God by being so completely detached and, as it were, destroyed and annihilated. . . . From this a truly spiritual soul should learn to understand the mystery of Christ as the door and way to union with God and realize that it unites itself the more intimately to God and accomplishes a greater work the more it annihilates itself in matters of sense as well as of spirit for the sake of God. When it is reduced to nothing in the most profound humiliation, then the spiritual union with God comes to pass, which is the highest stage the soul can reach on this earth. Hence this does not consist in spiritual refreshment, delights and feelings, but in a living death on the Cross according to sense as well as to spirit, externally as well as internally." [1]

(c) Creatures no Means to Union. Insufficiency of Natural and Supernatural Knowledge

Here we are at the heart of St John's message. He speaks of the great truth he has found and which he was sent to proclaim: our goal is union with God; our way, the crucified Christ with whom we are to be united on the Cross. The only adequate means to achieve this is faith. This is now proved by showing that there is no other way to bring it about, whether in the concrete or in the abstract sphere. For only that can be a means to union with God "which brings man into contact with God and has the greatest conformity with God". No created thing fulfils these conditions. It is true, all creatures have a certain relation to God and bear traces of him. "Yet there is no relation, no essential similarity between God and creatures. The distance between His divine Being and their being is infinite. Hence it is also impossible for the understanding wholly to penetrate into

[1] *Ibid.*, 2. 7.

God by means of creatures, be they heavenly or earthly. . . ." Even angels and saints are so far from the divine essence that the understanding cannot fully attain to God through them. This is true of all "the imagination can imagine and the understanding can grasp in this life".[1] Reason apprehends the natural world only through the forms and images perceived by the senses, but these do not lead a man to God. And even intimations of the supernatural world that are accessible to him on earth cannot help him to gain an exact knowledge of God. Hence reason cannot form an adequate idea of God by its understanding, memory cannot with the help of the imagination fashion forms and images that could reflect God; the will cannot taste a joy and bliss equal to that which God is in himself. Therefore, in order to attain to God one must "strive rather . . . not to understand than to understand, rather to become blind and be in darkness . . . than to open one's eyes". For this reason the Areopagite calls contemplation mystical theology, i.e. a secret knowledge of God and "a ray of darkness".[2]

As we already know, the darkness that leads to God is faith. It is the only means leading to union, for it presents God to us as he is: as the infinite, Triune One. Faith resembles God in that it blinds human reason and appears to it as darkness. "Hence the more faith a soul has, the more intimately it is united to God." Scripture indicates the darkness of God by the image of the cloud that veiled him in the revelations of the Old Testament, before Moses on the mountain[3] and in the Temple of Solomon.[4] This darkness hides the light of truth which will shine forth unveiled only when faith and life will end together.[5] But as long as we live on earth we can rely only on faith. Faith gives us contemplation, which is a dark and general knowledge; it is opposed not only to the natural activity of our reason but also to the diverse modes by which reason can receive separate and distinctly comprehensible forms of supernatural knowledge, such as visions, revelations, locutions and spiritual apprehensions. The bodily eyes may see forms from the other world such as angels, saints, or also some extraordinary brightness. A person may hear unusual words, smell sweet perfumes, enjoy sensible tastes or feel delightful touches. He should reject all this without examining whether it be good or evil. For God communicates himself to the spirit rather than to the senses; the soul is more secure and makes

---

[1] *Ascent*, 2. 8.   [2] *Mystical Theology*, 1. 1; *Ascent*, 2. 8.
[3] Exod. 19. 9, 16 and 24. 15f.   [4] 3 Kings 8.10–12.   [5] *Ascent*, 2. 9.

greater progress in the former, whereas experiences communicated to the senses are normally very dangerous. For in that case the senses would presume to judge spiritual things, whereas they are as ignorant of these as a donkey is of matters of reason. Here the devil, too, can easily practise deceit, because he can influence the senses. And even if visions are from God they are the less profitable to the spirit the more external they are; they nourish the spirit of prayer less and give the impression that they are more important and more apt to lead to God than faith. They also tempt the soul to have a high opinion of itself. Hence the devil likes to make use of them to harm souls. For all these reasons it is always best to reject such experiences. If they are from God the soul will lose nothing, probably because every communication that is from God "produces its first effect at the very moment it appears or is perceived, without leaving the soul time to reflect whether it wants it or not". In this they differ from diabolic visions, which "give the first suggestions to the will without moving it any further unless itself wants to", whereas divine visions "penetrate deeply into the soul, moving the will to love and thus produce their effect which the soul cannot resist even if it wants to". Yet despite these good effects the soul should not in the least desire such experiences: (1) because by prejudicing faith, which is superior to all sense perception, they deflect the soul from the only means of union with God; (2) they prevent the spirit from rising to invisible things; (3) they hinder the soul from attaining to true renunciation and spiritual detachment; (4) by causing it to cling to sensible things they render it less receptive to the spirit of devotion; (5) because if the soul longs for visions it loses the graces God wants to give it; (6) because the desire for them enables the devil to deceive it by similar visions. On the other hand, if the soul lives in the spirit of renunciation and is not inclined towards such experiences, "the devil leaves it, because he sees that he cannot harm it. Instead, God's prevenient love pours out his graces on such an humble and unselfish soul, making it a ruler over many things, as happened to that servant who was faithful in small things (Matt. 25. 21)". ". . . If the soul shows itself always faithful and lowly, the Lord will not rest until He has led it step by step to divine union and transformation." [1]

Like the perceptions of the external senses, so also the figments of the interior senses and of the imagination must always be rejected.

[1] *Ascent*, 2. 11.

The former seek to present images, the latter gives shape to what has been presented. Both are important for meditation, which is a consideration suggested by such images. (We can, e.g., imagine Christ on the Cross or bound to the pillar, or God on the throne of glory.) All these images are as unsuitable for being proximate means of union with God as are the external objects of the sense world, because "the imagination can create or represent nothing save what has come within the sphere of the exterior senses . . . at the most it can form objects similar to those that have been seen, heard or felt"; but these belong to no higher category than the ones perceived by the senses. "Now, since . . . all created things can have no proportion to the divine Being", nothing similar that may be imagined can be a proximate means to union with God. To incite beginners to love God it may be necessary to imagine him as a great fire or light or some other sensible thing like that. But even then these images are only a remote means; souls must "normally pass beyond them to reach the goal and the chamber of spiritual repose". But they may "only pass through them and not remain in them always, else they would never reach their goal".[1]

The right moment for leaving the stage of meditation has come when the three conditions known to us from the Dark Night of the Senses are present:[2] if the soul no longer finds joy and refreshment in discursive thought; if it is just as little disposed to occupy itself with other things; if it likes best to remain quietly with God in a general, loving knowledge of him. This loving knowledge is normally the fruit of many preceding meditations in which knowledge has been gained by laborious considerations and, by long practice, has become a permanent state. In some souls, however, God produces this state without much preceding practice, "by placing them at once in the state of contemplation and love". This loving general knowledge no longer allows distinctions and does not attend to detail. "When the soul in such a state begins to pray it drinks like one who has water at hand, delightfully and without labour, not needing to draw images and concepts by the aqueducts of preceding meditations. As soon as it approaches God there is at once effected that dark,

---

[1] *Ibid.*, 2. 12.
[2] In the *Ascent* (2.11f) they are set out in slightly different order. (The first condition in the *Night* is the second in the *Ascent*. The second in the *Night* is the third in the *Ascent*. The third sign in the *Night* is the first in the *Ascent*. In the *Night* these signs indicate the purifying action of God in the soul through the incipient infused contemplation.—Editors' Note.)

loving, satisfying and soothing knowledge in which the soul drinks wisdom, love and delight." All unrest and pain arise from misunderstanding this state and returning to a meditation that has become futile.

In contemplation the intellectual faculties of memory, understanding and will are all active together. In meditation and consideration, on the other hand, John of the Cross still sees an activity of the sensible faculties. The purer, simpler, more perfect, more spiritual and interior the general knowledge (and this is the case if it is poured into a very pure soul that is free from other impressions and particular kinds of knowledge), the freer and more delicate it will be, and the more easily it escapes notice. The soul is in a profound forgetfulness and lives, as it were, out of time. Prayer seems quite short to it, though it may last for hours. This short prayer "pierces the heavens, because such a soul has become unified in heavenly knowledge".[1] Its effect is a certain elevation of the mind to heavenly knowledge while alienating and detaching it from all things, forms and images. At the same time it is usually the will that is thus absorbed by the delight of love without quite knowing what is its object. The activity of the soul in this state consists purely in receiving "what is given it in the illuminations, revelations and inspirations of God". It is a clear and pure light that is infused into it. This light is unlike any other thing, and if the soul were now to turn to particular objects or considerations this "would . . . be an obstacle to the pure and simple spiritual light as if it were obstructed by clouds". "This light is never lacking in the soul; but because of the creaturely forms and veils with which the soul is covered and enveloped it cannot be poured into it. But as soon as it has completely stripped itself of these obstacles and covers and surrenders itself to perfect detachment and poverty of spirit, this soul, which itself is simple and pure, is transformed into the simple and pure Wisdom which is the Son of God." Then is poured into it "the calm and pure peace of God . . . with wondrous . . . knowledge of God that is enveloped in divine love".[2] In this sublime state of loving union God communicates himself to the soul no longer "under the veil of an imaginary vision or a parable or another image . . . but . . . from mouth to mouth . . . (Num. 12. 6ff) . . . i.e. in the pure, naked, divine Essence. This is, as it were, the mouth of God in love and communicates itself to the pure and naked essence of the soul through the will as the mouth of the soul in its

---

[1] *Ascent*, 2. 14. 11.　　[2] *Ibid.*, 2. 15. 2–5.

love for God." [1] But this goal can be reached only after a long ascent. God leads the soul step by step to this sublime summit. At first he adapts himself to its nature, communicating to it in the beginning "spiritual matters under exterior and palpable things," instructing it "through forms, images and ways of sense ... sometimes naturally, at other times supernaturally, also through its own use of reason, thus elevating it gradually to the supreme divine Spirit". Imaginary visions, too, have their place in this divine scheme of education. In these, however, one should attend only to "what is God's intention and will, namely the spirit of devotion. For He gives them for no other purpose. But whatever He would not give if this could be grasped spiritually without the help of the senses that should be disregarded." [2]

In the Old Covenant it was not only permitted but divinely ordered to desire visions and revelations and to be guided by them, because in this way God revealed mysteries of faith and made known his will. But what he then "spoke only in part to the prophets, He has now spoken completely by giving us the Whole, that is to say, His Son". Formerly, God spoke to promise Christ. Now he has given us all in him and has said: "Hear ye him" (Matt. 17. 5). Therefore it would be a lack of faith still to desire other revelations. "In him are hid all the treasures of wisdom and knowledge" (Col. 2. 3). "Thus we must be guided in all things by the teaching of our Lord Jesus Christ who has become Man, and of His Church and its ministers, according to a human and visible manner, and must be cured in this way of our ignorance and spiritual weakness. ... Nothing that is made known to us supernaturally is to be believed save only the doctrine of the God-man Jesus Christ and His human ministers. ... All else is of no avail and is to be believed only if it is in accordance with the doctrine of Christ." In the Old Covenant, too, not all men were allowed to ask God, and he did not answer all but only the priests and prophets. "God desires particularly that men should be guided by other men ... and that man should be governed by natural reason. Hence He earnestly desires that we should not give perfect credence to the truths He has communicated to us supernaturally ... as long as they have not reached us by the mouth of men. Hence as often as He communicates or reveals something to the soul" he gives it "a certain inclination to communicate it to those who have a right to know it". "For wherever there are several men together to speak about the

<hr>

[1] *Ibid.*, 2. 16. 9.   [2] *Ibid.*, 2. 17.

truth He comes to them and enlightens them and confirms them in the truth. . . ." [1]

Apart from what the understanding perceives through the outer or the inner senses there are also purely intellectual communications: they are offered to the understanding without the intervention of an outer or inner sense and without its own assistance: "clear and definite in a supernatural manner, in pure passivity, i.e. the soul does not do anything and contributes in no wise to them, at least not of its own accord". John distinguishes intellectual visions, revelations, locutions and apprehensions, but calls them all intellectual visions because in all of them the mind sees something. By vision in the narrower sense he means what is seen intellectually after the manner of bodily sight; in the same way we can call revelation what is grasped by the understanding after the manner of a sound that has never been heard before; what is perceived after the manner of hearing is called locution, and what is grasped after the manner of the other senses spiritual apprehension. In all these there is no form, image or shape, they are communications by supernatural intervention and mediation. Though these perceptions are of a higher kind and much more profitable than those received through the bodily senses or the imagination, men should not take any notice of them, for through them, too, "the understanding loses its keenness and obstructs . . . its way to solitude and detachment".[2] The visions can place material as well as immaterial beings before the spiritual eye. In a certain supernatural light the soul can see all bodily things that are in heaven and on earth. The immaterial beings (God, angels, souls) can be seen only in the light of glory, hence not in this life. "If God wanted to communicate them to a soul in their essence, it would at once have to leave its body and depart from this mortal life." These visions can only be communicated exceptionally "if God either suspends the natural functions or keeps them in action while completely loosing the spirit from nature, as, e.g., Paul was completely withdrawn from natural life in his vision of the third heaven" (2 Cor. 12. 2). These visions, however, are extremely rare and only given to those who, like Moses, Elias and Paul, are "sources of the spirit of the Church and of the divine law". In the normal course of things spiritual beings cannot here below "be seen by the understanding without veils and distinctly, but they can be felt in the inmost part of the soul, in a loving knowledge, together with the sweetest unions and touches of God". This "loving,

[1] *Ibid.*, 2. 22.   [2] *Ibid.*, 2. 23.

dark knowledge—that is, faith—leads to the divine union in this life, just as the light of glory is the means to the clear vision of God in the next".[1]

But this anticipates something that is to be treated later. At present we must discuss the intellectual visions of bodily things. They are seen by the understanding interiorly, by means of a supernatural light, just as the eyes see objects by means of the natural light. But the spiritual sight is much keener and more distinct than the bodily sight. It is like the flash of lightning which, in the darkness of night, makes objects appear for a moment quite clearly and distinctly. Under the influence of the spiritual light the objects are so deeply impressed on the soul that whenever, by the grace of God, it becomes aware of them again, it recognizes them as clearly as when they appeared for the first time. They elevate the soul to God, giving it tranquillity and clarity, heavenly joy, pure love and humility. These effects distinguish them from any counterfeits the devil may produce. Nevertheless, they, too, should be rejected. If the soul were to hoard them like treasures, these impressions, images and persons would clutter up its interior and be an obstacle in its way to God that leads through renunciation of all created things. It is true, the memory of such visions can produce a certain degree of love of God; but this can be done much more effectively by pure faith. If this takes root in the soul through detachment, darkness and spiritual poverty, hope and charity are infused into it at the same time, though this charity does not show itself by a certain tenderness in the feelings, but reveals itself in the soul by strength, greater courage and a hitherto unknown vigour. For God is incomprehensible and transcends all things. Therefore we "must journey to Him by the way of total detachment".[2]

Under the term revelation John combines two different kinds of spiritual communications: intellectual forms of knowledge by which hidden truths are revealed (they may concern material or spiritual matters) and revelations in the strict sense, by which mysteries are made known. The understanding of pure truths is quite different from the visions of bodily things discussed above. In it are known truths about the Creator or the creatures, and it is accompanied by incomparable and ineffable delight. "For these kinds of knowledge are directly concerned with God and penetrate deeply into one or other of his properties . . . and each one of these kinds of knowledge is permanently retained by the soul. Since this comes to pass in pure

---

[1] *Ibid.*, 2. 24.   [2] *Ibid.*, 2. 24. 9.

3*

contemplation, the soul recognizes clearly that it is utterly impossible to express any of it in words except perhaps in quite general terms. . . . But these are quite insufficient to convey what the soul has tasted and felt." If this concerns knowledge of God himself, nothing particular can be distinguished in it. "These sublime, loving manifestations of knowledge can only come to a soul that has attained to divine union, because they are nothing other than this union itself," a "kind of touch between the soul and the Divinity" that "penetrates the essence of the soul". Of some "kinds of knowledge and touches God works in the essence of the soul" a single one suffices "not only to purify the soul of all the imperfections that it would not have been able to cast off throughout its life, but also to overwhelm it with graces and virtues". They are so full of the most intimate delight that a single one "sufficiently repays the soul . . . for all the sufferings that it has endured throughout its life, even if these had been without number. . . ." It is impossible that the soul should attain to such exalted kinds of knowledge by its own activity. God alone produces them without its co-operation, often when it least thinks of or desires them. And because they are given to the soul so suddenly and without its own activity "it may neither seek nor refuse them; it should only accept them with humility and resignation, then God will do His work as and when it pleases Him".

Thus the saint does not counsel to reject these kinds of knowledge, because they are themselves part of the union to which he wants to guide men. For their sake a person should renounce all else and accept all sufferings "in humility and resignation, without thought of reward, purely from love of God. . . . For these graces . . . are only a proof of the very special love of God for this soul, because it, too, is quite unselfish in His regard. . . . God reveals Himself to the soul that surrenders itself to Him and loves Him truly." [1]

Very different from these kinds of knowledge are those others relating to actions and events among men. They concern prophecy and what St Paul calls "discernment of spirits" (1 Cor. 12. 10). They are deeply impressed on the soul and produce an unshakeable conviction of their truth. Nevertheless, they must be submitted to the judgement of the spiritual director, because the way of faith leads to union with God more securely than the way of understanding. Certain people come to know nature and its powers by supernatural means. Sometimes these are only isolated and transitory illuminations, but

[1] *Ibid.*, 2. 26.

in the case of the advanced they may also be general and lasting kinds of knowledge. Supernaturally enlightened men may also come to know what happens in the hearts of others from often quite insignificant signs. Further, they are informed of actions and adventures of absent persons without any co-operation of their own. It may happen that, without in the least thinking of it, a man suddenly understands quite clearly what he reads or hears, understanding even far more than is conveyed by the words themselves. He may even hear words in an unknown language yet understand their meaning perfectly. In this sphere (unlike the union experiences mentioned above) the devil has again much opportunity for deceit. In any case, these phenomena are of little value for the divine union and fraught with danger. Hence it is best to reject them all, while giving an account of them to the spiritual director and following his advice. These things are communicated to the soul passively and "always have only the effect God wants to bring about; there is no need for any action on the part of the soul".[1]

Revelations in the strict sense are concerned with the mysteries of faith: the Being of God (Trinity and Unity) and the divine action in creation. The latter includes the promises and threats of the prophets, as well as what "God sometimes reveals about the world in general and about particular kingdoms, provinces, states, families and individual persons". If the spirit is instructed in mysteries of faith this is, strictly speaking, no revelation, since these have already been revealed, but only a new presentation and interpretation of revealed truth. As all this is communicated through words and signs it can easily be faked by the devil. If, therefore, something were revealed that contradicts the faith it should on no account be accepted. And even in the case of a new presentation of truths already revealed the soul is "not to believe them because they are presented to it anew, but because they are already sufficiently revealed to the Church". It is "much better for it, if it does not want to see so clearly in matters of faith; then it will preserve the merit of faith in its purity and entirety, and only thus, in this night of the understanding, will it attain to the divine light of union with God". The soul will be wise to be careful about these communications; "only thus will it attain to the divine union through the night of faith, in purity and without the danger of error".[2]

The third group of purely spiritual communications are called

[1] *Ibid.*, 26. 18.   [2] *Ibid.*, 2. 27.

locutions or words. These are perceived by the understanding without the mediation of any bodily senses. John divides them into successive, formal and substantial words. The first are words and conclusions formed by the recollected spirit itself. This happens when it is "perfectly recollected and, as it were, wholly absorbed in some meditation". "It proceeds from one thought to the other, forms words and conclusions which exactly correspond to the subject and this quite easily and distinctly, and on matters which had been until then quite unknown to it." It seems to the mind as if someone else inside it answered and instructed it. In fact, however, it converses with itself, puts questions and answers, but in doing so it is the instrument of the Holy Spirit under whose influence it thinks. "For when the understanding is immersed in meditation it is united to the truth on which it reflects; and likewise the Holy Spirit is united with it in that truth, as it is always united with every truth. This results in a union of the understanding with the Holy Spirit through this truth. Then the other truths that are connected with that truth which is being considered are gradually derived from it in the inner mind, and the Holy Spirit is the teacher who opens the door and lets in the light." Despite this illumination error is not completely ruled out; first, because the light is so delicate and spiritual that the understanding is not quite at home with it; secondly, because the mind itself forms rational conclusions and may go astray. At first the understanding had, "as it were, the thread of truth firmly in its grasp; but then it at once adds something of its own: the skill or clumsiness of its own inferior insight. . . ." It may even happen that a naturally very lively and keen understanding attains to a similar activity without any supernatural aid and may then believe itself to be enlightened by God. There is another danger. The soul may think it has experienced something wonderful through these divine locutions and thus let itself be drawn away from the abyss of faith. Hence they should be received with care, even if they are due to the illumination of the Holy Spirit. For the understanding is enlightened by him according to the degree of its recollection, and it becomes most deeply recollected by faith. "The more purely and perfectly a soul walks in faith, the greater is the measure of infused love, and the Holy Spirit enlightens it and communicates His gifts to it according to the measure of its love." The light it receives by faith compares with that which it gains through illuminations on particular truths as the purest gold with ordinary metal, or an ocean with a drop of water. "For by reason you

receive insight into one, two or three truths; but in the light of faith
you receive the whole divine wisdom at once, namely the Son of God
Himself, who communicates Himself to the soul in faith." This fullness is diminished if we desire those supernatural communications.
We should rather sincerely and in simplicity of heart "direct the will
to the love of God", "firmly establish it in the power of humble love
and practise true virtue", i.e. "follow the Son of God in His life and
suffering and be mortified in all things. For this alone is the way to all
spiritual graces, rather than a multitude of interior locutions." These
may be produced not only by the activity of one's own nature but
also by the insinuations of the devil. It is true, they leave different
effects in the soul according to their origin, but it needs great experience in the inner life to distinguish between them with certainty.
Hence it is best not to attach importance to any of them. We should be
content "if we only know the mysteries and truths of the faith in
that simplicity and truth with which the Church presents them. This
is quite sufficient to inflame our will. . . ." [1]

Formal words are distinguished from successive ones by the fact that
the spirit receives them without its own co-operation, even without
being recollected and having thought about what it hears. Sometimes
they are clearly formulated, sometimes only like thoughts by which
we learn something. They may consist in a single word, but also in
several; even longer instructions are possible. These words do not
leave a deep impression, for they are normally only intended to enlighten the soul on a particular point. As a rule they also make a man
willing to do what they order. It may, however, also happen that the
soul has an aversion against what it is asked to do. God permits this
especially in the case of important actions which may bring it honour.
For ordinary and humiliating things, however, he grants ready consent. If the locutions come from the devil it is just the reverse. Then
the soul is very eager to do great and unusual things and feels repugnance for ordinary ones. Here, too, it is difficult to distinguish what
comes from the good and what from the evil spirit. Hence "the soul
should attach no greater importance to formal than to successive
locutions". Nor should a man undertake at once what is demanded
by the locutions, but should first discuss the matter with an experienced director and follow his advice. If no one with sufficient
experience is to be found, the best thing to do is to retain what is
certain and essential in the locutions, but not to give them any further

[1] *Ibid.*, 2. 29.

thought and to tell no one about them.[1] Like the formal locutions, the substantial words, too, are clearly and distinctly impressed on the soul; but they are distinguished from the former by their immediate substantial effect: they produce in the soul what they say. If the Lord says to it: Love me! and if this is a substantial word, the soul will at once possess and feel a true love of God. The words: Fear nothing! will at the same time give great courage and peace to a frightened soul. Such words are "life and strength and incomparable blessing. A single one of them effects in a moment more good in the soul than it has itself produced during its whole life." In such a case it need not do anything, desire anything or fear anything. Nor does it matter whether it desires such words or refuses them. The soul need not perform itself what it has heard; God himself does that. These locutions are given it without its desire. It "should only surrender to them in humble resignation. It need not reject them; for their effect is substantially in the soul: a fullness of divine grace. Since the soul experiences their effect purely receptively, its own activity is of little importance." Here a man need not fear deceptions from the understanding or the devil, because neither is able to produce such substantial effects. Only if a soul joined itself to the devil by free agreement could he impress on it his thoughts and words; but these would be evil effects, he could not possibly produce any similar to the divine ones.

"Thus these substantial words contribute greatly to the union of the soul with God. The more interior they are, the more they penetrate the substance and the greater is the progress they effect."[1]

The fourth and last kind of intellectual apprehensions are the spiritual feelings. There are two kinds of them, those that are rooted in the inclination of the will and those that have their seat in the substance of the soul. If they are from God, even the first are something very sublime. Those of the second kind "surpass all others and are of exceedingly great blessing and profit". Neither the soul nor its guide can understand how and why God gives it such graces. They do not depend on its meditations and works. It is true a man can make himself receptive to such graces, but God gives them "when He wills and as He wills and for what He wills". Some persons who have proved themselves in many works do not receive these touches whereas others, who have far fewer good works to their credit, have them abundantly and in the highest degree. Some of these touches are distinctly noticeable but pass quickly, others are less distinct but last longer. The understanding receives a certain knowledge of and insight into all these touches, those of the will as well as those in the substance of the soul. This knowledge consists normally in a most sublime perception of God that is a great delight to the understanding. But it is impossible to describe it distinctly, as little as the touch that is its source. The kinds of knowledge are more or less elevated and distinct, according to the difference of the divine touches from which flow the apprehensions and hence the knowledge. Both knowledge and apprehensions are given passively to the soul. "If all deception is to be ruled out, and if they are to have their profitable effects without hindrance, the understanding must not interfere with its own activity . . . for by its intervention it could easily destroy those delicate forms of knowledge altogether. . . . For they consist in a delectable supernatural intelligence which is quite above the reach of the natural understanding. . . . Neither should one have any desire for them, else the understanding might go further and form itself kinds of knowledge, or the door might even be opened to the devil to penetrate with all sorts of deceitful manifestations. . . ." The soul should "only be quite still, and be humble and resigned". God will communicate those graces to it "if He finds it humble and detached".[1]

(d) Stripping of the Memory

In the discussions reproduced above the saint was chiefly concerned to show how knowledge and faith are related to the goal of union with God. He has opened before us a vast spiritual realm revealing a great variety of psychological events unknown to ordinary experience, described them in masterly fashion and examined their importance for the spiritual life. It is beyond our scope even to indicate the wealth of problems and consequences resulting from this, but we shall emphasize those aspects that are important for our theme. Before doing this, however, we must follow the thought of the saint still further. He has already strongly stressed that the way of faith leads through the Dark Night and that it is a way of the Cross. Yet he has spoken so much of light and bliss that it might sometimes seem as if he had abandoned the subject of the Night and the Cross. But, apart from anticipating the description of the goal which must be known if the way is to be understood, this whole wealth of illuminations and

---

[1] *Ibid.*, 2. 32.

graces has only been described to show that it must be renounced. Only those who have possessed this wealth can realize how painful such voluntary deprivation must be, how dark it becomes when one closes one's eyes in bright daylight, and that it is a real crucifixion to suspend the life of the spirit and to take away from it all its refreshment. It has already been mentioned that this detachment does not only concern the understanding but also the other mental powers, memory and will. The last book of the *Ascent* is devoted to their preparation for the divine union.

Since "the soul must know God more through what He is not than through what He is ... it must reach Him by completely renouncing its apprehensions, the natural as well as the supernatural ones, rather than by admitting them".

We must first remove all natural barriers that constrain the memory and then raise it above itself; that is, above all distinctly defined knowledge and every sensual possession to the "highest hope of the incomprehensible God". Hence it must first be stripped of all the knowledge and images it has gained through the bodily senses. "As there is no form and no image by which the memory could grasp God" it must be freed from all forms except God; "as long as it is united with God it is ... as it were formless and imageless; the imagination is no longer active, the memory is completely concentrated on the highest Good in perfect oblivion, without the slightest remembrance of anything". Like the union itself in which it takes place, this complete emptying is not simply the fruit of one's own activity. "Something quite extraordinary" happens in it. "When God grants such touches of union to the memory it sometimes happens that suddenly in the brain ... there is a certain upheaval. This is sometimes so strong that one thinks that one is altogether going out of one's mind and losing reason and sense. Then the memory ... is emptied and purged of all knowledge. . . ." "The suspension of the imagination and the forgetfulness of the memory are sometimes so great that a long time elapses before the latter recovers and realizes what has happened during this time."[1] Such a suspension of the faculties, however, occurs only at the beginning of union, it does not happen to the perfect. They are completely guided by the Holy Spirit who reminds them at the right time of what they have to do, and so they are preserved from the external faults that are peculiar to the transition stage.

[1] *Ibid.*, 3. 2. 2–6.

Hence the perfect purification is experienced passively and is wholly due to God. The soul has only to prepare itself for it: whatever the senses may offer it, "of that nothing should be preserved in the memory but should at once be assigned to oblivion, and if necessary, it should think of other things.[1] No remembered image should be retained by the memory, which should behave as if these things had never existed. The memory should be left quite free and unencumbered and should on no account be led to any consideration of heavenly or earthly things. . . . One should . . . let these things sink into oblivion like something that is only a hindrance on the way. . . ."[2]

A spiritual soul that "would use reminiscences and natural ways of thought as a way to God" would have three disadvantages. The things of the world will cause it to suffer from manifold weaknesses, "e.g. deceptions, imperfections, desires, inclination to criticise, waste of time, etc. . . .". If a man suffers his memory to be occupied with what has been perceived by the senses he "meets imperfections at every step. For there always remains in the soul a certain inclination sometimes to sorrow and fear, sometimes to hatred, vain hopes and ambitions . . . all things that prevent the perfect purity of the soul and the pure union with God. . . . From these one best escapes once and for all by freeing the memory from all of them." However, "one need not renounce what is related only to God and contributes to this dark, general, pure and simple knowledge of God, but only what acquaints us with Him through images or by comparison with a creature". It is best "to calm and silence the powers of the soul so that God may speak to the soul".

Then "a stream of peace will be poured out over it . . . and . . . will deliver it of every anxiety and suspicion, of confusion and darkness which made it fear that it was already lost or on its way to perdition".[3]

Other disadvantages are caused by the devil. "He is able to bring the soul new impressions, forms of knowledge and thoughts, and with the help of these to arouse in it pride, avarice, envy, wrath, etc., to tempt it to unjust hatred or vain love. . . . By far the greatest number of deceptions and the greatest mischief the devil does to the soul come from the knowledge and thoughts of the memory. Hence if

---

[1] This seems to be a mistranslation in the German text. It contradicts what follows and in the translation of Allison Peers the passage reads: "He must allow himself to forget them immediately, and this he must accomplish, if need be with the same efficacy *as that with which others contrive to remember them*".—Translator.

[2] *Ibid.*, 3. 2. 14.   [3] *Ibid.*, 3. 3.

this faculty is shrouded in the complete darkness of oblivion and its activity is suspended, the door remains closed against the pernicious influence of the evil one . . . and this greatly profits the soul."[1]

A further disadvantage is that the natural contents of the memory can "hinder the moral good and deprive (the soul) of the spiritual good". The moral good "consists in the calming of the passions and the curbing of the unruly desires" as well as in the effects of this: calm, peace and tranquillity of the soul and, consequently, the moral virtues. On the other hand, all trouble and disturbance in the soul come from the contents of the memory. The soul that lives in unrest, unsupported by the moral good, is also "not capable of the spiritual good, which is at home only in a detached and peaceful soul". If the soul attaches importance to the contents of the memory and turns to them, "it cannot possibly be free for the incomprehensible, i.e. for God". If it would attain to God, "it must exchange the mutable and comprehensible for the immutable and incomprehensible".[2] Then, instead of the disadvantages just mentioned, it will gain the opposite advantages: calm and peace of the spirit, purity of conscience and soul, and thus it will be well prepared "for receiving wisdom human and divine as well as the virtues". It is kept safe from many insinuations, temptations and disturbances of the enemy who was helped by those thoughts, and becomes receptive to the suggestions and inspirations of the Holy Spirit.[3]

Like the natural sense perceptions, the supernatural visions, revelations, locutions and apprehensions also leave a very lively impression in the memory or the imagination. They, too, should be treated according to the principle that the soul should never think about clear and distinct objects so as to retain them in its memory. "The more the soul concerns itself with distinct and clear apprehensions . . . whether natural or supernatural, the less will it be able to penetrate into the abyss of faith which absorbs everything else. For . . . none of those forms and kinds of knowledge is God, nor have they any proportion to Him, hence they cannot be a proximate means for union with God." The memory must be freed from all of them in order "to be able to be united with God" in perfect mystical hope. For all possession is opposed to hope. . . . Hence, the more the memory exercises itself in renunciation, the more it gains in hope, and the more it grows in hope, the more intimately is the soul united to God. The possession of God

[1] Ibid., 3. 4.   [2] Ibid., 3. 5.   [3] Ibid., 3. 6.

in the divine union is perfect if the soul has perfectly dispossessed itself. . . ."[1]

The soul that is occupied with supernatural kinds of knowledge is at a disadvantage in five different ways: First, it is frequently mistaken in its judgements, believing a mere figment of the imagination to be a divine revelation, or taking divine things for a deceit of the devil and so forth. Hence the soul should "abstain from all judgement and even renounce the desire to know what is happening to it. . . . However great the value of these perceptions may be, they cannot contribute as much to the increase of love as the least act of living faith and hope, which is performed in perfect emptiness and renunciation of all these things".[2]

The second disadvantage is the danger of falling into pride and vanity. A man thinks he has advanced already very far because he receives such supernatural communications and behaves like a Pharisee, looking down on those who fail to experience such favours. In view of this, the soul must remember two things:

"1. Virtue consists neither in apprehensions and feelings of God, however exalted these may be, nor in anything one can feel in oneself, but rather in what cannot be felt in oneself. . . . It consists in profound humility and contempt of oneself and all one possesses . . . as well as in the desire that others should think the same of us. . . .

"2. One must be convinced that all visions, revelations and supernatural feelings . . . are of far less value than the least act of humility; for this contains the effects of charity, which does not esteem and seek its own, thinks evil only of itself and no good of itself but of others."[3]

The third disadvantage comes from the evil one. "He has the power to present to the memory and the imagination . . . false kinds of knowledge and images which are in appearance true and good. . . ." He appears to the soul as an angel of light. He is also capable of stirring up disorderly sensual and spiritual feelings even with regard to communications that are really from God, so as to make the soul fond of them and to plunge it into spiritual gluttony. Thus it is blinded by its pleasure and more concerned with sensual satisfaction than with love. It no longer desires the renunciation and charity demanded by the divine virtues. The cause of all these evils is "that the soul did not from the beginning suppress its joy in such supernatural apprehensions. . . ."[4]

[1] *Ibid.*, 3. 7.   [2] *Ibid.*, 7. 8.   [3] *Ibid.*, 3. 9.   [4] *Ibid.*, 3. 10.

The fourth disadvantage has repeatedly been mentioned before: namely that all possessions of the memory are a hindrance of its union with God through hope.

Finally, the perceptions and pictures of the imagination that are retained in the memory can result in "that one thinks of God's Being and majesty less highly and worthily than befits His incomprehensibility"; not "so sublimely as faith teaches, which says that God is incomparable and incomprehensible". In this life the soul can receive clearly and distinctly only what falls under the concepts of genus and species. Now God falls under neither, hence he cannot be compared with any creature on earth, with no image and no form of knowledge that can be grasped by the powers of the soul. "Hence whoever encumbers his memory and the other faculties with things they can grasp cannot esteem God as highly and think of Him in such a manner as is fitting."[1]

The advantages of perfect renunciation correspond to these disadvantages. The quiet and peace produced by the renunciation of natural perceptions are increased because a man is now also delivered from caring whether supernatural communications are good or evil. One "need not even spend time and energy on consultations with spiritual masters to ascertain it ... since one no longer attaches any importance to these things. Thus the time and strength of the soul can be spent on a far better and more salutary practice, namely the subjection of its will to the divine will, and the careful striving for self-denial and spiritual and material poverty", which means that the soul is truly anxious to do without any support from consolations and perceptions. Such a rejection of divine communications does not mean "quenching the spirit". By its own power the soul is capable only of natural activity, it cannot produce supernatural acts, since these are inspired by God alone. Hence "through its own activity it would only hinder the work of God which He performs in it by communicating the Spirit. The soul would be absorbed in its own activity, which is of quite a different kind and much baser than what God communicates to it; for what comes from God is passive and supernatural, what comes from the soul is active and natural. And this would mean quenching the spirit."

"The powers of the soul can, by their nature, reflect and act only if they make use of a concept, form or image, and this is but the rind

[1] *Ibid.* ,3. 12.

of the external appearance[1] (*corteza y accidente*) under which the real substance and spirit (*sustancia y espíritu*) are hidden. This real substance and spirit unite with the powers of the soul in true knowledge and love only if the powers suspend their activity. For the purpose and end of such activity is only that the soul should receive the Being that it knows and loves under these forms. Hence there is the same difference between active and passive operation . . . as between what one wants to do and what one has already done, and as between what one desires to attain and possess and what one has already attained and possessed." If, therefore, in the case of the supernatural perceptions we were to make an active use of the powers of the soul, this would mean ". . . to abandon the finished work and to do it all over again". The soul must direct its attention wholly to this: "in all perceptions that come to it from above . . . not to consider the letter and the rind, i.e. that which they mean or represent or give to understand; it must only consider and retain the divine love which they arouse interiorly in the soul. Only for this one purpose may one sometimes remember an image or apprehension that arouses love, in order to let the motives of love become active in the spirit. Even though the memory may not have the same effect as the first communication, yet each time . . . love is aroused anew and the mind is raised to God, especially if it is a recollection of supernatural images, forms or apprehensions, which are normally impressed on the soul like a seal, so that they last a long time and sometimes never disappear from it at all." Such memories "arouse nearly every time one remembers them divine effects of love, of sweetness, illumination etc. . . ., for this is why they are impressed on the soul. With this God grants the soul a great grace, since this memory is an inexhaustible source of good things for it." These images "are very much alive in the spiritual memory of the soul and do not resemble the other images and forms preserved in the imagination". Hence the soul has no need of the imagination to remember them, but "sees these forms in itself, as an image is seen in a mirror. If it remembers them to rouse its love they are no longer an obstacle "to the union of love in faith; but it must not be wholly absorbed by the image, but turn away from it as soon as love has been roused. . . . These formal images, however, are very rare, and for those who have no experience in these matters it is difficult to distinguish them from those that are only in the

[1] This is the literal rendering of the German *die Schale der äusseren Erscheinung* by which Edith Stein translates *corteza y accidente*.—Translator.

imagination. Of whatever kind they may be, it remains best for the soul if it seeks to know only one thing through them: God by faith in hope."[1]

The memory retains not only images but also purely spiritual kinds of knowledge. "If the soul has once received such apprehension, it can recall it whenever it desires," for the apprehension leaves in the soul a form, an image or a mental concept. This concerns those perceptions of uncreated perfections or of created things that have already been discussed. Memories of the second kind can be recalled to arouse love. "But if the recollection of them produces no good effect it should be removed from the memory. If, however, it concerns uncreated things one may direct one's attention to them as often as possible. . . . For they are touches and feelings of union with God, to which we want to lead the soul." They are not recalled through a form or shape, since they have nothing like that in them, but through their effects: illumination, love, delight, spiritual renewal. And as often as one thinks of them "one of these effects is renewed".[2]

In summarizing the saint once more reminds his readers that he is only concerned with leading the memory to union with God. Since one can only hope for what one does not possess, hope will be the more perfect the less one possesses. "Hence, the freer the soul keeps the memory from forms and things that are not God, the more deeply will it establish it in God, the better will it preserve it, in order to be able to hope that God will possess it completely." As often as definite images or forms of knowledge present themselves one should pass them by and turn to God. The soul may concern itself with memories only as far as its duties demand. Even then this should be done without attachment and pleasure, so that the soul may not be wholly absorbed by them.[3]

(e) Purification of the Will

"We should have done as good as nothing if we were to be content to purify the understanding in order to establish it in the virtue of faith and the memory to ground it in hope, if we were not also to purify the will for the sake of the third virtue, which is charity." All that is needed to fill this faculty with the love of God is perfectly expressed in the words of Deuteronomy: "Thou shalt love the Lord thy God with all thy heart, and with all thy soul and with all thy strength" (6. 5). "The strength of the soul consists in its faculties, passions and desires (*potencias, pasiones y apetitos*). All of these are subject to the

---

[1] *Ibid.*, 3. 13. 3f.   [2] *Ibid.*, 3. 14   [3] *Ibid.*, 3. 15.

dominion of the will. Now if the will directs all these faculties, passions and desires to God and turns them away from all that is not God, it preserves the strength of the soul for God and arrives at loving God with all its strength."

The principal obstacles to this are the four passions of the soul: joy, hope, grief and fear. "If reason thus orders these passions to God that the soul rejoices only in what furthers the honour and glory of God, that it hopes for nothing else and that it grieves for nothing save what concerns God and fears nothing but God: then it is clear that all the strength and capacity of the soul are preserved for God. The more the soul rejoices in something else, the less will its joy be in God. . . ." If the will is purged of its desires "the human and lower will is deified, i.e. it becomes one with the will of God". If the passions are not restrained they produce all kinds of imperfections in the soul, but as soon as they are well ordered and brought into subjection they will bring forth all virtues. All four are so closely connected that if one is made subject the others, too, are reduced to obedience. On the other hand, if the will rejoices in anything other than God it contains in germ hope, grief and fear with regard to this particular being. One passion takes captive the others as well as the will and the whole soul, preventing it from flying "to the freedom and repose of sweet contemplation and union".[1]

The subsequent discussion of *joy* is preceded by the enunciation *of this principle*: "The will should rejoice only in what is to the honour and glory of God. We can give no greater honour to God than by serving Him according to evangelical perfection. What is done apart from this perfection is of no value or profit to man."[2] Later a complementary explanation is given: ". . . Everything in which the will can rejoice in a certain manner is sweet and delightful, and nothing sweet or delightful is God: for as God is unattainable to the apprehensions of the other faculties He is so also to the desires and inclinations of the will. And since the soul is incapable of tasting God's essence in this life, no sweetness or delight that can be tasted, however sublime, can be God. Now the will can taste and desire something only in a definite form, inasmuch as it knows this or that thing. But since the will has never tasted God as He is, nor has apprehended Him through any apprehension of the faculty of desire, it does not know what God is, nor what it means to enjoy Him. . . . Hence it is clear that none of the definite objects in which the will may rejoice is God." It results from

[1] *Ibid.*, 3. 16.   [2] *Ibid.*, 3. 17. 2.

this that, in order to attain to union with God, the desire must be denied every enjoyment of natural as well as of supernatural things. Now union with God is possible only through love. "And since the delight, the sweetness and the enjoyment that can be given to the will is not love, it follows that none of these feelings can be a suitable means by which the will may be united to God. This can be done only by the operation of the will, and this is entirely different from its feelings. The will unites itself to God through its operation and has its end in Him in love; (it does not achieve union) through the feelings and apprehensions of its desire, which have their seat, goal and end in the soul. The feelings can only serve as motives for love . . ., but for nothing more." They do not lead "the soul out of itself to God, but want it to find its satisfaction in themselves. The operation of the will, on the other hand, consists in the love of God, directs the soul solely to Him, rises above all things and loves Him above all. Hence, if someone be excited to the love of God by a sweet feeling he ought to go beyond this sweet feeling and turn his love to God whom he cannot grasp by feeling." To turn to this feeling would mean "to give one's love to a creature . . . and to confuse the motive with the object and end. Thus the activity of the will would be perverted. The soul loves securely and truly in the spirit of faith only in darkness and emptiness of all that the will can feel and the understanding can comprehend. . . ." [1] Hence "it would be very stupid if one is without sweetness and spiritual delight to think that one is without God, or if one does feel such enjoyment, that for this reason one has Him. It would be even more foolish to seek such sweetness in God and rejoice in it, for this would mean that God would not be sought with a will established in the emptiness of faith but in spiritual enjoyment, which is something created . . . and thus God would no more be loved purely above all things: for this means to direct the whole power of the will solely to Him. . . . Hence it is impossible for the will to attain to the sweetness and delight of the divine union if the desire is not empty of every particular enjoyment. This is meant by the Psalm: *Dilata os tuum et implebo illud* ("Open thy mouth and I will fill it." Ps. 80. 11). This desire is the mouth of the will; and this mouth is opened if it is not hindered by a morsel of some enjoyment. . . . The mouth of the will must always be held open for God, empty of any

---

[1] *Ibid.*, 3. 45, hitherto unpublished. (So Edith Stein. According to Allison Peers, vol. I, note at end of *Ascent*, p. 334, this section does not belong to the work but is a letter, published by him in vol. III as n. 11, p. 278ff.—Translator.)

morsel of desire, so that God may fill it with the sweetness of His love. . . ." [1]

This is now proved with regard to the various objects in which the desire can seek satisfaction. Joy can be directed to temporal things: riches, honour, posterity and the like. These, it is true, need not necessarily lead to sin, but normally they will make a man unfaithful to God. He may rejoice in them only if they help him to serve God better or to reach eternal life more safely. But because one "cannot know clearly whether God is served better in this way, it is vanity to indulge in a definite joy in these things. . . ." [2] The main disadvantage of turning one's will to them is that, by doing so, one turns it away from God. This comes about in four stages, summarized in the words of Scripture: "The beloved grew fat and kicked; he grew fat and became swollen and gross. He forsook God his Maker and departed from God his salvation" (Deut. 32. 15). The growing fat signifies a blunting of the mind with regard to God. As soon as "the spiritual soul seeks its joy in anything, however little . . ., it is darkened as to God and its formerly unclouded judgement is dimmed. . . . Neither holiness nor sound judgement save a man from this evil if he gives way to concupiscence and joy in temporal things." [3] "He became swollen and gross"—this is the second stage, a "dilatation of the will, which now surrenders to temporal goods even more freely". Since the joy in them has not been curtailed from the beginning, the will becomes estranged from divine things and holy practices and no longer finds any taste in them. Finally a man gives up "his normal daily practices and all his mind is given to worldly things". Now it is no more only his reason and judgement that are darkened, "so that he can no longer recognize what is true and just, but in his great tepidity and sloth he even no longer cares to know it and to act accordingly. . . ." [4]

The third stage consists in a complete turning away from God. "He forsook God his Maker." Those who have come to this no longer care at all for the obligations of God's law. "They completely forget and neglect their salvation and give their whole attention to worldly things." These are the "children of this world" of whom the Lord says "that they are more prudent and efficient in their affairs than the children of light" (Luke 16. 8). These are the truly avaricious men who "cannot be satisfied. Their hunger and thirst increase in proportion as they recede from the source that alone can satisfy them, which

---

[1] See preceding note.   [2] *Ascent*, 3. 18. 3.   [3] *Ibid.*, 3. 19. 3f.
[4] *Ibid.*, 3. 19. 5f.

is God." They fall "into a thousand sins through their love of temporal things and suffer immeasurable loss". Thus one reaches the fourth stage, where the soul forgets God as if he did not exist at all. The cause of this complete forgetfulness of God is that "the heart, which should turn to God with its inmost being, is turned with its inmost being to money as if there were no other God". Such men make temporal goods their idols and sacrifice their lives to them if they are threatened with the loss of them. The idol gives them what it has: "despair and death. And even if it does not bring them to the utmost misery, to death, it causes them to live in perpetual fear of death. . . . But those, too, who . . . are harmed less, should greatly be pitied, for . . . they regress a great distance on the road to God." [1] If, on the other hand, a man rids himself of all attachment to temporal goods he will receive magnanimity, spiritual freedom, a clear understanding, profound peace and a quiet trust in God; he will worship God in truth and his will will be genuinely subject to the divine will. Even the joy in creatures is increased by renouncing them; it is a joy that the greedy man can never taste, because in his unrest he lacks the necessary freedom of spirit. The man who is free from possessions sees their true natural and supernatural worth. "He enjoys their truth, their better side and their essence . . ., whereas the man who regards them only with the senses enjoys their deceit, all that is worse and inessential in them." "He who keeps his heart free will not be troubled by cares whether in prayer or out of it. Without losing time he gathers a multitude of spiritual treasures, whereas another man, whose heart is caught in a snare and attached to creatures, will always move hither and thither. . . . Hence as soon as the spiritual soul perceives the first movement of joy in a creature it must try to suppress it. . . ." Thus the heart is preserved "free for God, and this is the essential condition for all graces God wants to bestow on a man. . . ." Even in this life God will repay a hundredfold "the renunciation of a single, however transitory joy for love of Him and of the perfection of the Gospel. . . ." On the other hand, "we must fear that as often as we let a vain joy arise in us God will prepare a great punishment for us proportionate to our fault. . . ." [2]

A second group are called natural goods: they are graces of body and soul, e.g. physical beauty and charm, a keen mind and sound judgement. They tempt those who possess them as well as others to attachment and vain pleasure. In order to avoid this, we should "reflect that beauty and all other natural gifts are but earth and will return to

[1] *Ibid.*, 3. 19. 8–11.   [2] *Ibid.*, 3. 20.

the earth whence they came; that grace and loveliness are smoke and vapour of this earth. . . ." Hence a man should keep his heart turned to God in joy and gladness, because in God there is all beauty and grace to the most sublime degree, infinitely exceeding all creatures.[1]

The particular disadvantages resulting from joy in natural goods are "vanity, presumption, pride and low esteem of our neighbour"; excitement of the sensuality and surrender to it; a craving for flattery and vain praise which also have a bad influence on others; a still greater blunting of the understanding and judgement than in the case of joy in temporal goods; tepidity and sloth of the spirit leading even to disgust with divine things. The saint stresses especially the dangers arising from desire for sensual enjoyment: "No pen can describe and no word can express them; it will always remain a dark and hidden secret how far one can go astray in this respect, and what misery arises from joy in natural beauty and graces." ". . . Even among the saints there will be only few that have not been enchanted and perturbed by the draught of joy and pleasure in natural beauty and graces." The wine of sensual enjoyment befogs the understanding. If one does not take an antidote at once, "the life of the soul will be in danger". "As soon as the heart feels attracted by vain joy in natural goods, it should remember that it is vain to rejoice in anything else save the service of God . . .; into what misery the angels were thrown because they looked with pleasure on their own beauty and natural gifts. For this joy was the cause of their fall into the terrible abyss."[2]

If the soul renounces all such joys "it prepares in itself a home for humility and a general charity towards its neighbour". If a man lets himself "be in no way attracted by the deceptive natural good things that appear to the eyes, he preserves his soul free and clear to love all reasonably and spiritually, as God commands it . . .; the more this love grows, the more grows also the love of God, and the more the love of God increases, the more grows also love for our neighbour". This renunciation also effects "a profound peace in the soul, frees it from distractions and produces recollection of the senses, especially of the eyes". If a man has gained some aptitude in this, impure things no longer make any impression on him. He acquires "purity of soul and body, i.e. in spirit and senses, and achieves an angelic conformity with God, so that soul and body become a worthy temple of the Holy

[1] *Ibid.*, 3. 21.   [2] *Ibid.*, 3. 22.

Spirit". Thus a man will gain "freedom of spirit, which is a very sublime quality of the soul necessary for the service of God. By this the soul conquers temptations, suffers trials patiently and increases more and more in the virtues".[1]

By the good things of sense John understands all that is perceived by the outer senses or acquired by the inner ones. Since God cannot be attained by any sense "it would at least be useless" to seek one's pleasure in objects of sense; the will could then "no longer be occupied with God and seek its joy with Him alone". But if a man does not stop short at this but directs his joy to God as soon as he feels enjoyment in such things, these impressions need not be rejected: "for there are souls which feel particularly attracted to God by means of such sensible objects". In many cases, however, the intention only *seems* to be directed to God, whereas actually "the effect is sensual satisfaction producing weakness and imperfection instead of turning a man to God". If, on the other hand, by the first movements of such joys a man is at once directed to God, he "does not take trouble to seek them; and if these joys come to him, the will frees itself at once from them, rejects them and turns to God".[2]

There are many other disadvantages in being attached to objects of sense. Joy in visible things results in "vanity of the soul, distraction of the spirit, unruly covetousness, immodesty, interior and exterior licence, impure thoughts and motions of envy. Joy in listening to useless words results directly in a distracted imagination, gossiping and envy, rash judgements, vacillating thoughts and many other very pernicious disadvantages. Joy in sweet scents breeds repugnance towards poor people, which is contrary to the spirit of Jesus Christ, dislike of rendering services to others, disinclination of the heart for humble things and spiritual insensibility, at least in comparison with covetousness.[3] Joy in delicious dishes leads directly to gluttony, wrath, discord and lack of charity towards one's neighbour and the poor.... From this result disorders of the body, diseases and evil motions; thus the incentives to dissipation are increased. This joy produces directly great spiritual torpor and spoils the taste for spiritual things.... Finally, this joy also results in distraction of the other senses and of the heart, and in discontent with many things." "Joy in the touch of pleasant things ... completely disorganizes mind and

---

[1] *Ibid.*, 3. 25.   [2] *Ibid.*, 3. 24.
[3] Literal translation of the German. Allison Peers is more intelligible: "at least to a degree proportionate with its desire for this joy" (I, p. 286).

senses and destroys their strength and vigour. From this develops the abominable vice of effeminacy . . .; it nourishes luxury, renders the soul soft and fearful, the senses . . . always ready for sin and evil. It fills the heart with vain dissipation and leads to lack of control of the tongue and to licence of the eyes. It hinders the power of judgement and tempts a man to silliness and spiritual futility; in the moral sphere it produces pusillanimity and fickleness, it darkens the soul, weakens the heart and makes it cowardly where it need fear nothing. Often this joy gives rise to the spirit of confusion and makes a man insensible to the voice of conscience and the spirit. Thus the understanding is greatly weakened and reduced to such a state that it can neither accept nor give good advice and becomes unreceptive to moral and spiritual goods; it is as useless as a broken vessel." [1] Now all these disadvantages do more or less harm according to the degree of passionate joy and the susceptibility of the various kinds of men.

"The advantages the soul gains from renouncing these joys are astonishing . . .: it grows strong in the struggle against distractions . . . and is once more recollected in God." The spirit preserves itself carefully and the acquired virtues increase and blossom again. Then a sublime transformation takes place: "We can truly say that what was sensual becomes spiritual, what was bestial rational; that man becomes similar to the angelic nature, what was earthly and human becomes divine and heavenly." Even in this life the will receives the hundredfold reward promised by our Lord (Matt. 19. 29). It exchanges sensual for spiritual joy and remains permanently united to God. Now all sense impressions serve to increase contemplation, as they did for our first parents in paradise. Finally, those who have renounced themselves will be rewarded in the life of glory in that "the physical gifts, such as agility and clarity, will be far more sublime than in those who have not renounced sensual joys; moreover, the essential increase of glory corresponding to the degree of charity . . . will produce immeasurable eternal glory (2 Cor. 4. 17) in the soul . . . for each temporal and transitory joy it has renounced." [2]

In contrast with the external, natural and sensual good things the moral ones have even in themselves some source of joy; moreover, they are means and instruments procuring benefits for men. The virtues deserve to be valued and loved for their own sake; they also bring temporal advantages. Therefore "humanly speaking, a man may rejoice in their possession and practise them for what they are in

---

[1] *Ibid.*, 3. 25.   [2] *Ibid.*, 3. 26.

themselves as well as for the sake of the blessings they bring him in human and temporal form". Thus did the princes and wise men of old. They esteemed and practised the virtues, and God rewarded them with temporal blessings since "they could not receive an eternal reward because of their lack of faith". "But, although the Christian should rejoice in this first way in the moral good and the good works he accomplishes in time, because they bring him the temporal blessings just described, he may yet not rest in them. . . . Because, having the light of faith, he hopes for eternal life, and since without this nothing either in this life or the next has any value for him, he should rather solely and essentially rejoice in the possession and practice of the moral good things according to the second manner, namely by accomplishing his works for the love of God and thus gaining eternal life. Hence he should turn his eyes and his joy solely to serving God, honouring Him by a good life and the practice of the virtues. Without this intention virtue has no value before God, as we see in the Ten Virgins of the Gospel. . . ." (Matt. 25. 1ff). "The Christian may not find his joy in doing good works and leading a good life, but in doing this without any other intention, solely for love of God." [1]

False joy in one's own good works produces Pharisaic pride and boasting, scant esteem for others and desire for human praise; thus the eternal reward is lost. Complacent joy in one's own work is unjust and amounts to denying God who is the Father of every good work. Such souls make no progress in perfection. If they no longer find satisfaction in their exercises, because God offers them the dry bread of the strong, they become discouraged and are unable to eat it: they "lose the constancy in which consists sweetness of spirit and interior consolation". Normally they also deceive themselves, preferring the practices and works that please them to those they dislike. But God is usually far better pleased with those works that require more self-denial, especially in the case of advanced souls. Finally, vain joy in one's own works renders a man "incapable of accepting good advice and reasonable instruction" about what ought to be done. "Such souls become very weak in their love for God and their neighbour, for the self-love produced by their works causes their charity to grow cold." [2]

By renouncing vain joy a man is preserved "from many temptations and deceits of the evil one, which are concealed in the joy in such works . . .". For the vain joy is itself deceit. There is another advantage

[1] *Ibid.*, 3. 27.   [2] *Ibid.*, 3. 28.

in "that the soul acts more deliberately and conscientiously in what it does". For the influence of reason is diminished by passionate joy, which makes the soul fickle in its resolutions and actions. In such a case a man is guided only by his own changeable tastes and leaves the most important works unfinished if he no longer feels attracted to them. But if the will renounces its natural satisfaction, it will persevere and reach its goal. Thus men also acquire the poverty of spirit our Lord calls blessed. They become meek, gentle and prudent in their behaviour, acting without violence and haste, and are incapable of arrogance. Renouncing vain joy makes them "pleasing to God and men, freeing the soul from avarice, spiritual gluttony and sloth, from spiritual envy and innumerable other vices".[1]

In a fifth group St John of the Cross treats the supernatural good things, i.e. "all the gifts and graces of God that transcend our natural capacity and power and . . . are called *dona gratis data*, e.g. the wisdom and knowledge which Solomon received and the graces of which St Paul speaks . . . : 'faith, gifts of healing, the working of miracles, prophecy, knowledge and discernment of spirits, interpretation of words and likewise the gift of tongues' (1 Cor. 12. 9f)". Their effects are related "to the salvation of men, and for this purpose . . . they are given by God". (On the other hand, the spiritual gifts discussed later concern the relation between God and the soul). The temporal effects of the supernatural gifts are the healing of diseases, the giving of sight to the blind, the raising of the dead and suchlike; the spiritual effects are that God is known and glorified by the person who does these signs or by the witnesses in whose presence they take place. Men should not rejoice in the supernatural works for the sake of their temporal effects, for thus they are not means of union with God. A man can "work them without having sanctifying grace and charity", though even so they may be given by God (as in the case of Balaam and Solomon), but they may also be performed with the help of Satan or of mysterious natural forces. St Paul teaches that all these gifts are nothing without charity (1 Cor. 13. 1f.). Then Christ will say to many who demand the eternal reward for their miracles: "Depart from me, ye workers of iniquity" (Matt. 7. 23). Hence we should only rejoice in the spiritual effects of these gifts, i.e. in "serving God in true charity, in which is the fruit of eternal life".[2]

Vain joy in supernatural things leads the soul into "deceiving others and being deceived itself"; it will become backward in the life of faith

---

[1] *Ibid.*, 3. 29.   [2] *Ibid.*, 3. 30.

and [become] a prey to vainglory or other vanities. These errors derive from the fact that only profound insight and divine enlightenment will tell a man whether such works "are genuine or spurious, and how and when they should be accomplished". Now a great esteem for them hinders such knowledge; judgement is darkened by complacency, and passion incites a man to procure this joy for himself as soon as possible, without waiting for the right moment. It is true, together with such gifts God also provides the necessary illumination on how and when to use them. Men, however, are imperfect, and do not heed the divine will nor care how and when the Lord wants these works to be done. Thus it is possible that the gifts bestowed by God may be used unjustly and perversely. Moreover, vain joy in miracles may lead men to perform them with the help of powers that are not from God. "For if the devil realizes that men are attached to such things he gives them much scope, offers them abundant material and intrudes in many ways." "Hence if someone receives such a gift of supernatural grace, he should suppress the passionate desire and joy in it when using it.... For God, who grants it in a supernatural way for the good of the Church and her children, will also move such persons supernaturally to use them when and as it is profitable...; for He wills ... that a man should take heed of the divine suggestion and the divine work in his heart, since every work must be accomplished with His power."

The damage done to faith by such works harms in the first place one's neighbour. A man who wants to perform a miracle though time and circumstances do not require it commits a grave sin, because he tempts God. If the attempt fails, this may weaken faith and expose it to contempt. But a man may also himself be harmed with regard to the merit of faith. "For ... the more signs and external proofs we have of a thing, the less is the merit of faith." All this indicates that God does not like to manifest himself through miracles. If he does so, this happens only "to lead someone to faith or for other purposes connected with the glorification of Himself and His saints". "Therefore those who take a special pleasure in these supernatural works lose much of the merit of faith." [1]

The soul that renounces such joys glorifies God and rises above itself. God is exalted in the soul when "the heart ... tears itself away from all that is not God...." But at the same time the soul, too, is exalted if it turns to God alone, for he reveals to it his majesty and

[1] *Ibid.*, 3. 31.

greatness and makes it realize what he is in himself. "If God is truly exalted when a man finds no joy in a creature, He is so even more if these . . . marvellous things . . . be disregarded. . . ." Further, God is the more glorified the more he is trusted and served without signs and wonders. "For then a man believes more about God than signs and wonders can manifest." In return, the soul will attain to a far purer faith which God infuses abundantly, thus increasing also hope and love. So it will enjoy "the most sublime divine knowledge through its dark and detached attitude of faith, the highest bliss of love through its charity, where the will finds joy in nothing save only in the living God; satisfaction in the will through hope.[1] All this is an admirable gain, leading directly and essentially to the perfect union of the soul with God."[2]

The good things of the spirit unite the soul to God more surely than all others. They are "those that influence and help the soul in divine things, in the intercourse of the soul with God and in God's communications to the soul". These good things may be pleasant or painful; they may concern things that are clearly and definitely known or others that are confused and dark. Here the saint wants to discuss only the pleasant communications referring to clear and distinct matters. (He reserves the others for a later chapter.)[3] With regard to these impressions the will is to follow the same rule as the understanding and the memory, since they can neither receive nor refuse anything without its co-operation. The will, too, ought not to have joy in anything from which these other two must be purified.[4]

The good things capable of giving the will a clear, conscious joy can be moving or encouraging, directing or perfecting.[5] To the moving kind belong the images and statues of the saints, oratories and ceremonies. "The images and statues . . . may be occasions of great vanity and vain joy", if men "consider the rarity and artistic value of a picture rather than what it represents". In such a case only the senses are captivated "and delight in it, while love and the satisfaction of the will remain unsatisfied". People even go so far as to adorn the saints with clothes appealing to contemporary taste, whereas the saints themselves "abhorred and still abhor such things". In this

---

[1] Thus in the text; we should rather expect memory, being the power that corresponds to hope. (Allison Peers follows a text that has memory, cf. vol. I, p. 307, note 2. —Translator.)

[2] *Ascent*, 3. 32.   [3] *Ibid.*, 3. 33.   [4] *Ibid.*, 3. 34.

[5] In Allison Peers's translation: "motive, provocative, directive and perfective", 3. 35. 1; vol. I, p. 309.—Translator.

way devotion is directed to the "adornment of the doll" and people are attached to it as to an idol. Some can "never have enough images and these must be of this or that shape . . . to satisfy the senses, while the devotion of the heart is left empty. . . . If properly used, however, images "are of great importance for the service of God, in order to excite the will to devotion". For this reason and to further the veneration of the saints the Church has approved their use. "Hence we should prefer those images which faithfully reproduce the living image and move the will to greater devotion." "The pious man will direct his devotion above all to what is invisible; he is satisfied with few images," preferring "those that express what is divine rather than what is human, in the ornaments of the images adapting himself rather to the divine, as did the saints of the past, and not to the fashion of the present". Such a person " is not attached to the images he uses and is not sad if they are taken away from him. He seeks the living image, Christ crucified, in himself . . . and gladly endures it if all others be taken away . . . even if they were means for him . . . to rise to God more easily. Being deprived of them does not take away his peace." "That which serves the mind to raise the heart to God . . . must be regarded lightly; it should not serve as a stimulant to the senses; for if I surrender to the delight I have in the stimulants, that which serves as a support for my imperfection will become a hindrance . . . just as attachment and inclination for anything else."

Even worse than the abuse of images is the imperfection "with which rosaries are commonly used. There are few who have not some weakness in their regard. One form is liked better than the other, this colour and this metal better than that. . . . Does God answer a prayer rather if one prays with this or that rosary? The point is only to pray with a simple and sincere heart, to have nothing else in view than to please God. . . ."[1]

Great, too, is the stupidity of those "who trust in one image more than in another and think God will hear their prayer if they venerate one rather than another, though both represent the same. . . . God looks only at the faith and purity of heart of him who prays." If he sometimes grants more graces through one image than through another, this is so because "the faithful are moved to devotion more by the one than by the other. If their devotion to one image were as great as that to the other (and even without the use of either) they would receive the same graces from God." If miracles once more rouse

[1] *Ibid.*, 3. 35.

sleeping devotion before a particular image, if the faithful are thereby inflamed to persistent prayer—"these are the conditions on which God grants our petitions—, then God, touched by the prayer and love of the faithful, deigns to use always the same image to bestow His graces and work His miracles . . .". "Experience teaches that God is wont to attach certain graces and miracles to statues which are not particularly well carved . . . so that the faithful should not ascribe anything to the artistic form. Often our Lord grants these graces through images venerated in lonely, far-off places, because love grows on the way there . . ., and also because we withdraw from the noise of the world in order to pray as the Lord did." "Therefore pilgrimages are best made without much company. If we set out with many people, we usually return more distracted than we left." " . . . Where there is devotion and faith, any image will suffice; where these are lacking, none will do. No other image was so truly living as our Saviour on earth, and yet those who did not believe in Him did not profit from the fact that they went about with Him and saw His miracles." [1] Yet even where there is devotion the use of images may involve dangers. The enemy likes to use them in order to bring careless souls into his power, e.g. by faking supernatural apparitions (that images begin to move, to make signs and suchlike). In order to avoid all harm we should seek in the images "only a motive for love and joy . . . in the living person they represent ". If an image should "rouse sensual or spiritual devotion or even give supernatural signs" the soul "ought not to pay attention to these irrelevant things . . . but only give such veneration to the image as is in accordance with the mind of the Church. Then it should raise its mind to what it represents and direct all the strength and joy of its will to God in devout interior prayer. . . ." [2]

Being attached to images or beautifully adorned oratories is perhaps even more dangerous than attachment to worldly things, because here we feel secure and free from faults. There are people who give the adornment of their oratories all the time "they ought to spend in prayer to God and interior recollection. . . . This satisfaction of their desires . . . causes them constant distractions, especially if anyone wants to take these things away from them." [3] True, for beginners it is "useful and salutary to find a certain sensible joy and pleasure in images, oratories and other visible objects of piety". This helps them to lose their taste for worldly things. The pure spirit, however, "knows only interior recollection and mental converse with God". Certainly,

[1] *Ibid.*, 3. 36.   [2] *Ibid.*, 3. 37.   [3] *Ibid.*, 3. 38.

we should pray in suitable surroundings; churches and silent places have the right atmosphere for prayer; yet, in order to adore God "in spirit and in truth" (John 4. 23) we should not select a place pleasing to the senses. "A lonely, rugged spot seems to be most suitable for the spirit to soar to God directly with its whole power and not to be hindered by visible things. ... For this reason our Saviour used to choose solitary places for prayer and such that did not appeal much to the senses (in order to give us an example), but which raised the soul to God, such as mountains that rise above the earth and are generally bare, offering no stimulus to the senses."[1] God uses three kinds of places to rouse the will to devotion: suitable scenery which incites spiritual feelings by the formation of its ground, its trees and its silent solitude. Nevertheless, men should " ... behave in such places as if they were not there, if they would be with God interiorly". Further, in certain places, whether solitary or not, God grants some persons special spiritual favours. Thus they become attached to such a place and long to go there again. There is nothing disorderly in this if it happens without selfish desire. For though God is not tied to a place it seems that he wants to be praised by the men more especially where he had granted them favours; there the soul is reminded more impressively of its duty of gratitude, and the memory is a great spur to its devotion. Finally, there are "places which God chooses in a special way to be invoked and served there. Such was Mount Sinai, where He gave the Law to Moses (Ex. 20. 2). ... Likewise Mount Horeb, where God told Elias to go so as to reveal Himself to him there (3 Kings 19. 8). ... The reason why God chose these places rather than others to be praised there is known to Him alone. As to us, it suffices to know that all is meant for our spiritual progress, and God hears us there and wherever we call on Him in perfect faith. And if we beseech Him in places that are dedicated to His special service, we have the more chance to be heard since the Church has appointed and dedicated them to this particular end."[2]

The aberrations so far discussed "are perhaps still to a certain extent tolerable and may be ascribed to innocent enthusiasm". But what is quite insufferable is the unlimited trust of many people "in various ceremonies which persons of little insight and lacking in the simplicity of faith have invented". They ascribe such power to certain practices that they imagine "all will be useless and God will not hear them if only a tittle be lacking or if they went beyond their limits. They trust

[1] *Ibid.*, 3. 39.   [2] *Ibid.*, 3. 42.

more in these practices than in the living spirit of prayer, and this greatly dishonours and offends God. Thus a Mass should be said with so many candles, neither more nor less; a certain priest must say it at such and such an hour, neither earlier nor later. . . . And if anything is lacking, all is in vain. . . . It is even worse and quite intolerable if others desire to feel an effect of their prayer in themselves or to receive what they ask, or to be assured that the granting of their request is a direct effect of their superstitious prayer."[1] "Such persons should realize that the more importance they attach to these vain external ceremonies the less they trust in God. Therefore they do not receive from God what they ask for. Many are far more concerned with the granting of their own desires than with the glory of God. . . ." "It would be far better for them to devote their energy to more important things, such as the perfect purification of their conscience or to understanding what concerns their salvation. . . . For this is our Lord's promise in the Gospel: 'Seek ye first the kingdom of God and His justice, and all these things shall be added unto you' (Matt. 6. 33). This petition for eternal salvation is most pleasing to God, and there is no better means to obtain the fulfilment of our hearts' desires than to direct all the energy of our prayer to what pleases God most. For then He will give us not only what we ask, that is eternal salvation, but also everything He knows to be good and profitable for us. . . . 'The Lord is near to all who call on Him; who call on Him in truth' (Ps. 144. 18). Now those call on Him in truth who ask Him for the highest, the true good things, such as concern salvation. . . . Thus the powers of the will and its joy in prayer must be directed to God and should not cling to our own inventions . . .; we ought not to introduce new practices, as if we knew these things better than the Holy Spirit and His Church. If God does not hear a simple prayer, let them not think that He will hear them however many inventions they may make." We shall obtain from God all we desire "if we agree with what is in harmony with Him; but if we pursue our own personal interest it is useless to turn to Him". ". . . When the disciples asked our Lord: 'Lord, teach us to pray', He surely taught them all that is necessary to be heard by the eternal Father. . . . He taught them only the seven petitions of the Our Father, in which all our spiritual and bodily needs are contained, and said nothing more of various forms of words and ceremonies. On the contrary, He urged them not to make many words when they prayed, since our Father in heaven knows well

[1] *Ibid.*, 3. 43.

what we need (Matt. 6. 7f). He only emphasized one thing in particular: that we should persevere in prayer. . . ." As to external ceremonies, he taught only two: ". . . when thou wilt pray, enter into thy
chamber and, having shut the door, pray to thy Father in secret"
(Matt. 6. 6). Further, we should retire to solitary places as he did,
and at the best and quietest time: at night. He says nothing of special
times and days, ceremonies and forms of speech.[1]

Finally, St John speaks of the preachers who may teach us to serve
the Lord. In order to be useful to his people and not himself to become
a victim of vain complacency, the preacher must realize "that preaching is a spiritual work and no mere talk". It is true, the effect of a
sermon presupposes a certain receptivity on the part of the hearers,
but the most important factor is the right attitude of the preacher.
Unless he is penetrated by the true spirit, the most sublime doctrine
and the most perfect style will be of no avail. The more exemplary
his life, the more useful he will be, even if his style should be poor and
his delivery simple. A fine style, sublime doctrine and a good delivery
will greatly stir the audience if they are animated by the spirit of
devotion. "But without this spirit only the senses and the understanding will find pleasure and satisfaction in it, whereas the will is
stirred and excited only little or not at all. . . . Well-sounding words
alone have no power to raise one who is dead from his grave." The
saint would in no way belittle a good style, sublime eloquence and well-
chosen words. All these "are very important for the preacher as for
every professional man, for the right word and a good style may please
and restore things that are fallen and spoilt, whereas badly chosen
expressions may ruin and destroy the best things. . . ."[2]

2. RECIPROCAL ILLUMINATION OF SPIRIT AND FAITH

(a) Retrospect and Prospect

Here the *Ascent of Mount Carmel* suddenly breaks off.[3] We do not
know whether the work was never finished or no complete manuscript has been preserved. The treatise on joy is incomplete, the other
passions have not been treated at all. The parts on passive purification
announced in the *Ascent* are worked out in the *Dark Night*. It is also

---

[1] *Ibid.,* 3. 44.   [2] *Ibid.,* 3. 45.
[3] In some manuscripts the two fragments first printed in *Ed. Crit.,* I, as chs. 45 and 46
follow here. We have used them in an earlier place, as the subject matter required it (at
the beginning of the preceding section on the purification of the will).

surprising that the poem placed in front of the work is actually commented on only at the beginning; later the presentation moves increasingly away from it in order to treat other questions arising from the context. This gap, too, is filled by the *Dark Night*. In the last part of this work the stanzas actually provide the leading ideas, though the commentary breaks off in the exposition of the first line of the third stanza as suddenly as the *Ascent* in the treatment of joy. The fragmentary and in some respects uneven character of these works is probably to be explained by the circumstances and the way in which they were written. John did not compose them as an author intent on creating a completely balanced whole. Nor was his aim to give a systematic theology of mysticism[1] or a philosophical and psychological doctrine of the affections. He wrote as a father and teacher for his spiritual sons and daughters in answer to their request for an interpretation of his spiritual canticles; hence he recalled the religious experience expressed in them and translated their imagery into the language of notional thought. He probably realized only while working on it that this needed preparatory considerations and a large amount of material which had to be gathered in many fields. So he may have become involved in more digressions than he had originally intended; yet he never lost sight of his goal, always firmly restraining his lively thought and the ideas that were crowding into his mind. It should further be borne in mind that he wrote his treatises just in those years when he was most burdened with offices and external business. He cannot have had sufficient leisure for quiet composition and subsequent corrections and polishing. It would also be quite probable that, after a considerable interruption, he could no longer take up the thread where he had left off but instead supplemented the first work by the second. All this had to be mentioned to enable us to give an adequate evaluation of the preceding discussions of the saint.

We have reproduced the teaching given in the *Ascent* on entering the night of the spirit so as better to understand what St John means

[1] *The treatise on the Dark Positive and Negative Knowledge of God* might be considered a short introduction to mysticism understood as a branch of theology. P. Gerardo was the first to print it in the Works of the saint (*Ed. crit.*, III, 287ff) and has given the several reasons that have been adduced for and against the authenticity of this work in his introduction (p. 271ff). In my view there are several internal reasons against the authenticity not mentioned by P. Gerardo. Hence I cannot assume that the work belongs to the saint himself and am obliged to use it only with great caution. The author certainly knew the writings of St John very well; he gives clear and precise summaries but, it seems to me, shifts the centre towards a purely natural and active spirituality, probably being himself without experience in the highest, purely passive, forms of prayer with which the saint is principally concerned.

by spirit and faith. For faith is the way leading through the night to
the goal of union with God. In it the spirit is painfully re-born and
transformed from natural into supernatural being. The discussions
on spirit and faith mutually illumine each other. Faith demands that
the natural activity of the spirit should be renounced; the active night
of faith, in which man imitates the Cross by his own initiative, is
characterized by this renunciation. The natural activity of the mind
must be discussed in order to explain this renunciation and, with it,
faith. On the other hand, faith proves by its very existence the
possibility of a being and activity superior to the natural ones; and
thus the discussion of faith leads to a new view of the spirit. This
explains why spirit must be discussed differently in different contexts.
A superficial reader might think this contradictory and betraying a
lack of balance. In fact it is due to the subject matter itself. For since
spiritual being implies life and change, its knowledge cannot be
pressed into rigid definitions but must itself be a forward movement
seeking a supple mode of expression. The same is true of faith. For
this, too, is spiritual being and hence movement, ascending into
increasingly incomprehensible heights and descending into ever
more mysterious depths. Thus, if the understanding would grasp it
as far as this is at all possible, it must do so by means of manifold
expressions.

(b) Natural Activity of the Spirit. The Soul, its Parts and Powers

In the first place, then, we must explain the natural activity of the
spirit. This results from the whole structure of psychic-intellectual
being. St John of the Cross seeks to define it with the help of traditional
concepts of scholastic pyschology which were certainly familiar to him
from his student days at Salamanca. The soul is an existing whole with
manifold powers, divided into inferior and superior, or sensual and
spiritual ones. Both in the lower and in the higher part of the soul the
powers are divided into intellective (= knowing) and appetitive
(= desiring) ones. This division is not explicitly stated, but presupposed in St John's works. The senses are organs of the body but
at the same time the windows of the soul, through which it gains
knowledge of the outside world. Hence sensuality is common to body
and soul, but John pays comparatively little attention to the former.
Apart from the impressions providing knowledge of the sense world,
the sphere of sensuality also contains enjoyment and desire, which are
caused in the soul by the impressions of sense. As has been stated

before, the Night of the Senses is pre-eminently concerned with sensuality in this second sense; in this Night the soul is both to free itself and to flame purified from the desire for sensual enjoyment. This restriction is fully justified, because enjoyment and desire are possible already at the stage of a purely sensual life of the soul (hence also in animals). Knowledge, on the other hand, even in the lower form of sense perception, is impossible without intellectual activity. Moreover, that which actually absorbs the soul is desire and enjoyment.

Sense knowledge is impossible without intellectual activity, and this suggests the close connexion between higher and lower psychic being. Now these expressions are not to be understood as referring, as it were, to floors built on top of each other. Higher and lower parts are only spatial images of something wholly non-spatial. St John says explicitly that in the case of "the soul as spirit one can speak neither of high nor of low . . . as in the case of extended bodies".[1] In the natural sphere sensual and spiritual activities are closely intertwined. Just as the windows of the senses cannot lead to a knowledge of the sense world unless there is a spirit to look through them, so, on the other hand, the spirit needs these windows in order to look into the world. Or, differently expressed: the senses provide the material for the activity of the spirit. In agreement with St Augustine[2] and differing from St Thomas, St John of the Cross places the memory as the third power of the mind beside understanding and will. This should not be regarded as a profound discrepancy, since there is no question of a real division of the soul but only of different modes of action; the one power of the soul is active in one direction or another. Both forms of dividing the powers of the soul can be supported by good reasons. Without the original achievement of the memory, the retaining faculty, neither a sense impression nor a spiritual activity would be possible.

For both take place in temporal succession, and this requires that the respective contents of the moment (broadly speaking) should not disappear but be preserved. It can be shown that the proper activity of the intellect (comparing, generalizing, concluding, etc.) also needs the other achievements of the memory such as remembering and freely modifying by means of the imagination. But this subject cannot be pursued here. We have only hinted at it, because it can thus be understood that in the case of the memory it is possible to distinguish between

---

[1] *Living Flame of Love*, 1. 10.   [2] *De Trinitate*, XII, 4 and 7.

sensible and intellectual activities and to include it in the other powers.[1] On the other hand, its achievements are not actually acts of knowledge but only aids towards them. (Something similar can be proved for the relation between memory and will). Hence we are justified in regarding the memory as a special power. Besides, for St Augustine the decisive factor in favour of the tripartite division of the soul was the trinitarian form of the spirit, for St John it was the mutual relation between the three spiritual powers and the three theological virtues. Here we touch the principal point in his doctrine of the spirit.

(c) *Supernatural Elevation of the Spirit. Faith and its Life*

In its natural activity the spirit is tied to the senses. It takes in what they offer it, preserves what has been perceived, recalls it when there is an occasion for doing so, combines it with other things, transforms it and, by means of comparing, generalizing, concluding, etc., arrives at its notional knowledge, at judgements and conclusions, the acts proper to the understanding. In the same way the will naturally acts on what it is offered by the senses, finds its joy in it, seeks to possess it, feels pain at its loss, hopes for possession and fears loss. But the spirit is not meant only to know and enjoy created things. It is a perversion of its original and true being that it should be ensnared in them. It must be disentangled from them and lifted up to the true being for which it has been created. Its intention must be directed towards the Creator, to whom it should surrender with all its powers. This is to be achieved by a progressive work of education and deprivation. God gives the impulse and perfects this work, but man must co-operate by his own spiritual activity. The spirit must be deprived of all that occupies it naturally. It must be educated to know God and rejoice in him alone. At first this is done by offering the natural powers something that will attract and satisfy them more than what they know and enjoy naturally. Faith directs the understanding towards the Creator who has given being to all things and who is himself infinitely greater, more exalted and more lovable than any of them. Faith also teaches it God's properties and tells it what God has done for man and

---

[1] St Thomas includes memory in the proper sense in sensuality because it recognizes past things as past, hence distinguishes them from the present: this, he affirms, is a concern of sensuality. But since the understanding not only knows what is present but also *that* it knows it and in such a way that it had this knowledge already formerly, the memory can also be counted as belonging to the spiritual part of the soul (*De Veritate*, 9, 10a, 2 corp. E. Stein, *Untersuchungen über die Wahrheit*, I, p. 266ff).

what man owes him. Now what is meant by faith in this connexion?
Evidently that which is offered us for our belief, the quintessence of
all revealed truths proclaimed by the Church: *fides quae creditur*. By
accepting what is presented to it without being able to grasp it by its
own insight, the understanding takes the first step into the dark night
of faith. Now this is *fides qua creditur*, a living act of the spirit and a
corresponding lasting habit (*habitus* or virtue of faith): the conviction
that God is (*credere Deum*) and the convinced acceptance of what God
teaches through the Church (*credere Deo*).[1] In this life of faith the
spirit rises above its natural activity, but it is as yet in no way detached
from it. Rather, in the new world opened up by faith the natural
powers of the mind are given a wealth of fresh material on which to
act. The activity of the mind by which it assimilates the contents of
faith is called meditation. Here the imagination looks upon the events
described in the Gospel, seeks to exhaust all their meaning and considers with the understanding their general significance and the
demands they make. The will is thereby inclined to love, resolving
henceforth to live in the spirit of faith. St John also knows a higher
form of meditation:[2] a naturally lively and highly gifted mind may
deeply penetrate into the truths of faith, consider them in all their
aspects, converse about them with itself, develop them to their
intellectual conclusions and discover their inner connexions. This
activity will become even more lively, easy and fruitful if the Holy
Spirit inspires the human mind and raises it above itself. Then it will
feel to be in the hands of a higher power enlightening it, so that it
seems no longer to be active itself, but to be instructed by divine
revelation.

Anything the spirit has acquired by meditation in one of these
forms becomes its permanent possession. Now this is more than a
mere treasure of stored-up truths to be produced from the memory
in case of need. Through its constant occupation with God the spirit
—and this means here not only the understanding but also the heart
—becomes familiar with him, it knows and loves him. This knowledge
and love have become part of its being; the relation between God and
man at this stage may be compared with that between two people
who have lived together for a long time and are on most intimate terms.
They no longer need to make enquiries and think about each other;

---

[1] To elucidate the variety of meanings contained in the term faith I here follow the
distinctions made by St Thomas in the *Quaestiones de Veritate* (q. 14, a. 7, ad 7;
Untersuchungen über die Wahrheit, II, p. 28).

[2] Cf. *Ascent*, 2. 26.

for they know one another thoroughly and are convinced that each is worthy of the other's love; they hardly need words to understand each other. True, each new meeting brings a fresh awakening and increase of love, perhaps even a knowledge of new minor traits of character, but this happens as it were by itself, without any conscious effort. This is a fairly adequate description of the communion of a soul with God after a long practice of the spiritual life. It need no longer meditate in order to learn to know and love God. The way has been left far behind, the soul is resting at its goal. As soon as it begins to pray it is with God and remains in his presence in loving surrender. Its silence is dearer to him than many words. This is what today is called "acquired contemplation". (John of the Cross does not use the term, but he knows the thing.[1]) It is the fruit of man's own activity, though inspired and supported by grace. For the message of faith, God's revealed truth, reaches us by grace, which also gives us the power to accept this message—even though we must do this by our own free decision—and thus to become faithful. Without the assistance of grace no prayer or meditation is possible. Yet all this is accomplished within the domain of our freedom with the help of our own powers. It also depends on us whether we begin to pray and how much time we spend in acquired contemplation. If we now consider this contemplation in itself, the quiet, loving surrender to God, we can affirm that this, too, is a form of faith, the *fides qua creditur*: not as *credere Deum* (though faith in God's existence is presupposed and included in it), neither as *credere Deo* (though this is the outcome of all we have accepted by faith as God's revealed truth), but as *credere in Deum*, believing as it were into God, entering into him by faith.

This is the highest achievement of the life of faith to be attained by man's own activity, if it results in the surrender of his own to the divine will and the ordering of his whole life in accordance with this. It also raises the human spirit far above the natural conditions of its being. Certainly, the truths of faith first acquaint us with God through images, parables and ideas taken from created things. But they also teach us that God transcends all these and surpasses all comprehension. Hence we must leave all creatures behind as well as our own faculties by which we grasp and apprehend them, and by faith raise ourselves

[1] Cf. *Ascent*, 2. 13. The *Short Treatise on the Dark Positive and Negative Knowledge of God*, Ed. *Crit.*, III, 287ff speaks of natural contemplation. (This short work is not generally recognized as genuine, as has been stated above.)

to God, the Incomprehensible.[1] Neither the senses nor the understanding are capable of this, if the latter be taken as the faculty of
notional thought. In our believing surrender to the incomprehensible
God we are pure spirit, detached from all images and notions, hence in
darkness, because the world we see in the daytime is built up from
images and notions. We are freed also from the mechanism of a variety
of diverse powers, and thus united and simple in a life which is knowledge, memory and love all in one. Only now are we on the threshold
of the mystical life, at the beginning of the transformation that is to
be achieved through the Night of the Spirit. We have reached what is
left untouched by the suspension of the faculties. For something must
be left, if the union and transformation in God is to be possible only
after the faculties have been suspended. And only this something that is
beyond sensuality and beyond the understanding tied to the senses
must be spirit in the proper sense. In this connexion John also speaks
of the essence of the soul. The soul is spirit according to its essence,
and in its inmost being receptive to all that is spiritual : for God, the
pure Spirit, and for all he has created and which is also spiritual in its
inmost being. But the soul is immersed in bodily existence and the
senses tied to the body are the organs by which it receives all that is
material. These organs which should have been servants have become
masters through the Fall. The spirit must first be freed from their
grasp if it is to regain strength for a purely spiritual life and action
as well as its dominion over the senses. We have pursued the activity
of faith in this process of deliverance up to a certain point: we
have seen how faith directs the spirit towards God and finally leads to
a purely spiritual intercourse with him. But this turning towards God
must be complemented by a turning away from all that is not God.
This is the chief work accomplished in the Active Night of the Spirit.

(d) Extraordinary Communications of Grace and Detachment

As has been seen, faith incites the powers of the soul to occupy
themselves with God and divine things; nevertheless, a man is still
far from having achieved detachment from the created world. Even
those who have seriously resolved to lead a spiritual life and persevere
in it devote only a greater or smaller portion of their day to prayer and
meditation. Apart from this, their feet are still firmly planted in the
created world. They strive to penetrate this world intellectually and

[1] (Only the negative contemplation is discussed here, which St John of the Cross
considers particularly, but not the way to positive contemplation.—Editors' note.)

to subject it, they want to acquire temporal goods and enjoy them. They still succumb to the magic of natural good things; they are not yet immune from the satisfactions of the senses, even though, under the influence of their prayer life they may already severely curb their desires in this direction. Hence their understanding is occupied with the things of this world which absorb its energy; their imagination is filled with them, their will is determined by them in its desires and tied to them by its passions. All this is a hindrance to the life of prayer and would finally destroy it altogether if God did not help the soul with his special grace. He does this not through the message of faith but through extraordinary communications capable of surpassing and neutralizing the attractions of the natural world. Senses and imagination are filled with images transcending all earthly beauty. Supernatural illuminations give the understanding insights which its own intellectual activity could never achieve. The heart is filled with heavenly consolation beside which all joys and pleasures of the world must pale. In this way the soul is prepared completely to turn away from the good things of earth and to rise to those of heaven.

But this is only half the work. We should never reach the goal of union with God if we were to stop short at the supernatural communications and rest in their enjoyment. Visions, revelations and sweet feelings are not God himself nor do they lead to him—excepting those highest, purely spiritual touches in which God himself communicates himself to the essence of the soul and thus grants it the mystical union. Hence the soul must also detach itself from all supernatural gifts of God in order to gain the Giver rather than his gifts. But how can it be induced willingly to surrender such great goods? This is once more achieved by faith which teaches the soul that God is nothing of all it can grasp and understand, inviting it to embark on the dark way which alone leads to the goal.[1] Yet faith would achieve but little if it only instructed the understanding. The powerful reality of the natural world and of the supernatural gifts of grace must be conquered by a still more powerful reality. This happens in the passive Night. Without this, as St John never fails to stress, the active Night would not achieve its end. The strong hand of the living God himself must intervene to free the soul from the snares of all created things and draw it to himself. This intervention is the dark, mystical contemplation, together with the privation of all that has hitherto given light, support and consolation.

[1] *Ascent*, 2. 3.

3. DEATH AND RESURRECTION

(a) Passive Night of the Spirit

Faith, Dark Contemplation, Detachment

We know from the Night of the Senses that there comes a time when the soul loses its taste for spiritual exercises as well as for all earthly things, when it is cast into complete darkness and emptiness with no other support than only faith. Faith offers it Christ, poor, humble, crucified, forsaken on the Cross even by his divine Father. In his poverty and desolation the soul recognizes its own. Aridity, distaste and pain are the "purely spiritual Cross" presented to it. If it accepts this, the soul will find that the yoke is sweet and the burden light; the Cross will become its staff by which it quickly mounts upward. For Christ accomplished his greatest work, the reconciliation and union of mankind with God, in the utmost humiliation and annihilation on the Cross. When the soul realizes this it will begin to understand that it, too, must be led to union with God through annihilation, a "living crucifixion, in the sensual as well as in the spiritual part".[1] As, in the desolation of his death, Jesus surrendered himself into the hands of the invisible and incomprehensible God, so the soul must enter the midnight darkness of faith, which is the only way to this God. Thus it will find mystical contemplation, the "ray of darkness".[2] the mysterious theology that gives dark and general knowledge: for this alone corresponds to the transcendent God who blinds the understanding, to which he appears as darkness. This contemplation invades the soul all the more purely the freer the soul is from all other impressions. For it is far more pure, delicate, spiritual and interior than anything known to the understanding from the natural life of the spirit; it is raised above the temporal and is a true beginning of eternal life in us. This contemplation is no mere acceptance of the message of faith that comes by hearing, no mere turning to God who is known only from hearsay; it is an interior touch and an experience of God capable of detaching the soul from all created things, of elevating it and at the same time immersing it in a love that does not know its object. We will not now decide whether this dark loving knowledge in which God touches the inmost sphere of the soul—from "mouth to mouth", from essence to essence—can still be regarded as faith.[3] The soul surrenders through the will (as its

---

[1] *Ibid.*, 2. 7.   [2] Dionysius the Areopagite, *Mystica Theologia*, 1. 1.

[3] St John himself speaks of the relation between faith and contemplation in different passages in a different way. We shall return to this at the end of this section.

mouth) to the loving approach of the still hidden God; its love is no
mere emotion; it is a love prepared for action and sacrifice, by which a
man surrenders his will to God to be led by him alone. If now the soul
is again granted definite particular illuminations, revelations and
consolations—as often happens in the normally very long period of
the Night of the Spirit—it will no longer want to rest in them. Thus
these supernatural communications will effect what God intended,
while the soul itself remains in the darkness of faith. For it knows
not only theoretically but by experience that these graces neither are
nor give God, whereas faith gives it all it needs: Christ himself who
is eternal Wisdom, and in him the incomprehensible God. It will be
the more ready for renunciation and perseverance in faith the more
thoroughly it has been purified by the dark night.

It has been stressed repeatedly that even after long practice of the
spiritual life the soul is still full of imperfections and in need of
thorough purification in order to be fit for the divine union. It has
also been shown that these imperfections can very well exist together
with all kinds of supernatural communications, indeed that the divine
gifts themselves can become an occasion for imperfection in the as yet
incompletely purified soul, in which they may cause pride, vanity and
spiritual gluttony. God heals all these weaknesses by the stripping
accomplished in the Dark Night, "by surrendering the understanding
to darkness, the will to aridity, the memory to emptiness and the
affections of the soul to extreme affliction, bitterness and strait-
ness. . . ."[1] Here spirit and senses are ultimately purified together,
after the transformation and curbing of the desires and the communion with God in the first Night have strengthened the senses
sufficiently to endure the much greater afflictions of this second purification. This, too, is the work of dark contemplation.

So far we have considered especially the advantages of contemplation, which directs man's spiritual powers to God and leads him to
detachment from all created things. This gain had become apparent
in the discussion of the Active Night of the Spirit in the *Ascent*; it is
once more briefly summarized in the new interpretation the saint gives
of the introductory stanza of the *Canticle of the Night* at the beginning
of the treatise on the *Dark Night of the Spirit*: "In poverty and
desolation, when my soul was void of all contents, i.e. in the darkness
of my understanding, in the constraint of my will, in the affliction
and anxiety of my memory, I have surrendered in darkness to pure

[1] *Dark Night of the Spirit*, 3. 3.

faith, this dark night for the said natural powers. While my will alone was filled with pain, sorrow and longing for the love of God, I went out from myself, that is from my lowly mode of knowledge, from my weak love and from my poor and limited manner of enjoying God, without being hindered in it by sensuality or the evil one. This was a great happiness . . . for me. For as soon as I had annihilated and calmed the powers, the passions, desires and inclinations of my soul, on account of which I had thought of God in such lowly manner and had found so little enjoyment in Him, I escaped from my poor, human way and operation and came to the way and operation of God, i.e. my understanding went forth from itself, and from a human and natural became a divine one. It united itself to God . . . and now no longer acts by its own natural power but through the divine wisdom to which it is united. My will, too, went forth from itself and became divine. United to divine love it no longer loves in a lowly manner with its natural power, but in the power and purity of the Holy Spirit. . . . In exactly the same way the memory, too, has changed and turned to apprehensions of eternal life. . . . All these energies and affections of the soul are wholly renewed through this night and purification of the old man (and enjoy) divine harmony and bliss."[1]

This purification, however, is not only night, but also pain and torment, and this for two reasons: "The first is the sublimity of divine wisdom, which transcends the capacity of the soul: therefore it is darkness. The second is the lowness and impurity of the soul; hence it is painful, afflicting and obscure."[2] Through the extraordinary, supernatural light "the natural intelligence of the soul is overwhelmed and extinguished". Thus it happens that God, "when He infuses this bright ray of His mysterious wisdom into the soul that is not yet transformed, causes thick darkness in the understanding". The pain and torment of the soul is caused by the fact that the "divine infused contemplation contains a wealth of sublime perfection. The soul which receives it and is not yet purified, however, is thrown into a sea of the most fearful distress, since contraries cannot exist together in one subject. . . ." Hence just in this bright light it feels itself "so impure and miserable that it seems to it that God is against it and it against God; it believes to be really cast out by God". It is tortured by the fear that it will never become worthy of God and that it has lost all its treasures of grace. For this divine and dark light shows the

---

[1] *Ibid.*, 4. 1f.   [2] *Ibid.*, 5. 2.

soul quite clearly all the misery of its sins, and it "recognizes perfectly that from itself it cannot have anything else".[1]

The soul is tormented in a different way because of its natural moral and spiritual weakness. When "the divine contemplation assails the soul with some strength in order to invigorate and govern it, it suffers so much in its weakness that it would almost despair. At certain times especially, when contemplation seizes it with extraordinary power, sense and spirit suffer as if they were thrown down under an immense, dark load"; they wish for death as a relief and favour. It is astonishing that "the soul is so weak and impure and for this reason feels the hand which is so kind and loving in itself as heavy and hostile, though this hand does not want to oppress and burden it, but only touches it in mercy . . . not to chastise it, but to grant it a favour".[2] When the two extremes, divine contemplation and the human soul, come into contact, "God consumes and destroys the spiritual substance of the soul and envelops it in such deep, black darkness that it . . . believes itself to be given over to destruction and dissolution by a cruel spiritual death. . . ." What the afflicted soul here feels most painfully "is the thought that God has apparently cast it out and thrown it into darkness as a creature to be abhorred. . . . It feels . . . shadows of death, groans of death and pains of hell. . . . This is the feeling of being without God, of being cast out by God in His great wrath . . . and then comes the fearful dread that, as far as it can see, it will always remain like this." Finally, the sublime greatness of this dark contemplation makes the soul conscious of its own bitter poverty and extreme misery. It feels a profound emptiness and poverty in temporal, natural and spiritual goods and sees itself cast "into the misery of its imperfections, into aridity, complete incapacity to apprehend anything with its faculties, and dark abandonment of the spirit. . . . It feels as if it were suspended in the air without being able to breathe. But God also purifies the soul by annihilating all its affections and habitual imperfections, emptying and destroying them as fire consumes rust and mouldiness in metal. Since these have struck deep root in the essence of the soul it usually has to suffer great affliction, destruction and interior torment, beside natural and spiritual poverty and stripping. . . ." To remove and destroy the rust of its affections the soul must in a certain sense "first annihilate and consume itself, since these passions and imperfections have, as it were, become its second nature". And it "feels this violent undoing of itself in its own substance . . . so

[1] *Ibid.*, 5. 3–5.   [2] *Ibid.*, 5. 6f.

that it almost swoons away for misery". "Here God greatly humbles the soul in order later to elevate it the more." If this state were to last, the soul "would quickly have to leave the body. But happily these feelings come to the fore with great violence only in short intervals. However, sometimes it perceives its abominable unworthiness so keenly that it seems to see hell open before its eyes. Such souls truly descend into the underworld, because they are purged here on earth in the same way as there. . . . And thus the soul that here suffers in this way either does not enter that place at all or is detained there only for a very short time, since it is here perfected more in one hour than there in many." [1]

The soul's sufferings are even intensified by its former happy state, for usually such souls "have found great sweetness in God before entering this night, and have done much in His service". But now they are far removed from this blissful state and can no more attain to it. Moreover, contemplation places the soul in such great loneliness and abandonment "that it cannot find comfort and support either in instruction or in a spiritual guide. For although it may be shown the most diverse reasons for comfort . . . it thinks that others do not see what it sees and feels itself or talk only without understanding the matter. And so, instead of being comforted it is, on the contrary, filled with new affliction since in its view all this cannot remedy its troubled state. And this is indeed so. For as long as the Lord has not completed the purification as it pleases Him there is no means or remedy to soothe its pain." This state lasts until the soul "is quite gentle, humble, purged in spirit and so keen, simple and delicate that it can become one with the Spirit of God, according to the degree of union of love that His mercy wills to grant. . . ." This degree determines the intensity and duration of the purging. Usually it lasts for years, but with interruptions, "in which, by the dispensation of God, the dark contemplation works in the soul not in a purging, but in an illuminating and pleasing way. The soul breathes in freedom and ease as if it had escaped from dungeon and fetters, feeling and enjoying the greatest delight of peace and of the loving friendship with God in readily abounding spiritual communication." Then a person thinks that all troubles are now over for ever, just as before the pain seemed to have no end. This is so, because "in the spirit, the present possession of something excludes by itself the present possession and feeling of its contrary. In the sensual part of the soul this is not so, because of the

[1] *Ibid.*, ch. 6.

weakness of its receptive powers. But because here the spirit is even yet not completely purged and cleansed from the affections the lower part has contracted, it is still subject to change in its afflictions . . . even though the spirit, as spirit, does not change." But the soul does not often imagine that all its pains are over. "For as long as the spiritual purification is not complete, it rarely receives the sweet communications of God in such abundance that they completely cover up the remaining root (of imperfection); the soul feels interiorly that it is still lacking something. . . . This feeling prevents it from completely enjoying that relief, since it still perceives an enemy within itself; though he is now hushed and asleep, it yet fears that he may rise again and continue his work. And this is truly so: when the soul feels itself quite secure and is inattentive, he seeks once more to devour it and to cast it down into even worse, darker and more painful sorrows than before. . . ." Again the soul believes that its former happiness is lost for ever, because the "present apprehension of the spirit . . . completely annihilates what is contrary to it". This is also the reason why the souls in purgatory doubt that their sufferings will ever end. It is true, they have the theological virtues and are aware of loving God, but they find no consolation in this, "because they cannot believe that God loves them or that they are worthy of it. . . . And though the soul perceives in this purification that it loves God and would give a thousand lives for Him . . . this gives it no comfort, but rather even greater sorrow. For it loves God so much that it is concerned about nothing else. . . . But since it sees itself so miserable it cannot believe that God loves it, nor that He has or will have reason to love it; it is rather convinced that it will quite justly be always abhorred not only by Him but by all creatures, and sorrowing it sees in itself the reason why it deserves to be cast out by Him whom it loves and desires so greatly." [1]

The weakening of the faculties in this distressing state brings it about that the soul can no longer raise its heart and mind to God in prayer as it did before. If it prays "it does so in such dryness, without strength and vigour, that it cannot help feeling that God does not hear it nor cares for its prayer. . . . And, indeed, now is not the time to speak to God in prayer but . . . to put one's mouth in the dust . . . and to bear this purification with patience. For it is God who is now working in the soul; therefore the soul can do nothing . . . neither pray nor assist at the divine offices attentively, much less can it attend

[1] *Ibid.*, ch. 7.

to other things and temporal affairs; not only that, it often suffers from such absentmindedness and such deep forgetfulness that many hours pass without its knowing what it has done or thought, nor what it is now doing or going to do. . . ." The reason for this is that the memory, too, must be purged of all thoughts and kinds of knowledge. The absentmindedness and coldness are due to the profound interior recollection in which the contemplation absorbs, as it were, the soul with all its powers in order to detach it from all affections for creatures and all ideas of created things. This state lasts longer or shorter, according to the intensity of contemplation. The simpler and purer the way in which the divine light penetrates the soul, the more the soul is darkened, emptied and annihilated. "And by thus emptying and darkening it" the divine ray of contemplation "purifies and illumines it", though the soul itself does not perceive that it receives the divine light. It rather remains in darkness, just as the ray of the sun "if it is pure and meets no object in its path remains invisible, even though it casts its light into the midst of a room. But if this spiritual light which penetrates the soul finds something on which it can strike such as the spiritual knowledge of perfection . . . or a judgement on it, whether it be false or true, the soul sees it at once and understands it much more clearly than before it had entered this darkness. The spiritual soul also distinctly perceives the light it has, so that it may easily recognize an imperfection that presents itself. . . ." "Because . . . this spiritual light is so simple, pure and general . . . and does not extend to any particular knowledge . . . it follows that the soul penetrates all the higher and lower things that present themselves to it . . .: 'The spirit searcheth all things, yea the deep things of God' (1 Cor. 2. 10), and 'Wisdom . . . reacheth everywhere by reason of its purity' (Sap. 7. 24), i.e. because it is not restricted to any particular object of the intellect or affection. And this is the property of the spirit that is purged and annihilated with regard to all particular affections and objects of knowledge, that it enjoys or understands nothing particular but remains in emptiness, darkness and obscurity, and thus is ready to embrace everything. . . ." [1]

Thus the blessed night darkens the spirit for no other purpose than "to enlighten it in all things", it places it "in lowliness and misery only to raise and lift it up . . . it deprives and empties it of every property and every natural affection so that it may expand divinely to taste and enjoy all earthly and heavenly things, in all-embracing

[1] *Ibid.*, ch. 8.

freedom of spirit". Because the natural understanding is incapable of grasping the divine light, contemplation must lead it into darkness. "This darkness must remain as long as is necessary to remove the habit the soul has long formed in the manner of its understanding. . . ." The destruction of the natural power of the understanding is profound, terrible and extremely painful. "For it is felt in the inmost substance of the spirit, and thus it seems a darkness that attacks the substance." The will, too, must be purged and annihilated so that in the union of love it may attain to that perfectly pure, divine, spiritual and exalted charity that transcends all natural affection and feeling and all desire of the will. "It must remain in aridity and affliction as long as its habitual attitude towards natural—divine or human—inclinations, requires." Thus "it must be withered, emptied and completely freed with regard to all evil influences in the fire of dark contemplation, so that its disposition may become pure and simple and its palate be purged and healed, in order to feel the sublime and rare touches of divine love. . . . The soul must also . . . be endowed with a certain glorious splendour for its communion with God, for this includes innumerable treasures and delights exceeding all the abundance the soul can grasp with its natural powers; for they cannot be received by such a weak and impure nature. . . . Therefore the soul must first become poor and empty in spirit . . . so that later, denuded of the old man, it may live the new, blessed life . . . of union with God. . . . The soul . . . must acquire a most sublime and delightful divine knowledge concerning all things divine and human . . . it regards things with eyes quite different from before, which difference is as great as that between the light and grace of the Holy Spirit and sense knowledge, between the divine and the human." For this reason the memory, too, must be freed, "the power of feeling must become much more interior and attuned to the abandonment of all things, when all will seem strange and different from what it was before. Thus this night draws the spirit away from its ordinary and lowly way of thinking about things to fill it with divine insight; this seems so strange to the soul and so different from all human ways of thought that it is quite beside itself. Sometimes the soul thinks it is under a spell or enraptured, it marvels at the things it sees or hears; they seem quite foreign and extraordinary to it, though they are the same as those with which it has normally to do."

"The soul must taste all these afflictions and purgings of the spirit to . . . be born anew to the life of the spirit. And in these pangs it brings forth the spirit of salvation. . . . Besides, by means of this night of contemplation the soul prepares for that tranquillity and peace which is so profound and full of bliss that it . . . surpasses all understanding (Phil. 4. 7). Therefore that former peace which was still full of imperfections must be completely removed from the soul," for this was "no peace, though it seemed a twofold peace to the soul". For it had already acquired the peace of sensual and spiritual knowledge and saw its senses and spirit surrounded by the fullness of this peace. But it must first undergo a purgation within the soul. The soul must surrender and destroy this peace and experience the fulfilment of the words: "And my soul is removed far off from peace" (Lam. 3. 17). In this state the soul suffers from many fears, struggles and imaginings. Through the feeling of being eternally lost "there arises in the innermost spirit such an acute pain and so deep sighing that they produce vehement spiritual cries and groans; sometimes, when the necessary strength and power are present, they express themselves in words and streams of tears. But this relief is rare." Like overflowing water "this roaring and these feelings of pain in the soul become so powerful that they overwhelm and penetrate it and fill all its inmost affections and powers with spiritual fears and sufferings without measure. Such are the effects this night produces in the soul by hiding all hope for the light of day." The will is as it were pierced by these pains, doubts and fears which seem to have no end. "This warfare and struggle are so deep because the hoped-for peace, too, must be very deep; and the spiritual pain is interiorly delicate and detached, because the love that the soul will possess must also be quite intimate and refined. The more interior and delicately polished a work is to be and to remain, the more intimate, careful and pure must be the labour. . . . Now because in the state of perfection towards which it journeys through the night the soul is to possess and enjoy innumerable treasures of graces and virtues" it must first see and feel itself stripped "empty and poor without them . . .; indeed, they must seem so far from it, that it cannot believe that it will ever come to possess them. . . ."[1]

Love and Transformation

In the mortal fears of the Night of the Spirit the imperfections of the soul have been burnt out as wood is freed by fire from all moisture so that it may itself be able to glow in the splendour of flame. Love is

[1] *Ibid.*, ch. 9.

the fire by which the soul is first purified and then enkindled. Thus
the second line of the Canticle of the Night has come true, the soul's
cares are "to loving ardours flushed". Though the love that has been
kindled is passionate, this burning is purely spiritual and as different
from that which is lit in the sensual part as spirit is from sense. It is an
infused love that shows itself in suffering rather than in action. It
"has already something in it of the union with God, and thus in some
way it also partakes of its properties", i.e. in the soul itself there are
now "more actions of God than of the soul itself, they are in it passively, the soul only gives its consent. But the heat and strength, the
temper and passion of love of the enkindling . . . are caused only by
the love of God which unites itself to the soul." Through the dark
purification the soul has been admirably prepared for the union. In
this state "the soul must love with the whole strength of all its
energies and spiritual and sensual affections". It is a tremendous fire
of love, because "God holds captive all the powers, faculties and
affections of the soul, the spiritual as well as the sensual ones, so that
all its powers and faculties may be occupied with this love in perfect
harmony and thus fulfil the first commandment in the fullest sense
of the word . . . (Deut. 6. 5)". "When the soul thus feels itself
inflamed and wounded by love and is yet still in darkness and doubts,
without the happy possession of love, there arises in it a yearning
that desires God most ardently." "In all things and thoughts it
finds in itself, in all matters and events that present themselves
to it, it is filled with love and longing in many ways and suffers
in its longing . . . at all times and in all places, finding rest in
nothing. . . ." "All becomes too narrow for the soul, it cannot
support itself and finds no place either in heaven or on earth, it
is penetrated by pains even unto darkness . . . i.e. it suffers pain
without comfort, even without that of a sure hope in some light or
spiritual good. . . ." Its yearning and pain are increased continually,
on the one hand by the spiritual darkness in which the soul finds
itself, on the other by its ardent love of God. Yet, in the midst of
its torments, it feels a strength which disappears as soon as the
burden of darkness vanishes. The reason for this is that this strength
of soul is devoured [1] without its co-operation by the dark fire of love
that has assailed it. If, now, this fire of love ceases, the darkness,
strength and warmth of love also cease in the soul." [2]

---

[1] German *verzehrt*. This does not seem to make sense; Allison Peers has "derived and
communicated".—Translator.   [2] *Ibid.*, ch. 11.

The purification of the soul through this dark, spiritual fire of love corresponds to the purification of the spirits in the next world through a dark material fire. The soul thus attains to purity of heart, which is nothing other than divine grace and love. Divine Wisdom itself purifies and illuminates the soul in this dark contemplation, which is the same Wisdom that frees also the angels from their ignorance. This divine Light illuminates the angels, gradually descending from the highest to the lowest, and finally reaching man. But man can only receive this loving contemplation "according to his own manner, which is limited and painful. For the divine Light illumines the angel in love, filling him with gentle tranquillity as befits a pure spirit prepared for such an infusion. But it enlightens man, who is impure and weak, naturally in such a way that it . . . leads him into darkness, pain and affliction, just as the sun irritates and gives pain to an eye that is weak. This lasts until the fire of love has spiritualized and refined a man with its purging, so that he can receive the infusion of this loving influence in gentle tranquillity like the angels."

The soul does not feel this ardent longing of love all the time, and normally not at the beginning of the purification but only after the divine fire has warmed it for some time. Sometimes the understanding is then "so delightfully and divinely enlightened by this mysterious and loving knowledge of God . . . that the will, helped by it, is marvellously enkindled and, without doing anything itself, burns brightly in this divine fire of love, so that now the soul seems to receive living fire with living understanding. . . . This common enkindling of love in the two united faculties . . . is something extremely precious and delightful for the soul, for it is certainly already a touch of the Divinity, a beginning of the perfect union of love for which it hopes." But it also happens in these communications of grace "that the will loves without the understanding being able to know, and also that the understanding knows, whereas the will does not love. For since this dark night of contemplation contains in itself divine light and divine love as fire contains light and warmth, it may well happen that this loving light . . . at times strikes more the will, enkindling it with love while leaving the understanding in darkness . . . and at another time fills the understanding with love[1] . . . while the will is left in aridity . . . : this is wrought by the Lord who communicates Himself as He wills."[2] For he is not tied by the laws of the natural life of the

[1] Allison Peers has "light" instead of "love", which seems more appropriate.—Trans.
[2] *Ibid.*, ch. 12.

soul. According to these it is indeed "impossible to love an object which one has not known before. But in the supernatural way God can well infuse love into the soul and increase it without infusing or increasing distinct knowledge in it. . . . This is the experience of many spiritual persons. . . ." Some "are not very far advanced in the knowledge of God, but excel all the more in will. Instead of intellectual knowledge they are content with faith, through which God infuses and increases love in them even though their knowledge is not increased." [1] The last words should, of course, not be understood in such a sense as if faith in general only aroused love without giving knowledge. On the contrary: it appeals in the first instance to the understanding, to which it reveals divine truth. But, on the other hand, this is done in a veiled manner, not in the way of natural knowledge. Further, it need not always present certain particular truths. To have faith may also mean to turn to the reality which all the truths of faith announce; that is, God; and to turn to him in such a way that he is not considered in the light of some particular truth of faith but that a man is surrendered to him, the Incomprehensible One who contains the essence of all truths of faith yet transcends them all in his very Incomprehensibility, in darkness and indistinction. If in this surrender the soul feels that it is seized by the dark and incomprehensible God, then this is the dark contemplation which God himself communicates to the soul both as light and love; it is "dark and indistinct for the understanding. . . . And just as this knowledge which God infuses is general and dark to the understanding, so the will also loves in a general way, without distinguishing any particular known thing."

Sometimes, however, "in this delicate communication God gives Himself more to the one faculty than to the others; often only understanding is noticed and not love, another time only love and not understanding. . . . For God can influence one power of the soul without affecting the other; and thus He can inflame the will with a touch of the heat of His love, though the understanding realizes nothing, just as someone can be warmed by a fire without seeing it." [2]

But when mystical knowledge is infused in the understanding, the soul "is full of light in the midst of this darkness, 'and the light shines in the darkness' (Jo. 1. 5). . . . Then the senses of the soul are in such delicate and delightful serene calm and simplicity that there is no name for it, and God is felt now in one manner now in another."

[1] *Spiritual Canticle*, B. 26. 8.   [2] *Living Flame of Love*, B. 3. 49.

Nevertheless, despite the simultaneous purification of understanding and will, contemplation is normally felt as love in the will before appearing as knowledge in the understanding. This is to be explained by the opposition between love as a passively experienced state (passion) and as a free act of the will. This "enkindling of love is a passion of love rather than a free act of the will". It "wounds the soul in its inmost substance and thus arouses passive affections. Hence this enkindling can be called a passion of love rather than a free act of the will: for it is called an act of the will in so far as it is free. But since the passions and affections belong to the will, if the soul is seized by an affection this is ascribed to the will; and this is truly so, for in this way the will lets itself be taken captive and loses its freedom, so that the violent power of passion carries it away with it: therefore we can say that this enkindling of love is in the will, i.e. it inflames the desire of the will; and thus, as has been said, it is called a passion of love rather than the free act of the will. But because the understanding can receive intelligence only in a detached and passive manner (and this can take place only when it has been purged), therefore, until this has happened, the soul feels the touch of intelligence less frequently than that of the passion of love. For this reason it is not necessary for the will to be so completely purged from the passions, because these help it to feel passionate love.

"Since, then, this enkindling and longing for love already come from the Holy Spirit, they are totally different from that which we have discussed in the Night of the Senses." They are felt in the spirit, even though the senses take their share in them. Here both what is possessed and what is lacking are felt so keenly that all the pain of the senses is nothing in comparison, though this is far greater than in the first Night of the Senses. "For the inner man recognizes the lack of a great good which can in no way be filled." Even in the beginning of this spiritual night, "before this enkindling of love is felt . . . God grants . . . the soul a love of esteem of Himself so great that the mere thought of having lost God or of being abandoned by Him is by far the worst of all the soul suffers and feels in the distress of this night. . . . And if, in this situation, it could know for certain that all is not lost and finished but that, on the contrary, this pain is for the best . . . and that God is not angry with it, it would count all these afflictions for nothing and even be happy in the knowledge of thus doing God a service. For its love of esteem for God . . . is so strong that it . . . would most gladly die for Him many times to please Him. But when once the fire of love has enkindled the soul and has united with the love of esteem for God which it already has, the soul normally acquires such strength and courage and is filled with such violent longing for God that, without heeding or considering anything else, it would in the strength and inebriation of love and desire perform the most extreme and extraordinary things to find Him whom it loves."

Through the sufferings of the Night of the Spirit the soul renews its youth like the eagle (cf. Ps. 102. 5). By supernatural illumination its human understanding is united with the divine intellect and thus becomes itself divine. The same happens to the will united to the divine will and love; the memory, too, and all affections and desires are divinely transformed. "Thus the soul becomes even now a soul of heaven . . . more divine than human." Hence, looking back on the night, it can exclaim: "O venture of delight." [1] It went forth "concealed from other eyes, when all my house at length in silence slept". The house signifies the ordinary behaviour of the soul, its wishes and desires, and all its powers. These are the inmates of the house that must be at rest so as not to hinder the union of love. Now the soul recognizes that it was "well protected in the darkness". For all errors come to it "through its desires of affections, its consideration or its understanding. . . . If, therefore, all these activities and motions are hindered it is clear that the soul is safe from being led astray by them. Thus it frees itself not only from itself, but also from . . . the world and the devil which, if the affections and activities of the soul are at rest, cannot make war upon it from any side or in any way." Now its desires and powers will no longer be occupied with useless and dangerous things; it feels safe "from vain and false joy and many other things. . . ." So, "through walking in dark faith it is by no means in danger of being lost, but . . . gains . . . in this state the virtues". That the dark night deprives the soul also of the enjoyment of good, even of supernatural and divine things, is due to the fact that the unpurged powers of the soul can receive supernatural things only in the ordinary and natural manner. Through "being weaned, purified and mortified . . . they lose their base and human way of acting and receiving, and thus all the faculties and desires of the soul are prepared and tempered in order to receive, feel and enjoy the divine and supernatural things in a pure and lofty manner. Now this is impossible unless the old man die first. If, therefore, these spiritual things are not communicated to the human will and desire from above, from the

[1] *Night of the Spirit*, ch. 13.

Father of lights, they cannot be tasted by a man in a divine and spiritual manner, however much he may turn . . . his powers to God, and however great enjoyment he may seem to find in Him. He will be able to taste God only in a human and natural manner, as he does the other things. For these spiritual blessings do not go from man to God, but come from God to man." Thus many find great pleasure in God and in spiritual things and "perhaps think this to be something supernatural and spiritual, whereas it is often only mere natural and human activities and desires". Hence the soul may regard aridity and darkness as happy signs, indicating that God is going to free it from itself; he deprives it of its own powers. It is true, the soul might have acquired many things through them, but it could never have acted so perfectly and securely as now, when God takes it by the hand. It is led by him like a blind man in dark ways without knowing where it goes—but even with the greatest good fortune it could never have found these ways with its own eyes and feet. Thus it makes great progress without realizing it, even thinking itself to be lost. For it does not yet know this new state and sees only "that it suffers loss in all it knew and enjoyed". But looking back it recognizes that it was "well protected in darkness". It was a secure way also because it was a way of suffering. "For the way of suffering is far more secure and profitable than the way of joy and action . . . because in suffering one receives strength from God, whereas in activity and enjoyment the weakness and imperfections of the soul are brought to light. Also . . . because virtues are practised and acquired in suffering, since the soul is purified and becomes wiser and more cautious." But the principal cause of this security is the dark Wisdom itself. "The Dark Night of contemplation embraces and veils the soul in such a way and brings it so near to God that He Himself takes it under His protection and frees it from all that is not God. For the soul is here subjected to a healing process destined to give it the health that is God Himself. Hence His Majesty causes it to practise a diet and to abstain from all things, taking away its desire for them all." It is "hidden in God's countenance from the disturbance of men" (cf. Ps. 30. 21), i.e. through dark contemplation it is "fortified against all the chances which may suddenly come upon it from men". It is also given security by "the fortitude by which the soul is at once inspired in these obscure and afflictive dark waters of God. Though they are dark, they are yet waters, hence they must refresh and strengthen the soul in what is most profitable for it. . . . Then the soul soon perceives in itself a firm determination and resolve on no account . . . to do anything it understands to be an offence against God, and to omit nothing by which it thinks it may serve Him. For this dark love infuses into the soul an extremely careful solicitude and an anxious attentiveness concerning what it should do or not do for God so as to please Him. . . . Now all efforts, desires and faculties of the soul, having been detached from all other things, are directed with all their power and might to the service of God." Thus the soul goes out from itself and all created things and walks "in darkness well protected" towards the sweet and delightful union of love with God: "in disguise up the secret stair".[1]

The Secret Ladder

The secret ladder is this dark contemplation: secret as the mystical theology that is mysteriously infused by love. How this is done "neither the soul itself nor anyone else understands, even the devil has no knowledge of it; for the master that teaches it is Himself substantially in the soul, where neither the enemy nor natural sense knowledge nor the understanding can penetrate". This wisdom is secret or hidden also in its effects: in the darkness and affliction of the soul's purification as well as in the subsequent illumination; the soul can "neither understand nor explain nor even name it". It "does not even desire to give it a name and finds . . . no means to express adequately such an exalted knowledge and such a delicate spiritual feeling . . . for that interior wisdom is so simple, general and spiritual that it enters the understanding without being defined by notions or represented by a symbol. . . . It is just as if somebody were to see something he has never seen before and the like of which he has never seen. . . . Despite all efforts he would not be able to give it a name nor to say what it is, even though he had perceived it with his senses. How much less will he then be able to speak about a thing he has not perceived with his senses?" Since God speaks to the soul wholly interiorly and spiritually this transcends all the capacities of the external as well as of the interior senses and makes them dumb; for they do not understand this language, they cannot reproduce it with words nor do they desire to hear it.

Mystical wisdom is called secret also "because it has the property of hiding the soul in itself. . . . It sometimes takes such hold of the soul and draws it into its hidden abyss in such a way that the soul can clearly see how far removed it is from all creatures. Thus it feels as if

[1] *Ibid.*, ch. 16.

it were placed in a very profound and vast solitude, whither no human creature can penetrate, in an immense desert without boundary on any side. This is the more pleasant, beneficial and lovely for the soul the deeper, wider and lonelier it is. There the soul feels the more hidden the higher it sees itself raised above every created being. And this abyss of wisdom greatly elevates and enriches the soul: it engulfs it in the science of love thus making it realize how base are the creatures compared with the sublime divine knowledge and feeling, and how base, insufficient and completely inept are all designations and words used in this life to speak about divine things, and how impossible it is in a natural way . . . to see them as they are." Only mystical theology can give enlightenment on this. Because "these things cannot be known after a human manner, they must be reached by human unknowing and divine ignorance; for, speaking mystically . . . these divine things and perfections are not known and understood as they are when they are being sought and practised, but only when they have been found and practised". ". . . The paths and footsteps in which God walks in the souls He wants to lead to Himself and to ennoble by uniting them with His Wisdom . . . cannot be known." [1]

The *Canticle of the Night* calls the dark contemplation a ladder; for "as men climb on a ladder to take the provisions, treasures and other things in a fortified city by storm, so the souls ascend by means of this hidden contemplation, without knowing how, to scale, know and possess the heavenly treasures and good things". Further: "Just as the same rungs of a ladder serve for ascending and descending, so the hidden contemplation humbles the soul by the same favours that . . . raise it to God. For all the favours that really come from God have this property that they both humble and exalt the soul." On this road the soul is subject to constant vicissitudes. Prosperity is always followed "at once by storms and afflictions, so that this well-being seems, as it were, to have been given only as a preparation and encouragement for the following misery; and misery and vexations are also followed by abundant enjoyment and well-being. Thus it seems to the soul as if each of its feasts were preceded by a vigil. And this is the normal procedure . . . in the state of contemplation. One never remains in the same state but always ascends and descends until the state of tranquillity is reached. The reason is this: since the state of perfection consists in perfect love of God and contempt of self, it

[1] *Ibid.*, ch. 17.

cannot exist without these two parts, i.e. without the knowledge of God and the knowledge of self. The soul must necessarily exercise itself first in the one and then in the other, it must now taste the one and be exalted by it and then again be tested and humiliated in the other, until it has reached perfection in the virtues. Then this ascending and descending will cease, because it has attained to God and been united to Him: He is at the top of the ladder, for the ladder rests and leans on Him."

Contemplation is called a ladder particularly because it "is a science of love, an infused, loving knowledge of God which simultaneously illumines and enkindles the soul with love till it ascends step by step to God its Creator. For it is love alone that unites and joins the soul with God." Following St Bernard and St Thomas, St John of the Cross distinguishes the steps of the ladder according to their effects: "For since this ladder of love . . . is so hidden that God alone can measure and weigh it, it would be impossible to know by natural means what these steps are in themselves." [1]

"The first step makes the soul sick for its salvation. . . . But this sickness is not unto death, but to the glory of God. For in it the soul dies to sin and to all that is not God, through God himself. . . . The second step causes the soul to seek God without ceasing. . . . On this step the soul walks so carefully that it seeks the Beloved in all things, and in all the affairs which press on it is concerned with and speaks of the Beloved. . . . The third step of the ladder of Love arouses the soul to action and incites it to fervour so that it does not grow tired. . . . On this step the soul considers the heroic works it has done for the Beloved as unimportant, many things as few, the long time it has spent in His service as short, because of the fire of love with which it is now burning. . . . In its great love of God the soul here takes little account of the greatest sorrows and pains it bears for God and, if it were allowed, its only consolation would be for His sake to be destroyed a thousand times. It therefore thinks itself useless in all it does, and feels that it loves in vain. From this derives a marvellous effect, the firm conviction that it is far worse than all other souls . . .; because its love gives it an ever greater understanding of what it owes to God and . . . because it recognizes the many works it does for God in this state as faulty and imperfect, they are to it but occasions for shame and pain, for it realizes how basely it works for such a great Lord. . . . The fourth step . . . causes the soul constant suffering for the sake of

[1] *Ibid.*, ch. 18.

the Beloved." Love leads it to "regard all great, difficult and burden-some things as nothing. . . . The spirit here gains so much strength that it keeps the flesh in complete subjection and thinks as little of it as a tree of one of its leaves. The soul here seeks in no way consola-tion and enjoyment, neither in God nor anywhere else, and has no desire or wish to ask favours of God, because it understands clearly that it has already received abundantly. It only cares to please God and to serve Him at least in something as is His due and as it owes it to Him for what it has received from Him; though even this it owes to Him. . . . This step of love is very exalted. For since the soul in this state is constantly drawn to God in sincere love and the desire to suffer for Him, His Majesty often grants it . . . the enjoyment of a delightful spiritual visit that is full of bliss. For the infinite love of the Word, Jesus Christ, cannot let the soul that loves Him suffer without coming to its aid. . . . The fifth step . . . causes the soul an impatient desire and longing for God. Here the yearning of the loving soul for the possession of the Beloved and union with Him is so violent that it thinks every delay, even the least, extremely long, wearisome and oppressive and only lives in the thought how it can find the Beloved. . . . On this step the loving soul must either gain possession of the Beloved or die. . . ."[1] "The sixth step causes the soul to run quickly to God and often to feel His nearness. Without growing tired it runs towards Him in hope, for, strengthened by love, it advances in swift flight. . . ." The agility here given to the soul is due to the fact that it has been greatly enlarged and that its perfect purification has almost been accomplished. Thus it soon reaches the seventh step. Here "the soul grows extremely bold. On this step love will not be persuaded by reason to wait, nor does it accept the counsel to draw back nor can it be hindered by shame. . . . Such souls receive from God what they ask of Him in the joy of their heart. . . . From the boldness and free-dom which God has given to the soul on the seventh step in order to be fearlessly familiar with Him in the whole strength of love follows the eighth step which gives the soul the possession of the Beloved and union with Him. . . : 'I have found Him whom my soul loves; I hold Him and will not let Him go'" (Cant. 3. 4). "On this step of union the longing of the soul is stilled, but with interruptions; some souls reach this union for a short time but are soon drawn away again; for . . . if they could remain longer on this step they would reach a certain kind of glory even in this life. . . . The ninth step . . .

[1] *Ibid.*, ch. 19.

is . . . the step of the perfect who burn in the sweet love of God. This sweet and delightful burning of love is wrought by the Holy Spirit through the union in which they are united with God. . . . The graces and riches of God to the enjoyment of which the soul is raised on this step cannot be expressed in words. Even if one were to write many books on it, the greater part would still be left unsaid." The tenth and last step of the hidden ladder of love does not belong to this life. "It assimilates the soul to God perfectly, through the clear vision of God which it possesses as soon as it leaves this body after it has reached the ninth step in this life. These souls, whose number is only very small, do not enter purgatory, because they are already perfectly purified by love. Hence it is written in St Matthew . . . 'Blessed are the clean of heart, for they shall see God' (Matt. 5. 8). This vision is . . . the cause of the perfect likeness of the soul to God. . . . Not because the soul embraces all things like God, for this is impossible; but because all the soul is will become like God. For this reason it will be called and will be God by participation. . . . On this highest step of the clear vision, the last step of the ladder . . . nothing will be any more hidden from the soul because of its perfect likeness to God. . . . But until that day, however far the soul may progress, there is still as much hidden from it as it lacks for the perfect similarity with God's essence. In this way, by the mystical theology and this secret love, the soul rises above all things and above itself and ascends to God. For this love resembles the fire that always rises upward, striving to be absorbed in the centre of its sphere." [1]

The Three-coloured Garment of the Soul

The soul has said that it has escaped by a secret ladder "in disguise". A person disguises himself, i.e. he hides his own clothes and form under that of another, "in order to reveal in this form and garment his love and affection for someone he loves and thus to gain his grace and goodwill; or, again, to hide from his adversaries in order to be better able to carry out his plan. . . . The soul, therefore, that . . . is burning with the love of Christ, its Spouse, escapes in a disguise that will most clearly express the affections of its spirit and in which it can walk most securely protected from its adversaries . . . the devil, the world and the flesh." For this reason its clothes are of three principal colours: white, green and red, which symbolize the three theological virtues. Through them the soul gains the grace of its Beloved and at the

[1] *Ibid.*, ch. 20.

same time walks quite secure from its three enemies. "For faith is a white undergarment of such dazzling brilliance that it blinds the sight of all understanding. If, therefore, the soul walks in the garment of faith the devil neither sees it nor dares to attack it. . . ." Nor is there a better garment than the dazzling whiteness of faith, the foundation of the other virtues, to gain the good pleasure of the Beloved and union with him. "This dazzling white splendour of faith the soul wears when it escapes", when it walks in the darkness and interior afflictions of the Dark Night. It is no longer satisfied with any natural knowledge nor refreshed by any supernatural enlightenment, since heaven seems closed to it; "but it suffers with constancy and perseverance, and passes through these trials without fainting and without forsaking the Beloved", who proves its faith by these afflictions and trials.

Over the white undergarment of faith the soul wears the green vestment of hope. In the strength of this virtue "the soul frees itself from the second enemy, the world, and protects itself against it. For this fresh green of living hope in God gives the soul such vigorous energy and boldness, it raises it so powerfully to the good things of eternal life, that, compared with what the soul hopes for, all the things of this world seem dry, faded, dead and worthless, as indeed they are. Here the soul strips and divests itself of all worldly vestments and clothes, nor does it set its heart on anything or hope in any of the things that are and will be in the world, but lives clothed only in the hope of eternal life. Since it has raised its mind so high above the world, this can no longer touch it or seize its heart, nor even attract its glance. And thus the soul journeys in this green livery and disguise well preserved from the second enemy, the world." It is "the proper task of hope to let the soul raise its eyes only to look upon God", so that it hopes for no good thing from anywhere else. In this garment it is so pleasing to the Beloved that it obtains from him as much as it hopes. Without this green livery it would "obtain nothing, since God is moved and conquered only by persistent hope".

"Over these white and green garments the soul wears as the crown and perfection of its whole vesture the third colour, a magnificent purple cloak", the symbol of love. This "protects and hides the soul from its third enemy, the flesh. (For where the love of God reigns, love of oneself and one's own things has no access.) That love . . . moreover strengthens also the other virtues, giving them life and vigour for the protection of the soul, granting them grace and beauty thus to please the Beloved. For without charity no virtue is pleasing to God."

This, then, is the disguise in which the soul ascends to God in the night of faith. Faith, hope and charity most fittingly prepare it for union: "Faith empties and darkens the understanding in all its natural knowledge and thus prepares it for union with divine Wisdom. Hope voids and separates the memory from all possession of created things . . . and gives it possession of what it hopes. . . . In the same way love empties all affections and desires of the will of all that is not God and directs them to Him alone. . . . Because . . . these virtues have the task of separating the soul from all that is less than God their effect is union with God." Without the garments of these three virtues, therefore, the soul "cannot possibly attain to the perfect love of God. . . . Hence it is a great and happy chance for the soul if it has acquired such clothing and wears it constantly until it has reached the desired and longed-for goal, the union of love. . . ." [1]

Now it is evident that it was "a happy enterprise" for the soul to have accomplished such a difficult work: it has freed itself from the devil, the world and its own sensuality, it has gained the precious freedom of the spirit, and, having been transformed from an earthly into a heavenly soul, its conversation is now in heaven. [2]

In Darkness and Hidden in Profound Peace

It was also a happy chance that the soul could escape "in darkness and hidden": in darkness it has journeyed secure from all wiles and craftiness of the devil. For infused contemplation is given it secretly without its own co-operation; all the faculties of its sensual parts remain in darkness. The devil, on the other hand, can realize and understand only by means of the sensual powers "what is in the soul and what happens in it. Hence, the more spiritual, interor and superior to the senses is the communication, the less the devil attains to its understanding. Thus such an interior communication with God is of the greatest importance for the security of the soul . . . so that the weakness of its sensual part should not hinder the liberty of its spirit and that an abundant spiritual communication may become possible." Further, in order to be safe from the enemy, the lower part of the soul is to know nothing of what happens in the higher part: "this is to remain a secret between God and the soul".

It is true, however, that the devil can conclude indirectly that the

[1] *Ibid.*, ch. 21.   [2] *Ibid.*, ch. 22.

soul is receiving interior and spiritual communications "from the great repose and silence which some of them cause in the senses and faculties of the soul. . . . If he then sees that he cannot prevent these graces in the inmost ground of the soul, he seeks with all his might to excite and disturb the sensual part into which he can penetrate, now by means of pains, now by terrifying images and fears, in order thus to trouble and disquiet the higher and spiritual part of the soul with regard to the blessing it then receives and enjoys. Often, however, when the communication of this contemplation is infused into the spirit in great purity and gives it strength, all the devil's efforts to disquiet the soul are of no avail; on the contrary, it receives a new gain, new love and a more profound peace. For as soon as the soul becomes aware of the disturbing presence of the enemy, at once—and this is very strange—without knowing how and without its own efforts, it retires ever more deeply into its inmost ground, feeling that it is in a secure refuge where it knows itself to be far away and hidden from the enemy. . . . All these fears attack it only from outside; the soul perceives quite distinctly and is happy to see how it can enjoy that quiet peace and sweetness of the Bridegroom in secret, that peace which the world and the devil can neither give nor take away. . . . At times, however, when the spiritual communications do not penetrate the spirit very deeply but touch also the sensual part, the enemy can trouble and disturb the spirit much more easily with these terrors by means of the senses. Then the torment and pain he causes in the spirit are very great, sometimes even indescribable. As this is a naked contact between spirit and spirit, the terrors the evil spirit causes in the good spirit, i.e. the soul, are intolerable once this disturbance takes hold of the soul. . . . At other times it happens that the devil perceives the favour God grants the soul by the mediation of a good angel; for God usually permits it that the enemy . . . recognizes these . . . favours . . . especially so that he may oppose the soul as is his due for the sake of justice . . . and that he may not be able to say he had no opportunity for gaining possession of the soul . . . as would be the case if God did not permit a certain equality between the two parties fighting for the soul, i.e. between the good and the bad angel. Thus the victory is the more honourable, and the victorious soul that has been proved faithful in temptation will be rewarded all the more gloriously. Therefore . . . God allows the devil to work on the soul in the same manner as He does Himself. If He gives it a true vision through His good angel . . . the evil spirit is allowed to present false

visions that are deceptively like the genuine ones." He can also fake
spiritual favours produced by good angels. But purely spiritual communications without form or shape cannot be faked by the devil.
"Thus, in order to attack the soul in the same way as it has been
favoured by God he presents himself with his fearful spirit in order to
fight and destroy spiritual things by spiritual weapons. If this happens
at a time when the good angel elevates the soul to a state of spiritual
contemplation, the soul cannot escape into the secret hiding-place of
contemplation fast enough not to be observed by the devil . . . . and
this results in a terror and disturbance of the spirit that are most
distressing for the soul. At times, however, it can withdraw instantly
without the evil spirit being able to produce an impression and cast
it into that terror; strengthened by the efficacious grace of the good
angel it hides within itself. At other times, however, the devil prevails
and the soul is seized with a disturbance and a terror that are much
more painful than any torment of this life. For since this dreadful
communication takes place directly between spirit and spirit, without
any bodily admixture, its torment surpasses all conception. However,
this does not last very long in the spirit, else it would be separated
from the body as a consequence of the fearful communication of the
other spirit. . . . All this . . . takes place in the soul without it being
able to do anything about it or to defend itself against it. . . ." But it
happens only "in order to purify the soul and by means of a spiritual
vigil to prepare it for a great feast and a spiritual favour. . . . In the
measure of the dark and terrible purification . . . the soul is made
happy by the marvellous . . . enjoyment, and this in so lofty a manner
that it cannot be expressed." The preceding terrors have made it very
receptive to it: "For these spiritual visions belong to the next life
rather than to this, and when one is seen this is a preparation for the
next." This, however, applies only to those graces that are mediated
by angels. If God himself visits the soul it remains completely "in
darkness and hidden", because "His Majesty dwells substantially in
the soul, where neither angel nor devil can attain to an understanding
of what takes place. Nor can they come to know the intimate and
mysterious intercourse between God and the soul. For these graces
are . . . wholly divine, exalted and as it were substantial touches
between God and the soul; in a single one of these touches which
constitute the highest degree of the life of prayer, the soul receives
more graces than in all the rest . . .; therefore it longs for such a
divine touch and esteems it more highly than all other graces that

God grants it. . . . If such favours are granted the soul in secret, i.e.
only in the spirit, it sees itself, without knowing how, so far withdrawn and separated according to the higher and spiritual part, from
the lower, sensual portion, that it recognizes in itself two parts so
different from one another that it imagines that there is no communication between the two. . . . And in a certain sense this is really so, for
all the soul operates here is wholly spiritual, and so in this it has
nothing more in common with its sensual part. Thus the soul becomes entirely spiritual, and in this hiding place of unitive contemplation its spiritual desires and passions become almost inactive." Therefore the soul, speaking of its higher part, can sing: "my house being
now profoundly at rest".[1]

Thereby it means to say: "Since the higher part of my soul as well
as the lower one with its desires and faculties were at rest, I escaped to
the divine union of love with God." Both the sensual and the spiritual
part had been attacked in the dark night; both had "to be brought to
rest and peace with their faculties and desires". For this reason this
line is repeated twice. "This repose and this peace of the spiritual
house the soul must make its own habitually and perfectly as far as
the state of this present life allows, by means of those as it were substantial touches of the divine union. . . ." Through them the soul must
be purified, calmed and strengthened so as to be able to enter that
union, "the divine marriage between the soul and the Son of God. As
soon as these two houses of the soul have been perfectly tranquillized
and strengthened together with all their inmates—the faculties and
desires of the soul—as soon as these are asleep and in silence with
regard to all heavenly and earthly things, the divine Wisdom
immediately unites Itself with the soul by a new bond of loving
possession. . . . No one can come to this union without a thorough
purification. . . . Hence if a man refuses to enter the Night in order to
seek the Beloved, to deny his self-will and die to himself, if he wants to
seek Him only on the bed of comfort . . . he will never find Him. . . ."[2]

In the blessed Night the soul has been granted undisturbed and
hidden contemplation. This is so foreign and unintelligible to the
sensual part that no creature can make contact with it and draw the
soul away from the union of love. The spiritual darkness of this
night threw all the powers of the higher part of the soul into obscurity.
Hence it could perceive and surrender to nothing save God and thus
was able to reach him. Now it is freed from all the forms, images and

[1] *Ibid.*, ch. 23.   [2] *Ibid.*, ch. 24.

perceptions that would hinder its permanent union with God. It is no longer supported by any illumination of the understanding or by any external guide in which to find comfort and satisfaction. "For the dark obscurities have deprived it of all these things. So love alone, which burns at this time and turns the heart to the Beloved, is the moving power and guide of the soul and raises it, it knows not how and in what manner, in solitary flight to God."[1]

Here the *Treatise of the Dark Night* breaks off, after commenting upon only six of the eight stanzas of the Canticle. This explanation has a double importance for us: it further elucidates the essence of the spirit and shows that dark contemplation is both death and resurrection to a new life. This new life of union, however, is no more described and clarified here than in the *Ascent*.

(b) The Soul in the Realm of Spirit and the Spirits

Structure of the Soul; the Spirit of God and Created Spirits

The soul as spirit belongs to the realm of the spirit and of spirits. Its own structure is peculiar: being the life-giving form of the body it is not only the interior of something external, but there is also an opposition between interior and exterior in itself.[2] It is properly at home in its inmost being, in the essence or the deepest ground of the soul. In the natural activity of its powers it goes out of itself to meet the external world, in a purely sensual activity it even descends below itself. That which it meets outside it absorbs and is absorbed by it. This determines what the soul is to do or not to do and in a certain sense limits its freedom; it cannot penetrate into the soul's innermost region, but it can keep the soul away from its own interior.

In its ascent to God the soul rises above itself or is raised above itself. Yet thus it actually reaches its own interior. This sounds contradictory, but it corresponds to the facts and is based on the relation between the realm of the spirit and God.

God is pure spirit and the archetype of all spiritual being.[3] Hence spirit can be properly understood only in relation to God; this means it is a mystery that attracts us constantly, because it is the mystery of

[1] *Ibid.*, ch. 25.
[2] Here we would remind the reader that in these distinctions a spatial image is used for something non-spatial. Actually the soul does not consist of "parts, and there is no difference in it between its inward and its outward being . . ." (*Living Flame of Love*, 1. 10).
[3] Here we can only hint at the problem of spiritual being; it is discussed at length in *Endliches und ewiges Sein*, E. Stein's Werke, vol. II (German ed.).

our own being. We have a certain access to it in that the latter, too, is spiritual being. We have also ways of approach from all other being, since all being, as meaningful and intellectually comprehensible, has some affinity to spiritual being. But it reveals itself more profoundly in the measure of our knowledge of God, without, however, unveiling itself completely, i.e. without ceasing to be a mystery.

The Spirit of God is completely transparent to itself. It can dispose of itself with absolute freedom (in that freedom from limitations implied in the Being-through-itself); it freely goes out of itself yet always remains within itself. The divine Spirit places all other being outside itself, embracing, penetrating and ruling it. Created spirit is a limited image of God in all the characteristics just mentioned: as image it is like to God, as limited it is opposed to him; it has a more or less extensive capacity for receiving God; in its highest form it is capable of being united to him in mutual, freely personal surrender.

We speak of a *realm* of spirit and spirits inasmuch as all spiritual being has at least the possibility of a relationship and is part of a whole. We call it realm *of the spirit*, because spirit contains more than all spirits, namely all spiritual being, and in a certain sense this means all that is. But we add: realm *of the spirits*, because in this realm the spirits, i.e. the personal-spiritual beings, play a predominant rôle.

God is the head of this realm, because he infinitely transcends all spiritual being and all spirits. A created spirit can ascend to him only by transcending itself. But as God calls all beings into being and preserves them in it he is also the ground of all. Whatever ascends to him sinks by this very fact into a secure position of rest.

The Soul's Communication with God and with Created Spirits

St John of the Cross calls God the deepest centre or point of rest of the soul, using a spatial image taken from the scientific ideas of his time.[1] According to these ideas, bodies are drawn most powerfully to the centre of the earth as the point of the strongest attraction. A stone in the interior of the earth would already be at a certain point of rest, but not yet in the deepest point, because as long as it were not in the centre it would still have capacity, strength and inclination to fall lower. Thus the soul has found its ultimate and deepest point of rest in God "when it knows, loves and enjoys God with all its powers". This can never be perfectly done in this life. If, therefore, by the grace of God it is in its centre, this is yet not the deepest centre, because it

---

[1] *Living Flame of Love*, I. 12.

can penetrate into God still further. For the power that draws it to God is love, and this can reach ever higher degrees here below. The higher its degree, the more deeply will the soul be anchored in God, the more intimately will it be seized by him. The soul ascends to God, that is, to union with him, by the steps of a ladder. The higher it ascends to him, the deeper it descends into itself: the union takes place in the innermost sphere of the soul, in its deepest ground. If this seems contradictory it should be remembered that these are only different spatial images supplementing each other and intended to indicate something utterly remote from space, which cannot be adequately represented by anything taken from the realm of natural experience.

God is in the innermost part of the soul, and nothing it contains is hidden from him. But no created spirit is by itself capable of entering this enclosed garden or of looking into it. The created spirits are the good and evil spirits (also called pure spirits, because they have no body), and the human souls. St John says little about the converse of human souls with each other. There is only one human relationship he frequently mentions, that of the spiritual soul to its director. But he is not interested in the notional means by which the communication is effected. He only observes on one occasion that men endowed with the gift of the discernment of spirits can deduce the interior state of others from small external indications.[1] This points to the normal way of knowledge that leads to the souls of others: it traverses the sensible expressions of the life of the soul and leads as far into the interior as this discloses itself. For all external going-out-of-oneself in bodily gestures, in sounds of emotion, words, deeds and works, presupposes an inner going-out-of-oneself, whether this be voluntary or involuntary, conscious or unconscious. If it comes from the interior, something of this sphere will also shine forth in it. But as long as we depend on the purely natural way, without the guidance of an extraordinary divine illumination, this will not be something that can be exactly defined and definitely grasped; it will rather remain shrouded in mystery. When the inner zone is closed, no human glance can penetrate it by its own power. Now the soul is in communication not only with others of its own kind but also with created pure spirits, good as well as evil ones. St John of the Cross, following the Areopagite, assumes that men receive divine illuminations through angelic mediation, though he does not hold that grace descends only through the orders of the Divine Hierarchies. He teaches a direct union of

[1] *Ascent*, 2. 26. 14.

God with the soul, and this is his chief concern. He is far more interested in the wiles of the devil than in the influences of the good
angels. He sees him constantly prowling around the souls to lure them
away from God. What means of communication are there between
human souls and pure, i.e. bodiless, spirits? Here, too, one possible
way of knowledge is through bodily expression and other sensible
manifestations. In the case of men this is possible inasmuch as pure spirits
have the power to communicate with them by means of visible apparitions or audible words. But this is a very dangerous way, because it
exposes the soul to manifold deceptions and errors: it may regard a
mere delusion or phantasm as the apparition of a spirit; the devil may
appear in the luminous form of a good angel, in order more easily to
seduce a man, and, for fear of being thus deluded, the soul may reject
genuine heavenly apparitions as deceit of the senses or the devil.

On the other hand, is it possible for the pure spirits to penetrate to
the interior by means of the external senses? The narratives of the books
of Job and Tobias can scarcely be interpreted otherwise than by
assuming that the devil and the angels closely watch and supervise the
external behaviour of men. Moreover, it agrees with the doctrine of
the Church that the angels have knowledge of the sense world and
thus of the human exterior, since their ministrations to men presuppose this.[1]

The fact that they do not need bodily senses for this indicates that
there must be yet other possibilities for the perception of bodily
nature, "a knowledge of the sensible without the senses".[2]

It is not our task to investigate these possibilities. It is certain that
for the pure spirits external appearances are not the only way of access
to the inner life; they also perceive interior, spiritual words and utterances. The guardian angel "hears" the prayer that ascends from the
heart without a sound. The devil observes certain movements of the
soul that might provide an opportunity for his insinuations. And
the spirits, too, are capable of communicating with souls in a spiritual
way: by means of silent words spoken interiorly without the instru-
mentality of the outer senses and heard interiorly, or through effects
perceived in oneself but as caused from outside, e.g. changes in mood
or impulses of the will that cannot be explained by the context of one's
own experiences. What does not fall within the sphere of the external
senses is not therefore necessarily free from all sensuality, and hence
need not be *purely* spiritual in the sense in which John of the Cross

[1] Cf. St Thomas, *De Veritate*, q. 8, a. 11, corp.   [2] Cf. q. 98, a. 8, ad 7.

speaks of pure spirituality. It is true, he calls memory, understanding and will spiritual powers, but their natural activity still depends on the senses, hence is sense life; only what happens in the inmost heart is purely spiritual, that is the life of the soul from and in God.[1] The created spirits have no access to this. The thoughts of the heart are hidden from them by nature, though they may be revealed by God.

The Interior of the Soul and the Thoughts of the Heart

The thoughts of the heart signify the original life of the soul in the ground of its being, in a depth that is beyond the division into diverse powers and activities. Here the soul lives as it is in itself, free from all creaturely influences. This inmost part is indeed the dwelling-place of God and the sphere where the union with him takes place; nevertheless, here flows the proper life of the soul before the union begins, even in cases where such a union is never accomplished. For every soul has its inmost sphere, whose being is its life. But this primeval life is hidden not only from other spirits but from the soul itself. There are several reasons for this. The primeval life of the soul is without form. The thoughts of the heart are as yet by no means thoughts in the ordinary sense, they are no circumscribed, organized and tangible creations of the thinking intellect. They must pass through several forms before they become such. First they must rise from the ground of the heart. Then they reach a first threshold, where they can be sensed. This sensing is a far more original mode of consciousness than rational knowledge; it still precedes the division into powers and activities. It lacks the clarity of purely rational understanding; on the other hand, it is richer than this. The things that rise up are felt to be invested with value, and on the strength of this it is decided whether that which rises up should be allowed to come to the surface or not. It should also be noted that what rises up and is sensed in a purely natural way is by now no longer the purely interior life of the soul but an answer to something that has set it in motion. But this leads in a direction which we cannot here pursue farther.

At the threshold where the rising motions are sensed begins the division of the faculties of the soul that can be known according to species as well as the formation of entities that can be apprehended. To these belong thoughts worked out by the understanding with their rational arrangement (these are interior words that can also be expressed in external words), movements of the mind and decisions of the

[1] Cf. *Living Flame of Love*, 2. 32.

will which enter the life of the soul as active forces. This life is now no longer the primeval life in the depth, but something that can be apprehended by interior perception. Now interior perception is a mode of apprehension totally different from that first sensing which rises from the depth. In the same way, the rising from the depth differs from the emergence of an object that has already been formed, that has been preserved in the memory and is now coming to life again.

Not all that rises up and becomes sensible is actually sensed. Much comes up, becoming an interior and exterior word, a desire, a will and an action "before one knows where one is". Only a person living perfectly recollected in his inner being watches faithfully even those first movements.

This brings us to the second reason why a man's inmost being is hidden from him. As has been said, here the soul is truly at home. But, strange though it may sound, it is normally *not* at home. There are but few souls that live in and from their inmost being; and even far fewer that are constantly living in and from it. Naturally, i.e. according to their *fallen* nature, men stay in the outer rooms of the castle of their soul. Whatever comes to them from outside draws them outward. God must call and draw them very perceptibly, indeed, if they are to be induced to "enter into themselves".[1]

Soul, Ego and Freedom

It is essential to understand as spiritually and unmetaphorically as possible what is here expressed in spatial imagery. These images can hardly be discarded, but they are equivocal and easy to misunderstand. What approaches the soul from outside belongs to the outer world, i.e. it does not belong to the soul itself; as a rule this includes also what does not belong to its body. For even though the body is called the soul's exterior, it is nevertheless *its* exterior, united to it in the unity of the same being and not external so as to be completely alien and separated from it.[2] Among these alien and separated things there is a difference between those that have a merely external—i.e. spatially extended—being, and those that have an interior, like the soul itself. On the other hand, we had to speak of an exterior and interior also in the soul itself. Though the soul be drawn outward, it does not go out from itself, it is only farther removed from its interior and thus

[1] In the chief mystical work, *The Interior Castle* (1. 1), St Teresa of Jesus compares the soul with a castle of seven mansions.
[2] St Teresa calls it the walls of the castle.

surrendered to the outer world. What approaches it from without has
a certain right to occupy it; and to the weight, the value and the
importance it has both in itself and for the soul, there corresponds a
certain depth in which it ought to be received in the soul. Thus it is
right that the soul should receive it according to this depth. But this
does not require the soul to surrender a more profound standpoint;
it is a spirit, and its castle is a spiritual kingdom, hence the laws in
force there are quite different from those valid in external space.
When the soul is in the deepest and most interior zone of this its
interior kingdom, it rules it completely and is free to visit every place
in it without leaving its own, the place of its repose. The soul's
capacity to move within is due to its being an ego (*Ichförmigkeit*).
The ego is that factor in the soul by which it possesses itself and which
moves in it as in its own space. The deepest point is also the place of
its freedom, where it can decide on its own being. Free decisions of
lesser moment can in a certain sense be made also from a more distant
point. But these are superficial decisions: it is mere chance if a decision
turns out to be adequate, for only in the most profound point are we
capable of judging all things by their ultimate standards. Nor will such
a decision be perfectly free, for if a man is not wholly master of himself he will not be able to dispose of anything with true freedom, but
will be subject to external influences.

Man is destined to live in his inmost being and to master himself
in a way that is possible only from this inmost sphere. A true relationship to the world is possible also only from here, and only from here
will he be able to find the place in the world that is allotted to him.
Yet he will never know his inmost being completely. This is a mystery
of God that only he can unveil as far as it pleases him. Nevertheless,
man is master of his inmost being, he can dispose of it in perfect
freedom, but it is also his duty to preserve it as a precious good
entrusted to him. It must be of great value in the realm of the spirits:
angels are appointed to protect it; evil spirits seek to make themselves
its masters; God himself has chosen it for his dwelling place. Neither
good nor bad spirits have free access to this inmost sphere of the soul.
The good spirits are as little capable as the evil ones of reading the
"thoughts of the heart", but God enlightens them on what they need
to know of these secrets. Moreover, there are spiritual means by which
the soul can communicate with other created spirits. It can address
another spirit through what has become an *interior word* to it. St
Thomas presents the language of the angels by which they are in

contact with each other as a wholly spiritual turning towards each other in order to communicate *one's own to the other*.[1] This applies also to the silent invocation of one's guardian angel or to an interior summons to the evil spirits. But even without our intention to communicate with them, the created spirits are, in a sense, aware of what happens within us: not indeed of what is hidden in our inmost soul, but of what has entered into us in comprehensible form. From this they can then draw conclusions with regard to what is hidden from their glance. In the case of the angels we must assume that they reverently protect the closed sanctuary. They only wish to lead the soul to withdraw there on its own account and then to hand it over to God. Satan, however, seeks to take God's property for himself. He cannot do this by his own power, but the soul itself can surrender to him. It will not do so if it has itself entered its interior and has come to know it as it does in the divine union. For then it is so deeply hidden in God that no temptation can approach it. But how is it possible that the soul should give itself up to the devil if it has not yet taken possession of itself, which it can do only when it has entered into its inmost centre? The only explanation is that it does so blindly, as it were from outside. It gives itself away without knowing what it surrenders. And even the devil cannot break the seal of this gift which he receives closed; he can only destroy what remains for ever hidden from him.

The soul has the right to decide its own fate; it is the great secret of personal freedom that God himself respects it. He wants his dominion over the created spirits to be a free gift of their love. He knows the thoughts of the heart, his glance penetrates the deepest layers and abysses of the soul that are hidden even from its own view unless God enlightens it in a special way. He will not possess it unless the soul itself wants it. But he does everything to obtain the free surrender of its will to his as a gift of its love so that he may lead it to blissful union. This is the Gospel that St John of the Cross proclaims and to which all his writings are dedicated.

What has just been said about the structure of the soul, especially of the relation of freedom to its most interior sphere, has not been taken from the works of the saint. We must therefore examine whether it agrees with his teaching and may even serve to throw a yet clearer light on it. (For only if this is the case can such an insertion be justified in this context.) At first glance some of what has been said may seem incompatible with certain statements of the saint.

[1] *De veritate*, q. 9, a. 4.

Every human being is free and is faced with decisions daily and hourly. Now, as long as the soul has not attained to the most perfect union of love the inmost part of it is the place where God dwells "all alone".[1] St Teresa calls it the seventh mansion, which is opened to the soul only in the mystical marriage.[2] This raises the question whether the soul can make truly free decisions only when it has reached the highest stage of perfection. Here we have to take into account that the soul's own activity evidently decreases in the measure as it approaches this inmost sphere. When it has reached it, God will work everything in the soul, itself will have to do no more than to receive.[3] Yet its share of freedom is expressed in just this receiving. Beyond this, however, freedom is involved even far more decisively, for in this state God works everything only because the soul surrenders itself to him perfectly. This surrender is itself the highest achievement of its freedom. St John himself describes the mystical marriage as the voluntary mutual surrender of God and the soul and attributes to the soul at this stage of perfection so great a power that it can dispose not only of itself, but even of God.[4] Hence, with regard to this highest stage of the personal life there is perfect agreement between the mystical doctrine of the two founders of the reformed Carmel and the view that the inmost region of the soul is the sphere of the most perfect freedom.

What, however, is the situation in the case of the great majority of men who do not attain to the mystical marriage? Can they enter into the interior and make decisions from there, or are they capable only of more or less superficial decisions? This question cannot be answered with a simple Yes or No.

It is an actual fact that the soul has a structure, is of greater or lesser depth, and has an inmost sphere. From this derives, also naturally, that the ego is able to move within this space and to take up its position in some place or another according to its inclinations. But these movements are made from the place in which it normally dwells. This is not the same for everyone, it differs according to the different types of men. The sensual man is mostly occupied with sensual enjoyment or means to achieve this; his standpoint is far removed from his interior zone. The seeker after truth lives predominantly in the sphere of rational research; if he is really concerned with truth itself, not only with amassing particular kinds of knowledge, he is probably nearer to God, who is Truth, than he himself realizes. We would add only one

---

[1] Cf. *Living Flame of Love*, 4. 14.   [2] *Interior Castle*, 7. 1.
[3] *Living Flame of Love*, 1. 9.   [4] *Ibid.*, 3. 78f.

more particularly important example, the egocentric man whose own self is all that matters to him. To the superficial observer it may seem as if such a man were especially near to his interior, yet for him the way there is perhaps strewn with more obstacles than for any other type. There will be something of this in every man until he has passed through the dark night. All these types must now be examined as to the possibilities of moving their ego, making free decisions and reaching their inmost sphere.

If a sensual man enjoying a pleasure is given the chance of procuring a greater pleasure, he will perhaps without further reflexion and choice pass at once from enjoyment to action. There is a movement, but not actually a free decision nor a penetration to greater depth if the stimuli are on the same plane. But the sensual man may also be approached by something belonging to an entirely different sphere of values; for no type is tied exclusively to one sphere, only one will always be more powerful than the other. He may, e.g., be asked to give up a pleasure in order to help someone else. Here the solution will hardly be effected without a free decision. In any case, the sensual man will not decide to make a sacrifice as if this were a matter of course but will have to make an effort. If he refuses, whether after some consideration or with an immediate "this is quite out of the question"—this refusal, too, involves a decision of the will. As a borderline case he may even remain in his enjoyment without refusing the sacrifice, if his spirit is so suffocated by the life of the senses that the demand cannot even reach it. The words are heard, perhaps their immediate meaning is still understood, but the deeper region where their true sense would be grasped is in ruins. In this borderline case there is not only no free decision, but freedom itself has been surrendered beforehand. In the case of the refusal the meaning has, indeed, been grasped, even though it has probably not been given its full weight. For this reason the decision is superficial, hence freedom is limited. Certain motives are not allowed to carry their full weight and good care is taken not to descend into that depth where they might gain force. In this way, however, a man suffers himself to be determined by one single sphere, he does not get a grip of himself, that is of all the deeper layers of his own being, and at the same time deprives himself of the possibility of facing the situation according to the actual facts, that is truly rationally and freely. Apart from this superficial refusal a more adequate one is also possible: the demand to give help is faced and allowed its full effect on the soul, but the person is compelled to reject it as unjustified after considering all the pros and cons. Such a refusal is on the same level as an acceptance after similar considerations. Both are possible only because the sensual man gives up his habitual attitude and passes on to the ethical attitude, which wants to understand and do what is morally right. This, however, means taking up a standpoint deep down in himself; so deep, indeed, that the transition resembles a veritable change and is perhaps not even possible in the natural way but only through an extraordinary awakening. Indeed, we may well say: an ultimately adequate decision is possible only in the very depths of the personality. For no man is naturally capable of surveying *all* reasons for and against which influence a decision. He can only decide to the best of his ability within his own sphere of vision. But the believer knows that there is One whose vision is not limited, but who embraces and penetrates everything. If a man lives in this certainty of faith his own conscience will not rest content with his own best ability. He must strive to recognize what is right in God's eyes. (This implies that only the religious attitude is truly ethical. There is, indeed, a natural seeking and longing for what is right and good, even a finding in individual cases, but it will become fully itself only in the search for the divine will.) For a man whom God himself has drawn into his own most intimate sphere and who has surrendered himself in the union of love, this question is solved once and for all. He need only let himself be directed by the palpable guidance of the Spirit of God and will then always be certain to do the right thing. In the one great decision which he has made in perfect freedom all future ones are included and can be made as it were automatically in any given case. But it is a long way from simply seeking for the right decision in a particular case to reaching this height—if there is a way from one to the other at all. If a man seeks what is right only here and now and decides according to his lights he is by this very fact on his way to God and to himself, even though he may not know it. But he is not yet perfectly master of himself. Hence he cannot fully dispose of himself nor decide with complete freedom on outside matters. If a man seeks to do the right thing on principle, i.e. if he wills to do it always and everywhere, he has decided about himself and placed his will within the divine will, even if it should not yet be clear to him that right is identical with what God wills. But if he is not clear about this, he has not yet found the safe way to what is right; and he has disposed of himself as if he were already master of himself, though he has not yet realized the depths of his own interior being. The ultimate decision is possible only before God.

But if a man's life of faith has reached the stage where he has completely decided for God and wants nothing save what God wills, has he then not arrived at the inmost sphere, and is there then still a difference between this state and the highest union of Love? It is very difficult here to draw the line, and it is also difficult to see how St John of the Cross draws it. Yet it seems necessary to me, both objectively and from his point of view, to acknowledge such a line and to make it clear. If, in blind faith, a man really wills nothing but what God wills he has reached the highest stage that can be attained by the grace of God: his will is completely purified and free from all earthly motives, he is united and fully surrendered to the divine will. Yet something decisive is still lacking to the highest union of love, the mystical marriage.

The Different Modes of Union with God

St John of the Cross has distinguished three modes of union with God.[1] By means of the first God dwells substantially in all created things and thus keeps them in being; by the second mode we understand the indwelling of grace in the soul, the third is the transforming, divinizing union through perfect love. In the passage just mentioned John sees only a difference in degree between the second and third modes. If, however, we consult other passages and consider the problem as a whole, it seems that there is a difference of kind, and within each mode there is, moreover, a series of steps. In the *Spiritual Canticle*, e.g., the saint mentions the same threefold division without speaking of a mere difference of degree between the presence of grace and the presence of love. On the contrary, he emphasizes the perceptible feeling of the highest Good present in the union of love and its effect: the burning desire for the unveiled beatific vision of God.[2]

St Teresa, too, has frequently treated this question. She says in the *Castle of the Soul*[3] that in the prayer of union she came to know the truth of faith that God is in every thing by his essence, his presence and his power. Before that she had known only his indwelling through grace. She then asked several theologians about her discovery. A "half-learned" man also knew only of the indwelling by grace. But others confirmed that what she had realized in the experience of union was a truth of faith. Perhaps we shall gain a clearer view of this when we compare the seemingly so different presentations of the two Carmelite saints.

[1] *Ascent*, 2. 5. [2] *Spiritual Canticle*, stanza II. [3] 5. 1.

They agree on the truth of faith which was familiar to John, the theologian, whereas Teresa had to discover it, that God the Creator is present in every thing and keeps it in being. He has foreseen each one of them beforehand and knows its destiny through and through in all its changes. In virtue of his omnipotence he can do what he pleases with everything at every moment. He can leave it to its own laws and the normal course of events, or he can intervene with extraordinary measures. In this way God also dwells in every human soul. He knows each one of them from all eternity, with all the mysteries of its being and all the vicissitudes of its life. It is in his power; he decides whether he will leave it to itself and the course of the world or powerfully intervene in its destiny. The rebirth of a soul by sanctifying grace is such a miracle of his omnipotence. John and Teresa agree again that God's indwelling by grace is different from the Presence by which he keeps his creatures in being, which is common to all. By "essence, presence and power" God can be in the soul without its knowing and willing it, even though it be hardened in sin and live far away from him, feeling no effect of his presence. The indwelling by grace is possible only in personal-spiritual being, for it presupposes the free acceptance of sanctifying grace by its recipient. (In infant baptism this free consent is given by adults representing the baptized child, and is later personally repeated throughout the life of faith of the baptized and in definite words in the renewal of the baptismal vows.) This implies that, in this second manner, God cannot dwell in a sinful soul that has turned away from him. For sanctifying grace derives its name precisely from the fact that it wipes out sin.

It is due to the very essence of grace that this indwelling is not possible in the case of impersonal, i.e. subhuman, beings. For it is a continuous infusion of the divine being and life into the soul. This being is personal life and can flow only where it is personally received; it is therefore impossible to receive grace without freely accepting it. Such a "being in each other" is possible only where there is truly interior, i.e. spiritual, being. Spiritual life can be received only by a being that lives spiritually. The soul in which God dwells by grace is no impersonal scene of the divine life but is itself drawn into this life. The divine life is three-personal life; it is overflowing love, in which the Father generates the Son and gives him his Being, while the Son embraces this Being and returns it to the Father; it is the love in which the Father and Son are one, both breathing the Holy Spirit. By grace this Spirit is shed abroad in men's hearts. Thus the soul lives its life of grace through the Holy Spirit, in him it loves the Father with the love of the Son and the Son with the love of the Father. The soul can share in this Trinitarian life without perceiving the indwelling of the Divine Persons. In fact only a small number of chosen ones attain to an experimental apprehension of the Triune God in their soul. A larger number is led by an enlightened faith to a living knowledge of this indwelling and to a loving communion with the three Persons in pure faith. Even if a man has not yet reached this high stage he is yet united to God in faith, hope and love, even though he does not realize that God lives in his inmost being, that he can find him there and that his whole life of grace and virtue is the effect of this divine life in himself and his participation in it. Living faith is the firm conviction that God exists, the belief that all he has revealed is true, and a loving readiness to be guided by the divine will. Being an infused supernatural knowledge of God it is a "beginning of eternal life in us" [1]—but only a beginning. It is placed into our soul as a seed destined to be carefully tended and to develop into a large tree bearing magnificent fruit. For it is the way that is to lead us to union with God even in this life, though ultimate perfection belongs to the next. We must now consider in what way the union of love is distinguished from the divine indwelling by grace. On this point St Teresa differs from St John of the Cross.

The Mother of Carmel believes that in the prayer of union she has experienced the first mode of indwelling, which is different from the indwelling by grace, whereas according to the *Ascent* the union of love is only a higher degree of the union by grace. Teresa, too, knows a mode of union with God that can be achieved solely by faithful co-operation with grace, mortification of one's nature and the perfect practice of the love of God and one's neighbour. She stresses this emphatically for the consolation of those who do not reach the "prayer of union". [2] But in a preceding passage she has stated with equal emphasis and all desirable clarity that the prayer of union can in no way be obtained by one's own efforts. [3] In it the soul is drawn so strongly to God that it becomes insensible to the things of the world while giving its whole attention to him. It is "as it were beside itself", so that it cannot think of anything. "Here it only loves, but does not even know . . . how it loves or what it loves. . . . The understanding wants to be wholly occupied with grasping something of what the soul feels; but as its powers are incapable of it, it is so utterly astonished

---

[1] *De veritate*, q. 19, a. 2, corp.   [2] Cf. *Interior Castle*, 5. 3.   [3] *Ibid.*, 5. 1 and 2.

that it can move neither hand nor foot. . . ." Here God works in the soul "without being hindered by anyone, not even by ourselves". And what he works surpasses all joys, delights and bliss of this earth. This state lasts only for a short time, scarcely more than half an hour. But the manner of God's presence in the soul is such that "when it returns to itself it cannot possibly doubt that it has been in God and God in it. It retains this truth with such certainty that it never forgets it and can never doubt it, even if God should not grant it this grace again for many years. And this is so, regardless of the effects left in the soul." As long as this mysterious experience lasted the soul did not perceive God. But afterwards it clearly recognized his presence. It did not actually see him, "but it retained a certainty that only God can give". This has nothing to do with the Body, as in the invisible Presence of Christ in the Most Holy Sacrament. Only the Divinity is present. "But how can we be so certain about something we do not see? That I do not know, for it is the work of God; but I do know that I am speaking the truth. . . . It suffices for us to know that He who gives these favours is almighty. However we may try, we are in no way capable of obtaining them by our own power; only God can give them. Therefore we will not attempt to understand them either."

Without intending to do so, St Teresa has yet made several attempts to interpret her experience. She did so when she understood this in-dwelling of God which she felt with such unshakable certainty as that which is common to all creatures. Another interpretation is con-tained in the remark: "If a person does not have this certainty I should say that not the whole soul has been united with God but only one of its powers, or that it has been granted one of the many other kinds of favours which God is wont to bestow on the soul." In the true union God is said to be united with the substance of the soul.

It is extremely valuable for us that Teresa has described her experience without restraint, regardless of the possibilities of a theoretical explanation and of possible criticisms. Her faithful des-cription may help us to ascertain with what kind of indwelling we are concerned and how to judge her own attempts at an interpretation. The soul has the certainty that it has been in God and God in it. This certainty has remained in it as an effect of this experience. It was essentially contained in this experience as one of its constituents, even though it could only be realized later. The consciousness of union is not added to the latter from outside but belongs to its essence. Where such a consciousness and subsequent certainty is impossible, as in the case of a stone or a plant, there cannot be the same kind of union or indwelling. Hence it is, indeed, a different kind of indwelling from that common to all creatures, which Teresa experienced in the prayer of union. Neither is this new kind of indwelling always actual where it is possible on principle. The saint herself expresses this when she says the soul was certain that God has been in it and it in God. It was a transitory state. On the other hand, the indwelling "by presence, essence and power" does not cease for a moment as long as a thing exists. Its interruption would mean that the thing sinks back into nothingness.

Thus we agree with St John of the Cross that the indwelling in the union of love is different from that which keeps all things in being. On the other hand, St Teresa's description shows quite clearly that this indwelling differs from that of grace not only in degree but in kind. She urges her daughters to make every effort to reach the highest stage of the life of grace that can be attained by faithful co-operation with it; i.e. the perfect union of the human with the divine will by the perfect practice of the love of God and one's neighbour. But she makes it equally clear that it is absurd to strive for that union which God alone can give. We shall never by our own efforts, even though supported by grace, come to feel God's presence and union with him as a living reality. The work of the will, aided by grace, can never produce the marvellous effect that is achieved in the short period of union, to transform the soul in such a way that it hardly recognizes itself, to change the worm into a butterfly. One's own efforts would need years of hard struggle to bring about a similar effect.

The prayer of union is not yet that form of union which St John always keeps in view as the goal of the Dark Night. It is only a preliminary. It serves to prepare the soul for perfect surrender to God and to rouse in it a burning desire that the union should be repeated and made permanent. This is clear from the fifth and sixth Mansions of the *Interior Castle* which describe the preparation and conclusion of the Spiritual Betrothal. A corresponding description is given in the explanation of the thirteenth and fourteenth stanzas of the *Spiritual Canticle*. In these two sections John and Teresa agree that the betrothal takes place in an ecstasy. God snatches the soul to himself so forcefully that nature nearly succumbs. Hence Teresa affirms that it needs great courage to effect this betrothal. And in the *Spiritual Canticle* the terrified bride asks the Beloved to turn away his eyes, when he suddenly grants her the glance she has so long desired. There is a certain contradiction between this passage and another, where St John says that the possession by grace and the possession by union are related to each other as betrothal to marriage. The one, he says, signifies what can be obtained by the will and grace, the perfect harmony of the human with the divine will through the perfect purification of the soul, the other the mutual complete surrender and union.[1] This contradiction can be partly explained by a difference of terminology: in both these passages the term betrothal is evidently used in a different sense. But beyond this there is an objective difference: in one passage the properly mystical experience seems to be restricted to the highest stage, whereas in the other it begins earlier.[2] It is decisive for the question under discussion that John here clearly states, at least with regard to the highest stage, that there is an essential difference between the mystical marriage and the utmost that can be achieved by grace and will. With this his presentation in the *Ascent* is evidently given up, for there he would admit only a difference of degree between the union by grace and the mystical union. Moreover, there are passages in all his writings which clearly show that properly mystical experience begins even at much lower stages. We would only recall those touches in the substance of the soul mentioned in the *Ascent*.[3] Of these the saint says that the understanding senses God in a sublime and delightful manner, that they are in no proportion to the works of the soul, that one can only prepare oneself for them, but that they are received in a purely passive manner and are meant to lead to union with God. All this points to something that is outside the normal way of grace: a transitory union that gives a foretaste of the permanent one.

How is it to be explained that St John of the Cross has not expressed himself unequivocally on this decisive question? To answer this with certainty we should have to know a little more about the personal life of the silent saint than he betrays in his writings or has confided to his contemporaries. We would only hint at some of the possibilities suggested by the history of his time and recent research on the textual history of his works.[4] The great religious controversies of his time, the heresies that were rampant, the dangers of an unhealthy pseudo-mysticism had led to a strict supervision of spiritual literature. Whoever wrote on questions of the interior life had to reckon with the

---

[1] *Living Flame of Love*, 3. 24.

[2] We shall see later that within the *Spiritual Canticle*, too, the presentation is not altogether consistent.　　　[3] 2. 32.

[4] Cf. Baruzi, vol. I, *The Texts*, as well as the Introductions in the latest critical edition by P. Silverio.

possibility that the Inquisition would seize him and his works. It is conceivable that John may have been anxious to distinguish his own teaching from illuminism (as he evidently does in some passages) and to bring the mystical development into the closest possible relation to the normal way of grace. The comparison of the older editions with the manuscripts and of the manuscripts among themselves has proved that there has been such an intention in the editing of his writings. The *Living Flame of Love* and the *Spiritual Canticle* are extant in two manuscript versions. The later versions show the desire to prevent misunderstandings by toning down bold expressions and by adding explanations. Have these alterations been made by the saint himself or by someone else? The *Ascent* and the *Dark Night* have been preserved only in one manuscript version. But the difference between these manuscripts and all the older printed editions down to the first critical one by P. Gerardo (also the difference between the old printed editions of the *Living Flame of Love* and the first manuscript version from which they were made) is so considerable that here the mutilation by other hands cannot be denied. *Ascent* and *Night* are extant only in fragments. Neither work contains those parts in which the union was to be treated in detail and the questions which occupy us at the moment were to be cleared up. Have these parts never been written or were they suppressed in the copies? (All four great treatises are extant only in copies, none in the original; only one copy of the *Spiritual Canticle* contains corrections in the saint's own hand.) And were these parts suppressed in accordance with the will of the author or of another? None of these questions can be answered.

In order to clarify these matters we have consulted the uninhibited descriptions of St Teresa. They give us certainty where the different formulations of St John of the Cross raise doubts. They are not only quite untampered invaluable accounts of facts and thus excellent material for arriving at a theoretical understanding; we have also the right to assume that, despite their difference of character, literary peculiarity, type of sanctity and esteem of the non-essential mystical graces, both saints were agreed on the fundamentals of the interior life. The *Interior Castle* and the works of St John of the Cross were written after both had for years been living in intimate spiritual communication at Avila. St Teresa then called her young collaborator the "father of her soul"[1] and St John has occasionally referred to her writings[2] to

---

[1] Letter to Anne of Jesus, Allison Peers, n. 261.   [2] *Spiritual Canticle,* 13. 7.

save himself explanations that could be found there. If, therefore, we find in her description of the different stages of the mystical union something that differs unmistakably from the union by grace, we may be convinced that St John of the Cross has approved it. By thus combining the teaching of both Carmelite saints we are confirmed in our view that the three modes of the divine indwelling are not only different in degree but in kind. We shall now try to work out the differences with greater precision.

It is the same God in three Persons who is present in all three modes; his unchangeable Being is the same in all of them. Yet his indwelling is different, because that wherein the same immutable Deity dwells is of a different kind in each case, and thus the indwelling itself is modified.[1] The first mode of indwelling, or rather the divine presence, because it is not yet an indwelling in the proper sense, requires from the being in which God is present only that it should be subject to his knowledge and power and owe its existence to the divine Being. This is common to all created being. Here divine and creaturely being remain completely separate; between them there is only the relation of a one-sided dependence, which is no actual "in-each-other", and for this reason no actual indwelling. For indwelling demands from both sides an interior being, i.e. a being that embraces itself interiorly (*das sich selbst innerlich umfasst*) and is capable of receiving another being within itself, so that a unity of being is effected without destroying the independence of either the receiving or the received being. This is possible only in the case of spiritual being: for only this both exists within itself and can receive other, also spiritual, being within itself. Only this is a true indwelling. The indwelling by grace is indeed something like this. If a man is subject to God's Being, knowledge and power, not without his own knowledge and will, but with his full consent, he will receive God into himself, and his being will be penetrated by the divine Being. But this penetration is not complete. It goes only so far as the receptive capacity of the other permits. The perfect union of love consists in being completely penetrated by the divine Being, and for this the soul must be free from all other being, empty of all other creatures and of itself, as St John of the Cross has so consistently emphasized. The highest fulfilment of love is union in free mutual surrender; this is the inter-Trinitarian divine life.

---

[1] If in one and the same creaturely being the indwelling is modified, this is indeed a modification, not an addition of one kind to another: if a soul receives sanctifying grace God does not then dwell in it in two different ways, but the indwelling by essence and that by grace are one.

Both the creatures' ascending, desiring love of God (*amor*, ἔρως), and God's mercifully descending love for his creatures (*caritas*, ἀγάπη), aim at this fulfilment. Where these two meet the union can progressively be achieved at the cost of what is still standing in its way and in the measure as this is destroyed. As has been shown, this takes place both actively and passively in the Dark Night. By purifying itself the human will enters more and more deeply into the divine will, but in such a way that the latter is not sensed as present reality but accepted in blind faith. In this there is indeed only a difference of degree between the indwelling by grace and the union of love. In the passively experienced purification by the consuming divine fire of love, on the other hand, the divine will increasingly penetrates the human will, at the same time making itself felt as a present reality. And here, in our view, we have a new mode of indwelling, different from that of grace not only in degree but in kind. This difference may be explained in connexion with St Augustine's exegesis of the words of St John's Gospel: "Many believed in his name.... But Jesus did not trust himself to them." [1]

Augustine applies this saying to the catechumens: they already confess Christ, but he does not yet give himself to them in the Blessed Sacrament. We may also refer it to the two modes of indwelling, the distinctive characteristics of which we want to grasp, and thus also to the difference between faith and contemplation. The indwelling by grace gives the virtue of faith, i.e. the power to accept as real what one does not perceive as present and to hold to be true what cannot be strictly proved by rational arguments. It is rather as if somebody had heard many fine things about a person who had also conferred benefits on him and given him presents; hence this man loves and is grateful to his benefactor and is more and more anxious to know him personally. But he has not yet entrusted himself to his protégé; he has not even granted him an interview, much less has he opened his soul to him or given him his heart. All this, however, God gives to a man, again in gradual ascent, in the third mode of indwelling, the mystical election: there God grants him a personal encounter by a touch in his inner being; he opens his own inner Being to him by special illuminations about his nature and his secret counsels; he gives him his heart, first as if by a sudden impulse during a personal meeting (in the prayer of union [2]), then as a permanent possession (in the mystical betrothal [3] and marriage [4]). All this is not face to face vision;

[1] John 2. 23f. Cf. Augustine, *Tract. in Joan.*, 11/12, Migne, *PL*, 35, 1484ff.
[2] Cf. *Interior Castle*, 5. 1; *Dark Night*, 2. 19; *Spiritual Canticle*, 13.
[3] *Interior Castle*, 13 and 14.   [4] *Interior Castle*, 7. 1; *Spiritual Canticle*, 22.

in this the comparison with the progressive approach between human beings is inadequate. But even at the lowest stage there is a meeting between two persons, hence an experimental knowledge. God touches the inmost sphere of the soul (which St John of the Cross also calls its essence) with his own essence. Now God's essence is nothing else but his Being and his self; he himself is Person, his Being is personal Being, and the inmost sphere of the soul is the heart and source of its personal life and at the same time the true place of its meeting with other personal life. A contact between persons is possible only in the most interior sphere; through such a touch one person makes known its presence to another.[1] Hence, if we feel ourselves touched in such a way, we are in living contact with a Person. This is not yet union, only an approach to it. But compared with the indwelling by grace it is already the beginning of something new: there, divine Being is communicated to the soul, but the personal source remains hidden and does not enter into this communication of being; here, the source of divine life (in so far as it can be called such) touches the source of the life of the human soul in its being and thus is perceived as present, though it still remains in darkness and hidden. In the illuminations of divine mysteries the closed interior of God is opened: in the infusion of the Divine Being the soul experiences an elevation of its own being and enters into the former. In the union (with its various stages) is accomplished a "oneing" that is derived from the personal source of life by mutual personal surrender.

Here several things should be noted. The mere touch in the interior does not necessarily presuppose the indwelling by grace. It may be given in the case of a complete unbeliever to awaken him to faith and prepare him for the reception of sanctifying grace. It may also serve as a means to make an unbeliever a fit instrument for various ends. Both apply also to particular illuminations. The union as a mutual surrender, however, cannot take place without faith and love, i.e. without sanctifying grace. If this should be given to a soul not in the state of grace it would at the same time also have to receive sanctifying grace and perfect contrition as a condition. These possibilities confirm the essential difference between the union by grace and the mystical union and between the corresponding modes of indwelling. There are here two different ways of ascent. But this does not exclude the

---

[1] We cannot here examine in how far this applies also to the communications among human persons.

possibility that the life of grace can prepare the way for the mystical union.

The fact that the inmost sphere of the soul is basically the place of personal meeting and union makes it understandable—insofar as we can speak of understanding in the case of divine mysteries—that God has chosen the inmost part of the soul as his dwelling. For if union with him is the end for which souls have been created the situation that makes this union possible must exist from the beginning.

It is equally intelligible that the soul can freely dispose of this inmost sphere, because loving surrender is possible only for a free being. Is this loving surrender in the mystical marriage different also on the part of the soul from the unconditional surrender of its will to the divine will? Evidently yes. It is different from the point of view of knowledge: if God surrenders to it in the mystical marriage, the soul comes to know God in a way in which it did not know him before, and in which it cannot know him by any other means; it also had not known its own last depths before. Hence it did not yet know, as it knows then, to whom it surrenders its will, what it surrenders and what kind of surrender this divine will may demand from it. It is different also from the point of view of the will: as regards the end, for the surrender of the will envisages the union of one's own will with the will of God, not with his heart, nor with the divine Persons; as regards the starting point, for only then has it reached the deepest source and does the will wholly embrace itself, because it embraces the whole person from its personal centre; as regards the accomplishment, for in the bridal surrender not only one's own will is sub- and co-ordinated to the divine will, but the divine surrender is also received. Hence in the surrender of his own person a man simultaneously takes possession of God in the boldest way imaginable, surpassing all human understanding. St John of the Cross expresses this very clearly when he says that the soul can now give more to God than it is in itself: it gives God to himself in God.[1] Thus there is here something essentially different from the union by grace: the soul is most profoundly drawn into the divine Being and thus itself divinized. The persons become one in a way that does not destroy their independence, which is, on the contrary, the condition of this union; they penetrate each other in a way surpassed only by the circumincession of the divine Persons themselves which is its archetype. This is the union which St John unmistakably envisages as the end in all his writings, even though

[1] *Living Flame of Love*, 3. 77ff.

he often uses the word in a different sense and thus does not always differentiate it from the other kinds as precisely as has been attempted here. Anticipating, we have already stated that the mystical marriage is the union with the Triune God. As long as God touches the soul only in darkness and concealment it can sense the personal touch only as such, without perceiving whether it is being touched by one Person or by several. But if it has been drawn into the divine life in the perfect union of love it also realizes that this is a tri-personal life, and it must come into contact with all three Divine Persons.[1]

Faith and Contemplation. Death and Resurrection

The difference between the indwelling of God through grace and through the mystical union also seems to us a suitable basis from which to reach a clear distinction between faith and contemplation. St John of the Cross mentions them very frequently, but he does not make a definite comparison between them in such a way as to provide a univocal definition of their mutual relation. His discussions frequently sound as if there were no definite borderline at all: both are called the way to union, both a dark and loving knowledge. The *Ascent of Mount Carmel*[2] treats above all of the darkness of faith; for here faith is called a midnight darkness, because the light of natural knowledge must be wholly surrendered in order to gain its light. John often designates contemplation by the terms of the Areopagite as mystical theology (hidden knowledge of God) and ray of darkness.[3] Both come very near to each other if he says that God veils himself in darkness when communicating himself to the soul.[4] On the other hand, it becomes clear especially in the discussions of the *Ascent* that faith and contemplation cannot be simply identical, because the author says that the night of faith guides the soul to the delights of pure contemplation and union. A difference is presupposed also when he says in the preface to the *Spiritual Canticle* that mystical wisdom does not require distinct understanding and in this is similar to faith, by which we also love God without grasping him distinctly.[5] If both were identical he could

---

[1] We shall meet this presently when discussing the *Living Flame of Love*. St Teresa describes the descent of the Blessed Trinity to the mystical marriage in the *Interior Castle*, 7. 1.

[2] *Ascent*, 2. 1ff.

[3] E.g. *ibid.*, 8. 6. Dionysius uses the term 'ray of darkness' in the first chapter of his *Mystical Theology* (Migne, *PG*, 3. 999f).

[4] *Ascent*, ch. 9.

[5] Here we have at the same time a proof of the presentation of faith as loving knowledge; for contemplation cf. esp. *Ascent*, 2. 14f.

not speak of similarity. Both distinction and relationship are perhaps most clearly expressed in a passage where contemplation as an indistinct, dark and general knowledge is opposed to the supernatural, clearly recognizable particular kinds of rational knowledge. "The dark and general knowledge is but one: this is the contemplation that is given in faith."[1]

To understand this sentence and the relation between faith and contemplation we must remember what has been said above on the many meanings of the term faith as well as on the ambiguity of contemplation. Faith can mean the content of the divine revelation and our acceptance of it as well as the loving surrender to God of whom revelation speaks and to whom we owe it. The content of faith provides the material for meditation, in which the powers of the soul work on what has been received by faith, presenting it in images, rational considerations and acts of the will. The fruit of meditation is a permanent state of loving knowledge.[2] Then the soul rests in quiet, peaceful and loving surrender in the presence of God whom it has come to know by faith, without meditating on any separate truth. This is acquired contemplation, the result of meditation. As regards its experienced content it is not distinguished from faith in the third sense: *credere in Deum*, by which the soul enters into God by faith and love. But usually St John of the Cross means something different when he speaks of contemplation. God can grant to the soul a dark, loving knowledge of himself even without a preceding exercise of meditation. He can place it suddenly in the state of contemplation and love. He can infuse contemplation. This, too, will happen in connection with faith. As a rule it will be granted to souls who have been prepared for it by a fervent life of faith. But if an unbeliever should be seized by it, the teaching of faith which he had not yet accepted would nevertheless help him to know what has seized him. And the faithfully loving soul will always return from the darkness of contemplation to the secure clarity of the doctrines of the faith, in order to understand from there what is happening to it.[3] Despite all similarity, this is something basically different from acquired contemplation and surrender to God in mere faith, the content of which is largely identical with acquired contemplation. What is new is that the soul is now seized by the felt presence of God, or, in those experiences of the Dark Night in which the soul is deprived of this felt presence, that it is painfully wounded

---

[1] *Ascent*, 2. 10. 4.   [2] Cf. *ibid.*, 2. 14.
[3] *Spiritual Canticle*, stanza 11.

with the fervent desire that remains if God withdraws from the soul. Both are mystical experiences, caused by the kind of indwelling that is a contact between two persons in the inmost sphere of the soul. Faith, on the other hand, and all that belongs to its life, is based on the indwelling by grace.

The contrast between God's felt presence and his felt absence in mystical contemplation points to something else that may serve to distinguish faith from contemplation. Faith is in the first place a concern of reason. It is true, the acceptance of faith involves a participation of the will, yet it is the acceptance of a kind of knowledge. The darkness of faith relates to a peculiarity of this knowledge. Contemplation, on the other hand, is a matter of the heart, i.e. of the inmost part of the soul and thus of all its powers. The presence and apparent absence of God are felt in the heart, giving blissful happiness or a most painful longing. Now here in its most interior sphere the soul also senses itself and its state;[1] and as long as it has not been perfectly purified it feels this as painful because it is opposed to the holiness of God experienced as present within it. Thus the night of contemplation signifies not only the obscurity of knowledge but also the darkness of impurity and purifying torment.

God takes hold of the soul both in faith and in contemplation. Revealed truth is not simply accepted by a natural decision of the will. The message of faith comes to many who do not receive it. This may also be due to natural motives, but there are cases in which there is a mysterious incapacity: the hour of grace has not yet come. The indwelling by grace has not yet begun. But in contemplation the soul meets God himself who takes hold of it.

God is love; therefore to be seized by God is to be inflamed by love, if the spirit is ready for it. Eternal love is a consuming fire for all that is finite, that is for all the motions caused in the soul by creatures. If it turns to them it withdraws from divine love, but it cannot escape it. Then this love becomes a consuming fire for it. The human spirit is designed for everlasting being. This is indicated by the immutability it ascribes to its own states, expecting its own temporary situation to remain for ever.[2] This is a deception, for its temporal being is subject

---

[1] This sensing itself in the depth is different from the simple self-knowledge which St Teresa assigns to the first Mansion. It is a becoming aware of oneself without facing oneself, in which one's own being remains as mysterious as God's presence within it. The interior is here not restricted to the seventh mansion, where the marriage takes place, but applied to the whole sphere of mystical experience.

[2] *Night of the Spirit*, 7, 4f.

to change. But this deception shows that the spirit is conscious that its being is not confined to the temporal sphere, but has its roots in eternity. By its nature the spirit cannot crumble away like material things. But if it clings to the temporal in free surrender it will feel the hand of the living God who, by his omnipotence, can either destroy it, consuming it with the avenging fire of scorned divine love, or preserve it in eternal destruction like the fallen angels. This second and most real death would be the lot of us all if, by his Passion and death, Christ did not stand between us and divine justice, opening a way for the mercy of God.

In virtue of his nature as well as his free decision there was nothing in Christ that resisted love. He lived at every moment completely surrendered to divine love. But in the Incarnation he assumed mankind's whole burden of sin, embracing it with his merciful love and hiding it in his soul. This he did in the *Ecce venio!* with which he began his earthly life, explicitly renewed in his baptism, and in the *Fiat* of Gethsemani. Thus the expiatory fire was burning within him, indeed in his whole, lifelong Passion, but most bitterly in the garden of Olives and on the Cross, because there the felt beatitude of the indestructible union ceased in order to surrender him wholly to suffering, even to the most profound experience of being abandoned by God. The end of the expiatory burning is announced in the *Consummatum est* and the final return to the eternal, unclouded union of love in the "Father, into thy hands I commend my spirit".

In the Passion and death of Christ our sins have been consumed by fire. If we accept this by faith, and if we accept the whole Christ in faithful self-giving, that is to say by choosing and walking in the way of the imitation of Christ, he will lead us "through his Passion and Cross to the glory of the Resurrection". It is exactly this that is experienced in contemplation: man passes through the atoning fire to the blissful union of love. This explains its twofold character. It is death and resurrection. After the Dark Night there shines forth the Living Flame of Love.

§3. THE GLORY OF THE RESURRECTION

I. IN THE FLAMES OF THE DIVINE LOVE[1]

LLAMA DE AMOR VIVA

LIVING FLAME OF LOVE

I

Oh llama de amor viva,
Que tiernamente hieres
De mi alma en el más profundo centro!
Pues ya no eres esquiva,
Acaba ya si quieres,
Rompe la tela deste dulce encuentro.

I

Oh flame of love so living,
How tenderly you force
To my soul's inmost core your fiery probe!
Since now you've no misgiving,
End it, pursue your course
And for our sweet encounter, tear the robe!

II

Oh cauterio suave!
Oh regalada llaga!
Oh mano blanda! Oh toque delicado,
Que a vida eterna sabe,
Y toda deuda paga!
Matando, muerte en vida la has trocado.

II

Oh cautery most tender!
Oh gash that is my guerdon!
Oh gentle hand! Oh touch how softly thrilling!
Eternal life you render,
Raise of all debts the burden,
And change my death to life, even while killing!

III

Oh lámparas de fuego,
En cuyos resplandores
Las profundas cavernas del sentido,
Que estaba oscuro y ciego,
Con extraños primores
Calor y luz dan junto a su querido!

III

Oh lamps of fiery blaze
To whose refulgent fuel
The deepest caverns of my soul grow bright,
Late blind with gloom and haze,
But in this strange renewal
Giving to the belov'd both heat and light.

IV

Cuán manso y amoroso
Recuerdas en mi seno,
Donde secretamente solo moras:
Y en tu aspirar sabroso
De bien y gloria lleno
Cuán delicadamente me enamoras!

IV

What peace, with love enwreathing,
You conjure to my breast
Which only you your dwelling place may call:
While with delicious breathings
In glory, grace and rest
So daintily in love you make me fall!

[1] N.3 in Allison Peers and Campbell.

(a) *On the Threshold of Eternal Life*

The soul has escaped from the Night. What is now taking place in it is far more powerful than words can express. The longing cries of "Oh" and "How" seek to make this clear. Therefore the saint hesitated to comply with the request of Ana de Peñalosa, his spiritual daughter, to explain the four verses. He felt that words were quite inadequate to convey something so spiritual and interior. After some time, however, it seemed to him that the Lord "had in some way opened his understanding and given him some fervour", indeed, had himself encouraged him to begin the work.[1]

"Some fervour!" Not only the four verses of the Canticle but the whole interpretation, too, seem to be an eruption of the Living Flame of Love. Thus we, too, can approach these divine secrets of a chosen soul with holy fear and reverence. But once the veil has been lifted we are no longer allowed to be silent about it. For here we have what is lacking in the *Ascent* and the *Night* in the form in which they have come down to us, that is to say, a description of the soul at the end of its long way of the Cross, in the blessed state of union.

It has been said before that even the first works were evidently written by someone who had already arrived at the goal. The *Canticle of the Dark Night* can hardly be understood otherwise. But when interpreting the poem St John went back in thought to the time of the Night and described it as if he were still surrounded by it. He discussed the goal only by anticipating. Now, however, he is immersed in the radiant light of the morning of the resurrection. If he still speaks of the Cross and the Night he does so only in retrospect. Just this makes the work so important in our context: the new life is born from death, the glory of the resurrection is the reward for having faithfully endured the Night and the Cross. Thus the soul "pays every debt".

It feels that "out of its belly flow rivers of living water"[2] and it seems to it as if it "were already so effectively transformed into God, so powerfully possessed by Him and so abundantly adorned with gifts and virtues that only a slight web separates it from eternal beatitude". When this tender flame of love that is burning in it seizes the soul, it is each time "as it were transfigured in sweet and powerful glory . . ." and thinks the web of this earthly life is being broken and only very little lacking to the possession of eternal bliss and life. Thus it is wholly filled with violent longing and asks to be delivered from this mortal veil.[3]

---

[1] *Living Flame of Love*, Prologue.   [2] John 7. 38.   [3] *Living Flame*, I. I.

The Living Flame of Love is the Holy Spirit "whom the soul now feels in itself . . . like a fire consuming and transforming it in blissful love", but also "as a fire that burns out from it and . . . breaks out in flames. As often as this flame flares up it immerses the soul in bliss and enkindles it with a kind of divine life." The Holy Spirit works in the soul as a burning of love in which the will of the soul has become one sole love with the divine flame. The transformation in love is the *habitus*, the permanent state in which the soul has been placed. Its acts "are the flame that breaks forth from the fire of love and flares up the more violently, the more intensely the fire of union is burning." In this state the soul cannot act itself. All its acts are inspired and performed by the Holy Spirit and for this reason are wholly divine. Thus, whenever the flame flares up it seems to the soul that it is now granted eternal life: "For it is raised to a divine operation in God." When the soul is thus transformed into a flame of love, the Father, the Son and the Holy Spirit communicate themselves to it and it approaches so closely to God that it snatches a ray of eternal life; it has the feeling as if this were eternal life.[1]

The flame of the divine life touches the soul with the very tenderness of this life and wounds it so deeply in its inmost being that it wholly dissolves in love. How can this still be called a wounding? Indeed, these wounds are "like the brightest flames of tenderest love", the playing of eternal Wisdom, "flames of the tenderest touches whereby the soul is incessantly stirred by that fire of love which is never inactive. . . ."[2]

This happens in the deepest ground of the soul where neither the devil nor the senses are able to penetrate, hence entirely undisturbed, substantially and delightfully. "The lovelier and more interior a thing is the purer it is, and the greater the purity, the more abundantly, frequently and perfectly does God communicate Himself, and the more profound is the delight and joy of the soul. . . . It is God who works all this, the soul gives nothing of its own." For of itself it can act only with the help of the bodily senses; but the soul in this state is completely removed from them and thus "contents itself with only receiving from God; He alone can accomplish His work in the ground of the soul . . . without the mediation of the senses, and can move the soul". Thus all the movements of the soul are divine and God's acts, yet also the acts of the soul. "For God performs them with it in it, since it gives its will and consent."

[1] *Ibid.*, 1. 3.   [2] *Ibid.*, 1. 7f.

If the soul says that the Holy Spirit wounds it in its depth it means by this that there are in it also spheres that are less deep, according to the degrees of its love of God; but now its very essence, its operation and its power are touched and seized. The soul would not assert "that this is taking place as essentially and perfectly as in the beatific vision in the next life"; it only speaks in this way "to express the abundance of delight and bliss which it feels in these favours of the Holy Spirit. This delight is the greater and more interior, the more powerfully and essentially the soul is transformed into God." Here this does not happen as perfectly as in the next life. "Indeed, the habitual love of the soul may perhaps be as perfect in this life as in the next, but not its fruit and activity." But its state becomes so similar to life in the other world that the soul, convinced that this is the case, dares to say: in the deepest ground of my soul. If a person has no experience of these things he may think this exaggerated. But "the Father of lights, whose hand is not shortened and . . . bestows blessings abundantly . . . does not hesitate in a soul that has already been . . . tested, proved, purified and found faithful in love, for the sake of this faithfulness to fulfil even in this life what the Son of God has promised, namely that if anyone loved Him, the most Holy Trinity would come and dwell in Him (John 14. 23). This happens when the understanding is divinely enlightened in the wisdom of the Son, the will is filled with the delight of the Holy Spirit, and the Father powerfully and intensely plunges the soul into the abyss of His love." Now in the soul burning with the living flame of love the Holy Spirit works something even far more sublime than this communication and transformation of love. "The one is like a burning coal, the other is like a coal in which the fire not only glows but flares up as a living flame." The simple union resembles the "fire of God in Sion" (Is. 31. 9), i.e. in the Church militant, in which the fire of love does not burn to the utmost, whereas the union of love in which love flares up resembles "the furnace of God in Jerusalem" the vision of peace in the Church triumphant, where this fire burns in perfect love like a furnace. Though the soul has not yet reached the perfection of heaven, it burns like a furnace in a peaceful, glorious and loving vision. It perceives how the "flame of love gives it all blessings after a living manner". Therefore it cries: "O flame of living love that tenderly woundest me", by which it means to say: "O burning love, that tenderly glorifies my soul with its movements of love according to its greater capacity and power! You give me a divine knowledge, corresponding to the whole ability and capacity of my understanding, you give me a love that corresponds to the enlarged power of my will and you fill the essence of my soul by your divine touch and substantial union with a stream of delight, as it can be received only by the purity of my essence and the receptivity and capacity of my memory." When all the powers are completely purified "the divine Wisdom . . . causes the soul with its divine flame to be absorbed in an unfathomable, subtle and sublime manner and in this absorption of the soul in wisdom the Holy Spirit sends out the blissful wings of His flame".[1] It is the same fire that was dark and painful to the soul in the state of purification. Now, however, it is shining brightly, lovely and blissful. Therefore the soul says: "Since thou art no longer oppressive." Formerly the divine Light only showed the soul its own darkness; now, when it is enlightened and transformed, the soul sees the light in itself. Formerly the flame was a terror to the will, because it made it painfully aware of its own hardness and aridity. The will could not sense the delicacy and loveliness of the flame, nor could it taste its sweetness, because its taste had been spoiled by perverse inclinations. The soul was incapable of grasping the infinite treasures and delights of the flame of love under whose influence it only realized its own poverty and misery. All this it now remembers and means to express in those brief words: "Now you are no longer darkness to my understanding as aforetime, but a divine light wherewith I can see you. You no longer cause my weakness to faint, but you will rather be the strength of my will under whose influence, altogether transformed into divine love, I can love and enjoy you. Now you are no longer a burden to the substance of my soul, but rather bliss, delight and enlargement."[2] And because the soul now knows itself to be so near the goal it asks for the ultimate grace: "Perfect me, if it be thy will."

This is the request for the perfect mystical marriage in the beatific vision. It is true, at this stage the soul is perfectly resigned and almost without desire: it would not ask for anything else. But since it is still living in hope and is not yet a child of God in the fullest sense it longs for the consummation, all the more as it has already a foretaste of it and enjoys it as far as is possible on earth. It possesses it to such a degree that it thinks its nature ought to dissolve, since its lower part is incapable of enduring such a mighty and sublime fire. And it would, indeed, cease to exist if God did not aid its weak nature and support it with his right hand. Besides, the brief glimpses of con-

[1] *Living Flame*, 1. 9ff.   [2] *Ibid.*, 1. 26.

templation are such "that it would be a proof of feeble love if it refrained from asking to enter into that perfection and consummation of love". The soul also perceives that the Holy Spirit himself invites it to beatitude, somewhat like the bride in the Canticle: "Rise up and make haste, my love, my dove, my beautiful one and come" (2. 10). "Perfect me—if it be thy will", with this the soul pronounces "those two petitions the Spouse teaches in the Gospel: Thy kingdom come, Thy will be done".[1]

For the perfect union every web that separates God from the soul must be removed. This can be of three kinds: "A temporal one comprising all creatures; a natural one embracing all natural activities and inclinations . . . a sensual one that includes the union of the soul with the body, the sensual and animal life. . . ." The first and second webs must already have been broken, else the mystical union could not have been reached. This has been accomplished "by the fearful encounter with that flame when it was still terrible". Now there is only the third web of the sensual life to be torn, and owing to union with God this already is as thin and delicate as a veil. When this has been broken the soul can speak of a sweet encounter. For the natural desires of such souls are quite different from those of others, though the natural conditions of death are similar. "If they die of illness or old age, their soul tears itself away with great violence and in a far more exalted movement of love . . .; for this movement of love has . . . power to break the web and to bear away the precious jewel of the soul. For this reason the death of such souls is lovelier and sweeter than was their spiritual life throughout their earthly existence. Their death is caused by the most sublime impulses and the most delightful encounters of love, just as the swan sings most beautifully when it is about to die. Hence David says: 'Precious in the eyes of God is the death of His saints' (Ps. 115. 15). For here are united all the riches of the soul and its rivers of love enter the sea . . . so rich and silent . . . that they seem already to be seas." The soul sees itself "on the threshold of entering on the fullness of bliss . . . fully to possess its kingdom. . . . It sees itself pure and rich, full of virtue and well prepared to take possession. . . . For in this state God lets the soul see its own beauty. . . . Then all is changed into love and praise without a vestige of presumption or vanity, since all the leaven of imperfection has been taken away. . . . Now the soul sees that nothing is lacking to it save that the frail web of its natural life should be broken. . . . Thus it

---

[1] *Ibid.*, 1. 27f.

desires to be dissolved and be with Christ and feels it as a torment
that such miserable and feeble life should prevent it from possessing
that other life, so sublime and without end." Therefore it begs: "For
this sweet encounter break the web." [1]

Since the soul now "feels the power of the life to come . . . it also
becomes aware . . . of the weakness of this life. It seems to it . . . like
an extremely thin web, similar to a spider's net (Ps. 89. 9) . . . indeed
. . . even much less." For it now knows the things as God knows
them. "They are nothing to its eyes, and itself, too, is nothing, God
alone is its all."

It asks that the web be broken, not cut: in the first place, because
this is better suited to the idea of a meeting; secondly, "because love
delights in the force of love and in strong, impetuous contact. . . .
Thirdly, because love longs for the act to be accomplished in the
shortest possible time. . . ." For it has the greater "force and value,
the shorter and more spiritual it is. For force is more powerful united
than if it is split up." The acts that are performed in the soul in an
instant are infused by God; those that come from the soul itself are
rather preparatory desires and never become perfect acts of love unless,
as has been said, God sometimes "forms and perfects them quite
quickly in the spirit". "The act of love is instantaneously infused into
the soul that is prepared for it, for the spark seizes its dry food at the
first contact. Therefore the soul inflamed by love desires a quick
breaking." It does not want delay and cannot await the natural end.
"The power of love and the preparation which it perceives in itself
arouse in it . . . the desire that its life should be ended as soon as
possible by some encounter or supernatural impulse of love." It
knows that "God likes to take away those souls He loves particularly
before their time, in order quickly to perfect them by this love."
"Therefore it is an important task for the soul to practise acts of love
in this life, that it may attain to the vision of God in a short time,
without staying here or there."

The soul calls the vehement interior movement in which it is seized
by the Holy Spirit a meeting or an encounter. God assaults it with
this supernatural violence in order to raise it above the flesh and to
lead it towards the consummation it desires. These are true encounters
in which the Holy Spirit penetrates the substance of the soul, transforming and divinizing it. "Thereby the divine Being absorbs the
being of the soul above all being." Here the soul is granted a lively

[1] *Ibid.*, 1. 29ff.

taste of God and it calls this meeting sweet above all other touches and encounters, because it is more sublime than they. Thus God prepares the soul for perfect beatitude and himself inspires the petition to break this delicate web that henceforth it might love God without limits and without end in the fullness and contentment for which it longs.[1]

(b) United to the Triune God

Oh cautery most tender!
Oh gash that is my guerdon!
Oh gentle hand! Oh touch how softly thrilling!
Eternal life you render,
Raise of all debts the burden
And change my death to life, even while killing!

In the first stanza the union was considered mainly as the work of the Holy Spirit. The fact that all three Persons make their habitation in the soul was mentioned only briefly. Now St John attempts to describe the share of each of the three divine Persons in the "divine work of union". Burn or cautery, hand and touch are the same thing as to their essence; but the names are distinguished according to the effect. "The Holy Spirit is the burn,[2] the hand is the Father and the touch is the Son." Each grants the soul a special gift: to the Holy Spirit, the sweet burn, it owes the delightful wound; the delicate touch of the Son causes it to taste eternal life; the gentle Hand of the Father transforms it into God. Yet it addresses only the one Godhead, "for all three Persons work in union, and it attributes all to one and all to all".[3]

The Holy Spirit has already been called a consuming fire (Deut. 4. 24), a "fire of love which can consume and transform into itself the soul it touches in a sublime manner surpassing every concept. . . . When this divine fire has transformed the soul it not only feels the burn but is completely turned into a vehemently burning furnace. It is marvellous . . . that this vehement and consuming fire of God that could much more easily consume a thousand worlds than the earthly fire consumes one straw . . . should not destroy and annihilate the soul . . . but . . . deify and delight it. . . ." It "has obtained the rare good fortune that it knows all, tastes all and does all it wants; it succeeds in all things, nothing can harm or touch it". Of this soul the words of the Apostle are true: "The spiritual man judgeth all things, yet he himself is judged of no man" (1 Cor. 2. 15); and again: "The

---

[1] Thus ends the exposition of stanza 1 (32ff).
[2] We follow the rendering of Alison Peers.—Translator.   [3] Ibid., 2. 1.

6*

spiritual man searcheth all things, even the deep things of God" (1 Cor. 2. 10). For it is the property of love to search out all the treasures of the Beloved."[1]

The sweet burn causes a delectable wound; "for since it is a fire of sweet love, it will also be a wound of sweet love, sweetly refreshing the soul". As the material fire changes the wounds it touches into burns, so the firebrand of love touches the wounds caused by misery and sin, healing them and changing them into wounds of love. Differing from material fire, it also heals the wounds it causes, which, indeed, cannot be healed in any other way. But it heals them only to inflict new wounds. "As often as the burn of love touches the wound of love it enlarges it and thus cures and heals the soul the better the more intensely it wounds it . . . , until the wound is so large that the soul becomes wholly absorbed in the wound of love. And thus . . . as it were turned into a wound of love, it is made quite whole in love, i.e. transformed in love . . . ; it is wholly wounded and wholly healed." Yet the burn ceases not to work, but, like a good physician, gives the soul its loving treatment.

This highest kind of wounding by love "is caused by the direct touch of the Godhead in the soul without any intellectual or imaginary form and shape. . . ." But there are still other, very sublime, kinds of burn, in which a spiritual form co-operates. The saint here gives a very detailed description of how the soul can be wounded by a seraph with a burning arrow or spear. This can scarcely refer to anything else but the wounding of the heart of St Teresa. But his description has some notable traits not contained in Teresa's own account.[2] This is not surprising, since she had revealed her whole soul to John and thus must have spoken more freely than in her literary presentation. The soul, he tells us, "feels the delicate wound and the healing herb with which the point of the dart was effectively sharpened, as a living point in the substance of the spirit, as it were in the heart of the pierced soul. And in this most intimate point of the wound that seems to be in the very centre of the heart of the spirit where the most delicate delight is tasted—who can express this fittingly?—the soul feels a tiny grain of mustard seed full of life and fire, which radiates a living and glowing fire to its circumference. The soul feels as if this fire, which originates in the essence and power of this living point wherein is the substance and power of the herb, were diffused in a sublime manner into all its spiritual and substantial veins . . . thus feeling the heat of love greatly

[1] *Ibid.*, 2. 2–4.   [2] *Life*, ch. 29. Allison Peers, vol. I, 192f.

increasing and growing. In this heat love is purified to such an extent that it seems to the soul as if a whole sea of love-inflamed fire were in it, flowing up and down for abundance, filling all with love. In this fire the whole universe seems a sea of love; immersed in it, the soul sees no limits and end of love, while it perceives in itself . . . the living centre of love. Of the delight the soul here enjoys one can only say that it experiences how truly the Gospel compares the kingdom of heaven with a grain of mustard seed which, though it is quite small, grows into a large tree because of its great power (Matt. 13. 31f). For the soul perceives that it has itself become an immense fire of love which breaks forth from the glowing point in the heart of the spirit.

Few progress thus far, but some have reached this stage, especially those whose virtue and spirit must be transmitted to their descendants. For God filled the heads of families . . . the first-fruits of the spirit with riches and strength, according to the greater or lesser number of those that were to make their doctrine and spirit their own." (This remark, too, points to St Teresa.)

In some cases the interior wound becomes visible also externally in the body. John here refers to the stigmata of St Francis, which the seraph "impressed also on the body . . . as he had inflicted them on his soul by the wound of love.[1] For God normally grants no favour to the body that he has not first and principally bestowed on the soul." The greater the delight and power of love because of the interior wound, "the more intense is also the external pain in the wound of the body. And one grows together with the other." For "that which is pain and torment to the corruptible body gives delight and sweetness to the purified souls that are strengthened in God. . . . But if the wound is inflicted only on the soul . . . the delight can be far more intense and sublime; for the flesh bridles the spirit, and if it is given a share in spiritual graces it draws the rein and bridles the fiery energy of the nimble spiritual steed; for if it were to use its strength, the rein would break."[2]

The short digression on the forms of the wound of love is remarkable because it shows how carefully the saint supplements his own interior experience by his knowledge of other souls, but how firmly he also retains his principle: however sublime the wound of love that is received in a visionary experience—nothing can match the purely spiritual events in the substance of the soul. This corresponds to the

[1] John wrote this about two years after St Teresa's death. He did not yet know that the wound of love had left visible marks in her heart.
[2] *Living Flame of Love*, 2. 6–13.

very characteristic view of the relation between body and soul indicated in this passage: the soul, being spirit, is essentially the governing principle, though after the Fall it is burdened by the body even in the highest elevation possible in this life and dragged down by its earthly covering; the order of grace adapts itself to this original order of nature, granting its gifts principally to the soul and only secondarily and not necessarily to the body by means of the soul.

The hand that inflicts the wound is the loving and almighty Father, "a hand . . . that, as generous and liberal as it is powerful and rich, communicates its precious gifts to the soul when it is opened to distribute its grace. . . ." The soul feels its loving condescension and touch as all the more gentle, since this same hand could thrust the whole world into the abyss if it should be laid on it a little harder. It kills and gives life and no one can escape from it. "But you kill, O divine life, only to grant life. . . . When you chastize you touch softly, but this suffices to destroy the whole world. But when you refresh the soul you show yourself wonderfully condescending, and the consolations of your sweetness are without number. You have wounded me in order to heal me, O divine Hand; you have killed that in me which held me captive under the tree of death, far from the divine life. . . . You have accomplished this with the liberality of your generous love in that touch by which you touched me in the splendour of your glory and with the image of your substance (Heb. 1. 3). This is your only-begotten Son; in him, who is your Wisdom, your power extends from one end to the other (Wisd. 8. 1). And this your only-begotten Son, O merciful Hand of the Father, is the delicate touch with which you have touched and wounded me in the power of your burn.

"O delicate touch, Word, Son of God, who in the tenderness of your divine being penetrate sublimely the substance of my soul! And while you touch it very gently, you cause it to be perfectly absorbed in you, in divine sweetness and bliss such as has never been heard of in the land of Chanaan nor seen in Theman (Bar. 3. 22). O delicate touch of the Word and wholly unique to me! By the shadow of thy might and power that went before you, you have overthrown the mountains and crushed the rocks on Mount Horeb, and revealed yourself very softly and palpably to the prophet in the whisper of a gentle air (3 Kings 19. 11f). O delicate and gentle air, tell me, how you were such a soft and gentle air; how you can touch so lightly, since you, the Word of God, are so terrible and powerful. O blessed and thrice blessed the soul which you, who are so terrible and powerful, touch so gently and delicately. Announce it to the world—or no, do not say it, for it has no understanding for this gentle air. . . . O my God and life! Only they will recognize and perceive you in this gentle touch who have themselves become delicate by detachment from the world, because only what is delicate meets the delicate; and thus they can feel and enjoy it. . . . Again, delicate, and most delicate touch, the stronger and more powerful for being more delicate. For with the strength of your delicacy you free . . . the soul from all touches of creatures, unite it to yourself and make it your own. You leave in the soul an affect and a feeling that are so beneficent that every touch of creatures . . . seems gross and deceitful to it. . . . Their very sight disgusts it and it is a great pain and torment for it to speak about them or to come into contact with them."

The power of perception grows together with the delicacy, the abundance of communications with the simplicity and subtlety of the soul. The Word is infinitely simple and delicate, the soul in this state of purity and simplicity is a vessel of great capacity and content. The more delicate and gentle the touch, the more delight it gives. This divine touch is without form and shape, because the divine Word fits into no mode or manner. The touch is substantial, i.e. it takes place in the soul through God's simple Substance, hence it is ineffable. This touch is infinite and therefore also infinitely delicate.[1] Thus it "can give a taste of eternal life". This is not impossible when God's substance touches the soul in its substance. The delight that is then felt is indescribable. "Therefore I will not speak of it so that it may not be supposed that this does not surpass anything that can be expressed in word." Souls have their own terminology for these sublime things that can be understood only by those who are granted these experiences: they rejoice in them and keep them secret. It is with these terms as with the names on the white stone: no one knows them save those who receive them (Apoc. 2. 17). Thus the divine touch bestows a foretaste of eternal life, even though the joy is not yet so perfect as in eternal glory. Here the soul "tastes all divine riches communicated to it, strength, wisdom and love, beauty, grace, goodness and so forth. And because God is all this, the soul tastes it in a single divine touch, and this with all its faculties and substance. From this blissful enjoyment of the soul the unction of the Holy Spirit sometimes overflows into the body. The whole sensual nature shares in this enjoyment, it is tasted by all its members, by its bones and even by the marrow of the bones

[1] *Ibid.*, 2. 16–20.

... with the feeling of great delight and glory that can be perceived even to the remotest joints of hands and feet." [1] In this foretaste of eternal life the soul feels rewarded far beyond its due for all its former pains, sorrows, trials and penances. And thus is "paid every debt".

If so few "attain to this exalted state of perfect union with God" this is not due to God, for he wants to see all men perfect. But he finds only few vessels capable of enduring "so high and sublime a work". Most men "refuse to take upon themselves minor desolations and mortifications and will not work with patient perseverance. . . . And thus he does not lead them on, so as to purify them by the work of purgation and raise them up from the dust of earth. . . . O you souls who want to walk in the spiritual life in security and consolations, if you knew how necessary sufferings are that you may attain to security and comfort. . . . Take . . . up your cross and, bound to it, drink gall and unmixed vinegar. Count this a great happiness, for if you thus die to the world and to yourselves, you will attain to a divine life in the delight of the Spirit." He who "is given the quite special grace of interior trial" must do God many services, display much patience and constancy and greatly please the Lord in his life and world. For this reason "only few deserve to reach perfection by suffering".[2]

Looking back, the soul then realizes that all has been for its good and that its present light corresponds to its past darkness. Not only is all paid back to it; but it has been freed from all imperfect desires wanting to deprive it of the spiritual life. Thus, by doing to death, God's hand has changed death to life.

Life is here to be understood in a twofold sense: it is the beatific vision of God to which we can attain only through natural death, and also the perfect spiritual life in loving union with God: this is achieved by the mortification of all vices and desires. What the soul here calls death is "the whole old man, . . . the use of memory, understanding and will that are occupied with the things of this world . . ., and the desires and affections which are directed towards creatures". The old life consists in all this, which means death to the new spiritual life. In this new life of union all desires and powers of the soul, all its inclinations and activities are divinized. It lives "a life of God, and thus its death has been changed into life, its sensual into a spiritual life". Its understanding is transformed into a divine understanding, its will, memory and natural desires are all deified. "The substance of the soul is not, indeed, the divine Substance, since it cannot be sub-

[1] *Ibid.*, 2. 21f.   [2] *Ibid.*, 2. 27f.

stantially changed into God, but by being united to God and drawn
into Him it is God by participation." Thus the soul can now say with
full justification: "I live, now not I, but Christ liveth in me" (Gal. 2.
20). It is now "inwardly and outwardly keeping festival, and often
jubilant joy rises up to God from the mouth of its spirit, like an ever-
new song in joy, love and knowledge of its blessed state". God, who
makes all things new, also constantly renews the soul. He does not
suffer it to decline, as formerly, but increases its merits. "Apart from
being conscious of the sublime grace it has received, the soul feels
that God wants to make it happy with His delicate, tender and loving
words and to exalt it now by this, now by another favour; and thus
it seems to it as if He had no other soul in the world to favour and
nothing else to occupy Him but is there only for this soul. Because it
feels this, it utters the words of the bride in the Canticle: 'My Beloved
to me and I to Him' (Cant. 2. 16)." [1]

(c) *In the Splendours of the Divine Glory*

Oh lamps of fiery blaze
To whose refulgent fuel
The deepest caverns of my soul grow bright,
Late blind with gloom and haze,
But in this strange renewal
Giving to the belov'd both heat and light.

The soul overflows with gratitude for the graces it has received
through the union. Its mind and faculties, once blind and in darkness,
are now flaming brightly in the knowledge of love. Thus it can give
back light and love to the Beloved, which makes it intensely happy.

In the substantial union with God the soul knows the splendours
and powers of all divine attributes that are included in the simple
divine Being: his omnipotence, wisdom, goodness, mercy etc. "Each
of these attributes is the same Being of God in one single Person, [2] . . .
in the Father, in the Son or in the Holy Spirit; and thus each one of
these perfections is God Himself. And since God is an infinite divine
Light and an infinite divine Fire . . . each of His innumerable properties and powers gives light and burns like God Himself. Thus each
of these properties is a lamp which enlightens the soul and fills it with
the fire of love." In one sole act of union the soul receives the knowledge of the various properties, and thus "the same God is to it a

---

[1] *Ibid.*, 2. 29–36.
[2] *"In einer einzigen Person"*, Allison Peers, *ibid.*, p. 161: "In one sole substance",
which would seem the correct translation.—Translator.

multitude of lamps together, which illumine it with wisdom and fill it with the fire of love in various ways". Thus the soul is enkindled by each of these lamps separately and by all of them together. "For all these properties are one being . . . ; and thus all these lamps, too, are but one lamp which, according to its powers and properties, gives light and burns like many lamps." The splendour of the lamp of the divine Being, insofar as it is almighty, gives it the light and heat of the love of God inasmuch as he is almighty. But he also fills it with splendour as the All-Wise and thus is a lamp of wisdom. It is the same with all other properties revealed to the soul at the same time. The soul receives marvellous delight from the fire and light of these lamps in infinite abundance, since they come from so many lamps and each is burning with love. "And the fire of one increases the fire of the other, the flame of one the flame of the other and the light of one that of the other. For any individual perfection is known by any other. And thus all together become one light and one fire. . . ." The soul is completely immersed in these delicate flames, most tenderly wounded in love by each one of them and still more wounded by all of them together in the love that comes from life, and "it is well able to see that this love comes from life eternal and comprises all blessing in itself". God gives the soul his love and benefits together with all his attributes: he gives it grace and love with omnipotence and wisdom, in goodness and holiness, in justice and mercy, purity and simplicity, etc. He esteems it very highly, desiring to place it on the same level as himself, and therefore shows himself to it gladly in the knowledge of union. He pours upon it torrents of love, and it is gladdened in perfect harmony of soul and body, transformed into a paradise perfectly cultivated by God. The infinite fire is so beautiful that it is like the waters of life which with their vehemence quench the thirst of the spirit. This is indicated by the marvellous event narrated in the Books of the Machabees: the sacred fire which had been hidden in a cistern had there been changed into water, but on the altar of sacrifice it was once more transformed into fire.[1] The Spirit of God is like a sweet, delightful water as long as he is hidden in the veins of the soul; but when he is revealed in the sacrifice of divine love he is a living flame of fire. Because here the soul is enkindled and acts in loving surrender it speaks of lamps rather than of water.

Yet all these are but poor attempts to express what really happens: "For the transformation of the soul in God is something ineffable."[2]

<hr/>

[1] 2 Mach. 1. 20–22.   [2] *Living Flame*, 3. 2–8.

The splendours in which the soul shines forth signify its knowledge of the divine perfections which inflames it with love. United to these the soul is transformed into rays of light glowing with love and shines like these. The radiance of the divine rays of light is quite different from that of material lamps. These illuminate with their flames the things outside them; whereas that other radiance causes the things to light up in the interior of the rays. For the soul is within these splendours which have transformed it and has itself become a flame of light: it resembles the air within the flame, which is enkindled and transformed into fire. The movements of the flame, its vibrations and flares come from the soul and the Holy Spirit together; "they are not only splendours but also a transfiguration of the soul, the graceful games and festivities of the Holy Spirit in the soul" that have been mentioned above. It seems that he thus wishes to give the soul eternal life and perfect glory. This is the end of all preceding and subsequent graces. But however powerful the effect of the inspirations of the Holy Spirit, the absorption in the fullness of beatitude is possible only when the soul "leaves the sphere of this mortal life and can enter into the innermost depths of the spirit, of the perfect life in Christ".

The aforementioned movements of the flame cannot actually be ascribed to God but are movements of the soul. For God is immovable; it only seems as if he were moving in it.

The fullness of splendour can also be called an overshadowing, as was done by the angel at the Annunciation (Luke 1. 35). For to overshadow or give shadow means to "protect, favour and bestow benefits". For as soon as the shadow of a person falls on someone this is a sign that he is near to give protection and assistance. Now the shadow cast by an object agrees with its nature. "If it is opaque and dark it casts a dark shadow, if it is bright and transparent the shadow, too, will be bright and transparent." Thus the shadows of the divine lamps of fire are splendours: the shadow the lamp of beauty casts on the soul produces another beauty, the lamp of strength another strength, and the shadow of the wisdom of God is again wisdom. Or, better: the wisdom, beauty and strength of God are veiled in shadow, because the soul cannot perfectly comprehend them here below. But as this shadow completely corresponds to God, his essence and properties, the soul distinctly recognizes the majesty of God in this shadow. God's omnipotence and wisdom, his infinite goodness and his beatitude "pass by in bright, fiery shadows of these bright and burning lamps" and are thus recognized and tasted by it. Thus the soul knows and tastes all the riches that are united in the infinite unity and simplicity of the divine Being. The knowledge of one does not hinder the knowledge and enjoyment of the other; rather each beauty and virtue is a light that reveals yet another grandeur. The purity of the divine wisdom brings it about that many things are seen in it as one.[1]

All this splendour fills "the deep caverns of sense", that is the faculties of the soul, memory, understanding and will. "These are the deeper, the greater the blessings they can receive." Only the infinite can fill them. When they are filled with God their bliss is as great as was the pain they suffered when they were empty. As long as they had not been emptied and purged of all attachment to creatures they could not feel the immense void of their capacity. The slightest trifle to which they are attached renders them insensible, so that they "do not feel their shadow, fail to realize the loss of the blessings of grace and cannot recognize their own capacity. . . . Despite their capacity for infinite blessings the least thing is capable of ensnaring them so that they cannot receive those blessings. . . . But if they are empty and purged the thirst, hunger and longing of the spiritual sense is intolerable. For each of these caverns has a very deep bowel, and thus they also feel deep pain, for the food they lack is unfathomable, which is . . . God Himself. This deep sensation (of hunger and thirst) commonly appears towards the end of the illumination and purification of the soul. . . ." If the spiritual desire is pure of all creatures and all attachment to them the soul has exchanged its natural for the divine mode of being and possesses a well-prepared empty space. But since the divine Being does not yet communicate itself in the mystical union it feels "a pain that is greater than death, especially if a divine ray penetrates through some opening or gap, though God does not communicate Himself to it. These are the souls that suffer from the vehemence of love and are unable long to remain in this state: they must either receive what they desire or die."[2]

The first cavern is the understanding, its emptiness is the thirst for God that longs for divine Wisdom. The second cavern is the will that hungers for God and desires the perfection of love. The third cavern is the memory. It is devoured by the desire for the possession of God. All these caverns are capable of receiving God. And because God is deep and infinite, their capacity, too, is in a certain sense infinite, their thirst and hunger are infinite, the process of their destruction and their pain are an unending death. Even though this pain is not yet so pro-

[1] *Ibid.*, 3. 9–17.   [2] *Ibid.*, 3. 18.

found as that in the next life, it yet gives a good idea of it, because the soul is already prepared to receive the fullness of eternal life. But because this distress is rooted in love it cannot be alleviated. "For the greater the love, the more impatiently the soul desires to possess God; for this it hopes every moment with the most ardent desires."[1]

But if the soul truly desires God it already possesses him whom it loves, and thus it seems that it can no longer feel pain. "For the desire of the angels to see the Son of God . . . (1 Peter 1. 12) is free from pain and anxious longing since they already possess Him. . . . Now the possession of God gives delight and satisfaction. Hence in this desire the soul must feel the more satisfaction and delight the more vehement it is, since it lives all the more in the possession of God; therefore it feels neither grief nor pain."

Here it should be noted that the possession of God has a double meaning: it may refer to the possession by grace or by union. Both are related to each other as, say, betrothal[2] and marriage. At the betrothal an agreement is made, the bride and bridegroom sometimes visit each other and exchange presents, but a mutual communication and union of the persons takes place only in marriage. Thus, in the perfect purification of the soul the will of God and the human will have become one by free consent; the soul then possesses "all that can be attained through will and grace; that is to say: God has placed His true being[3] and the fullness of His grace in the being of the soul. This is the sublime state of the spiritual betrothal of the soul with the Word of God; here the Bridegroom gives it great graces and often visits it most lovingly." But the sublime favours the soul is granted in this state cannot be compared with those of the mystical marriage; they are but a preparation for it. For the mystical marriage requires not only the purging of all attachments to creatures, but also the preparation by visits and gifts, so that the soul may become ever more beautiful, pure and simple, and worthy of such an exalted union. This takes more or less time according to the different cases. The soul is prepared by the unctions of the Holy Spirit. If these "are already very exalted . . . the longing of the caverns of the soul normally becomes most intense and delicate; . . . for as they unite the soul more intimately to God, hence make it more desirous of Him and draw it to Him with more delicate affection, the longing, too, becomes more delicate and

---

[1] *Ibid.*, 3. 19-22.

[2] It has been pointed out above that betrothal is here not used in the strict sense of the mystical betrothal, in contrast with the *Spiritual Canticle*, stanzas 13 and 14.

[3] Allison Peers, III, p. 174, has "consent" instead of "being".—Translator.

deep. For the desire for God is the preparation for union with Him."[1]
The unctions of the Holy Spirit "are so lofty and delicate that they
penetrate the innermost substance of the ground of the soul . . . and
cause it to dissolve in sweetness; then the pain and the longing swoon-
ing away in the immense emptiness of the caverns is almost infinite".
But the more delicate the preparation, the more perfectly will the
sense of the soul enjoy the possession in the marriage. "By the sense
of the soul is understood the capacity and vigour of the substance of
the soul with which it enjoys the objects of the spiritual faculties; thus
it tastes the wisdom, love and communication of God." The soul calls
its faculties "deep caverns of sense" because it tastes in them the
majesty of the wisdom and the perfections of God. And "if it feels
that they contain the profound kinds of knowledge and the splendours
of the lamps of fire, it realizes that they have such a capacity and depth
as corresponds to the various things it receives from God: kinds of
knowledge, sweetnesses, delights, enjoyments, etc." As the common
sense of the imagination is the store house and archive for the images
and forms of sense, "so also the common sense of the soul, which is
the store house and archive for the grandeurs of God, is enlightened
and enriched in proportion as it receives a share in this sublime and
magnificent possession".[2] Once it was blind and dark, before the soul
had been illumined by God. The bodily eye cannot see when it is
blind or in darkness. Thus also the soul, despite the most excellent
powers of vision, cannot perceive anything unless God, its light,
enlightens it. Conversely: if its spiritual eye has become blind through
sin or the desire for a creature, the divine light strikes upon it in vain.
It does not recognize its own darkness, i.e. its ignorance. Darkness
is to be distinguished from the obscurity of sin; the former is the
guiltless ignorance of natural or supernatural things. Thus, before the
union, the sense of the soul was in darkness in a twofold sense. "For
until the Lord spoke the word 'Let there be light!' there was darkness
upon the caverns of this sense. The more profound the sense of the
soul and its caverns, the deeper and more intense is also the darkness
with regard to the supernatural things unless God, its light, illumines it.
It is impossible for this sense to raise its eyes to the light, nor can it
grasp it by thought. For it does not know the light, since it has never
seen it, and so it cannot even desire it. It would rather desire darkness,
since it knows what it is." But when God has granted the soul the light
of grace, the eye of its spirit is enlightened and opened to the divine

---

[1] *Living Flame of Love*, 3. 23–6.   [2] *Ibid.*, 3. 68f.

light. And as before one abyss of darkness called to the other (Ps. 18. 3), so now one abyss of grace calls for the other, namely for the transformation of the soul in God. Then the light of God becomes wholly one with the light of the soul, the natural light of the soul unites itself to the supernatural light of God until only the supernatural light shines forth from the soul.

The sense of the soul was blind also because it delighted in something other than God. Desire lay before the eye of reason like a cataract or a cloud; it was blind to the sublime beauties and riches of God. The smallest object placed directly in front of the eye prevents it from looking at other things that are farther away. Thus a slight desire suffices to prevent the soul from seeing all the glories of God. In such a state "the eye of judgement" sees only the cloud, sometimes of one colour, sometimes of another. It thinks that the cloud is God because it covers the senses; but God does not fall within the sphere of sense. Those who have not yet stripped themselves of all desires and affections should therefore be convinced that their judgement is faulty. They imagine that to be great which is common and negligible for the spirit but satisfies the senses, whereas they despise what is sublime for the spirit but appeals less to the senses. In the case of a sensual man, i.e. one who lives wholly according to his natural desires and affections, even the desires that have their origin in the spirit become merely natural. Even if the soul desires God this longing is not always supernatural, but only if it is infused and strengthened by God.

Thus the sense of the soul with its desires and affections was dark and blind.[1] But now, being supernaturally united to God it is enlightened, even more, together with its faculties it is itself a brightly shining light "in this strange renewal giving to the belov'd both heat and light".

The caverns of the powers of the soul are filled with the light of the divine lamps. They themselves are not burning and send up to God in God the fullness of the splendour they have received, in loving bliss, as glass reflects the sunlight that falls on it, only much more sublimely, because the will co-operates with them. This happens in quite unique abundance transcending all normal thought and cannot be expressed in words. The understanding that is united to God reflects wisdom as fully as it receives it. And the will that is united to divine goodness gives it back to God in God with equal perfection. For the soul receives only to give back: it returns to the Beloved all the light

[1] *Ibid.*, 3. 71–6.

and warmth of love he communicates to it. Through the substantial transformation it has become a shadow of God and "thus it does in God and through God that which He does through Himself in the soul, and in the same way as He does it. . . . As . . . God communicates Himself with a free and gracious will, so also the will of the soul— and the more freely and generously the more intimately it is united to God—gives God in God to God Himself. . . . In this state the soul sees that God truly belongs to it, that, as an adopted child with the right of ownership it has entered on its inheritance. . . . As He is its property . . . it can give Him to whom it wills. . . . And thus it gives Him to its Beloved, . . . God Himself . . . who has surrendered Himself to it. And it feels . . . ineffable bliss and satisfaction when it perceives that it gives God its property and that it is worthy of the infinite Being of God. . . . God is fully satisfied with this gift of the soul. . . . He could not be satisfied with anything less, and He receives it gladly and gratefully from the soul as something that belongs to it. . . . In this surrender to God the soul loves Him in a new way, and He liberally gives Himself to the soul anew. . . . Thus there is truly established between God and the soul a mutual love founded on the conformity of union and surrender of marriage, wherein both possess the property of both, which is the divine Essence, by voluntary surrender to each other and by union with each other. . . . It gives the greatest satisfaction and joy to the soul that it can give God more than it is and can do of itself, when it so liberally gives God to Himself as its property. . . . In the next life this is achieved through the light of glory, in this life through perfectly enlightened faith." Thus "the deep caverns of sense . . . with strange brightness, give heat and light together to their Beloved". Together—for Father, Son and Holy Spirit communicate themselves to the soul in union and are its light and fire of love.

The love between God and the soul is of quite extraordinary perfection as is also the enjoyment it finds in it and the praise and thanksgiving it offers to God. "The soul here loves God not through itself, but through God Himself . . . : through the Holy Spirit, as the Father loves the Son. . . ." Further, the soul loves God *in* God: "In this vehement union the soul is absorbed in the love of God and God, too, gives Himself to the soul with great vehemence." Finally, "the soul here loves God for His own sake. It loves Him not only because He is so bountiful, good and glorious . . . to it, but even far more intensely because it is all this essentially in itself."

The enjoyment of it is so sublime because it is an enjoyment of God through himself. For according to its understanding the soul is here united to the omnipotence, wisdom and goodness of God; and though this does not happen so clearly as in the next life, yet its joy in all these things that are distinctly understood is extremely great. In addition, the soul now takes its pleasure only in God without any interference from a creature. It enjoys God only through what he is in himself, without the admixture of its own taste.

Its praise is so excellent because the soul offers it according to duty: for it understands that God has created it for his praise. It also praises him for the graces it receives and for the delight it feels in his praise. But above all it praises him for what he is in himself, "for even if the soul were to feel no delight, it would yet praise Him for Himself".[1]

(d) The Hidden Life of Love

How gently and lovingly
Thou awakenest in my bosom,
Where thou dwellest secretly and lone!
And in thy sweet breathing,
Full of blessing and glory,
How delicately thou inspirest my love!

The soul here describes a marvellous effect God sometimes produces in it. It uses the image of a man awakening from his sleep and sighing with relief, for it really has the feeling that something similar takes place in it.

"God awakens in the soul in many ways. If we would enumerate them all we should never end. But this awakening of the Son of God to which the soul here points is extremely sublime and carries the greatest blessing with it. It is a movement caused by the Word in the substance of the soul, and it is of such greatness, power and glory and of such intimate sweetness that it seems to the soul as if all the balms and perfumed spices and flowers of the whole world were scattered abroad . . ., as if all the kingdoms and dominions of the world and all the powers and virtues of heaven were in motion . . . as if all virtues and essences, all perfections and charms of all created things were shining forth and made the same movement aiming at one thing. . . . If then this great Sovereign, on whose shoulder is the government of the threefold edifice of the world . . . and who bears it all by the word of His power, wants to make Himself felt in the soul, it seems that everything begins to move at once, just as when the earth moves all the material things

[1] *Ibid.*, 3. 77–85.

that are upon it also move as if they were not. . . . This comparison, however, is quite insufficient, since here all things not only seem to move but also reveal all the grace of their being, their power, beauty and charms as well as the innermost ground of their existence and life. Here the soul sees how all creatures of higher and lower orders have their life, strength and existence in Him . . ., but that God, in His own Being, is infinitely superior to all these things, so that it understands them better in His being than in themselves. And this is the great delight of this awakening that it knows the creatures through God and no longer God through the creatures. . . . But how this movement can take place in the soul, since God is immovable, is a wondrous thing. For though God does not really move yet it seems to the soul that He is, indeed, moving; for as the soul is changed and moved by God in order to perceive this supernatural sight, there is revealed to it in quite a new light this divine life and the being and harmony of all creation in Him with their movements in God; and thus it seems to the soul that God is moving and thus the cause appropriates the name of the effect it produces. . . ." Thus the soul is aroused from the sleep of natural vision to the supernatural vision: "In my opinion this awakening and vision of the soul happens in this way: since the soul, like every creature, is in God with its own substantial being, God takes away some of the many veils and covers hanging in front of it, so that it may see of what nature He is. Then His face that is full of grace shines through and is perceived, even though in some darkness, since not all the veils have been taken away. And since He moves all things by His power, there appears together with Him all He does, so that He seems in continual motion in them and they in Him. Hence the soul has the impression that God moves and awakens, whereas that which has moved and awakened is itself. . . . Thus men ascribe to God what is in themselves. Hence those that are lazy and sleepy say that God rises and awakens, though He is never asleep. . . . But as in truth all good things come from God and man can do nothing good of his own power, it is true to say that our awakening is an awakening of God and our uprising an uprising of God. . . . And because the soul has sunk into a sleep from which it has never been able to wake up by itself, and because only God could open its eyes and cause it to wake up, the soul calls this awakening in a real sense an awakening of God. . . .

"It is quite indescribable what the soul knows and feels in this awakening of the glory of God." This glory communicates itself to the essence of the soul (which it calls its bosom) and reveals itself with immense power, with the voice "of thousands upon thousands of virtues of God which no one can number. Among these the soul remains immovable . . . terrible and firm like the ranks of an army and at the same time lovely and gracious, endowed with all the charms of the creatures." Though still in the weakness of the flesh, the soul does not faint in such glorious awakening nor die of fear, because it is already in the state of perfection. The inferior part is perfectly purified and conformed to the spirit so that it no longer suffers loss and pain in these spiritual communications, as it did before. Moreover, God shows himself "gentle and full of love". He sees to it that the soul suffers no harm and protects its natural part while communicating his glory to the spirit. Hence the soul feels in him as much love and gentleness as power, glory and majesty. Its delight is as powerful as his loving, gentle protection so that it is able to bear this overwhelming delight. Thus the soul grows strong and vigorous rather than weak. The King of Heaven shows himself to it as an equal and a brother. He descends from his throne, bends down to it and embraces it. He clothes it with royal garments, the marvellous virtues of God, he surrounds it with the golden splendour of love and causes the knowledge of higher and lower beings to shine in it like precious jewels.[1] All this happens in its inmost being, where he "dwells secretly and alone". Now God dwells indeed in all things secretly and hidden, else they could not subsist. But in some he dwells alone, in others he is not alone; in the ones he dwells with pleasure, in the others with disgust. In some he dwells as in his own house, directing and governing all things, in others like a stranger who is not allowed to command or do anything. The less a soul is absorbed by its own desires and affections, the more he is alone in it and as if in his own house, and the more alone, the more hidden does he dwell in it. In a soul that is free from all desires, stripped of all forms, images and creaturely affections, he dwells quite secretly and in the most intimate embrace. Neither the devil nor human reason can understand what happens there. But this is not hidden from the soul itself, since at this stage of perfection it is always aware of the divine indwelling. But even then there is still the difference between sleeping and waking. Sometimes it is as if the Beloved were reposing in it so that no exchange of love and knowledge is possible, at other times it is as if he awakened. Happy the soul that always has the lively feeling that God reposes and finds refreshment in it. It must preserve itself in infinitely quiet peace so that no movement

[1] *Ibid.*, 4. 1–13.

or noise may disturb the Beloved. If he were always to remain awake in it, communicating to it his treasures of knowledge and love, it would already be in the state of glory. In souls that have not yet attained to the union of love he mostly remains hidden. They do not normally perceive him but only when he rouses them with delight. This awakening is different from that in the state of perfection. Here not everything is so hidden from the devil and from human reason as there, for in these souls everything is not yet wholly spiritual; they still suffer from movements of the sensuality. But in that awakening which is effected by the Spouse himself, in the perfect soul, all is perfect, because he accomplishes it. The breathing and awakening of the soul is like that of a man who wakes up and draws his breath; the soul feels in itself the breathing of God.[1] Therefore it says:

> And in thy sweet breathing,
> Full of blessing and glory,
> How delicately thou inspirest love!

"Of this breathing of God I did not and I do not want to speak; for I see clearly that I cannot express it properly, and it would seem less than it is if I were to speak of it. For it is a breathing of God Himself. In it the Holy Spirit breathes into the soul in that awakening of the most sublime knowledge of the Godhead; and according to the measure of knowledge in which it is profoundly absorbed by the Holy Ghost, it is most delightfully inflamed in love, according to what it has seen. And as this breath is full of grace and glory, the Holy Spirit fills the soul with happiness and bliss, so that it is beside itself with love and is drawn into the depth of God in an ineffable and incomprehensible manner; therefore I here break off."[2]

(e) Characteristics of the "Living Flame of Love" compared with the Earlier Writings

If the saint is forced to keep silence because he feels unable to express the inexpressible, how can we dare to add an explanation to his words? We can only thank him that he has allowed us a glance at a marvellous country, an earthly paradise on the threshold of the heavenly one. Yet we must attempt to connect what he has here opened up to us with things that are already known. Love of souls has unsealed his lips: he wants to encourage them to walk in the hard way of the Cross that is indeed steep and narrow but ends in such luminous, blissful heights.

Thus we have briefly expressed the interior relationship between

[1] *Ibid.*, 4. 14–17.   [2] End of *Living Flame of Love*, first recension, Allison Peers, III, p. 113.

the *Living Flame of Love* and the two works whose subject was the way of the Cross itself, i.e. *Ascent* and *Dark Night*. A proper comparison of the ideas of these writings would only be possible if we had before us those parts of them that are lost or were never written. However, we may say this much: comparing certain passages on the mystical union in these two works with the *Living Flame*, we have the impression that we are faced with a new basis of experience. The fundamental attitude has remained the same: there is no other way to union save through the Cross and the Night, the death of the old man. Nor are we going back on what has repeatedly been emphasized, viz. that the author and interpreter of the Canticle of the Night had already attained to union. But this union seems to take place in the night, even on the Cross. Only later does the saint seem to have had the blissful experience how far heaven can open even in this life.

The external fate of the last work, too, was happier than that of its predecessors. This does not only mean that it was finished and preserved as a whole. *If* the others actually did remain unfinished—we have always left this open—the reason may have been that there the interpretation was written later, not only at a temporal, but also at an interior distance from the Canticle itself. The interpretations of the *Ascent* and the *Dark Night* are far more didactic than those of the *Living Flame of Love*. The thinker confronts the poem, the outcome of his original experience, as if it were something alien, or at least simply a given object. He is so carried away by his desire to give a rational interpretation of its basic ideas and governing images that, in the case of the *Ascent*, he soon abandons altogether his original intention to explain the poem stanza by stanza and line by line, whereas in the *Dark Night* this is done only later. In the *Living Flame of Love*, on the other hand, both poem and interpretation are one. It is true, some time elapsed between the two, but this had not harmed their unity, on the contrary. St John hesitated to undertake the interpretation because this seemed to surpass the powers of the natural understanding. He decided to do so when the flame of love had once more flared up, flooding him with heavenly light. The meaning of what he had written before then revealed itself more profoundly, and he could easily follow the sequence of thought expressed in the four stanzas. The unity of the whole is broken only in one place by a lively discussion on ignorant spiritual directors.[1] Apart from this the work

[1] *Living Flame of Love*, 3. 53–67. We have left out this insertion here so as not to break up the context. It will be used in Part III.

is all of a piece, penetrated by poetic and mystic enthusiasm as none of the others. The super-abundance of light also involves a peculiarity of style. The saint lived in the Scriptures, the images and comparisons of which constantly suggested themselves to his mind. He liked to make use of them to confirm and stress what his own experience had taught him. But in the *Living Flame* the harmony between this experience and the revealed Word of God is particularly impressive.[1] The reader realizes that now the saint has seen the veils lifted, that everything becomes transparent to him, revealing the secret intercourse between God and the soul. What to the unenlightened mind of the ordinary reader is but an external event becomes for him, as it were naturally, the expression of a mystical happening. To give only one example: Mardochai, who has saved the life of King Assuerus, is for John the image of the soul that faithfully serves its master without receiving a reward. But suddenly it, "as once Mardochai, is rewarded for its pains and services. For not only is it allowed to enter the interior of the palace and to stand before the king clothed in regal vesture, it also receives the crown, the sceptre and the throne of the king as well as the royal ring, so that it may do all it desires in the kingdom of its Spouse."[2]

2. THE BRIDAL SONG OF THE SOUL

(a) *The Spiritual Canticle in its Relation to the Other Writings*

Where John has spoken of the union of the soul with God he has done so in all his writings in the words of the Canticle. But at the time when his own soul was probably moved most strongly by all the pains and delights of love, in the months spent in the dungeon of Toledo, the old bridal song was re-born in his heart. It has been preserved in two versions; the difference between which is important for our subject.

---

[1] Our account of the Living *Flame of Love* gives only a very faint impression of this, because we have reproduced very few of the many Scriptural examples (this is true also of the other writings). To gain the right impression of it the works of the saint must themselves be consulted.

[2] *Living Flame*, 2. 31.

CANCIONES ENTRE EL ALMA Y EL ESPOSO[1]	SONGS BETWEEN THE SOUL AND THE SPOUSE

I

Esposa

1

A dónde te escondiste,
Amado, y me dejaste con gemido?
Como el ciervo huiste,
Habiéndome herido;
Salí tras tí clamando, y ya eras ido.

2

Pastores, los que fuerdes
allá por las majadas al otero,
Si por ventura vierdes
Aquel que yo más quiero,
Decidle que adolezco, peno y muero.

3

Buscando mis amores,
Iré por esos montes y riberas,
Ni cogeré las flores,
Ni temeré las fieras,
Y pasaré los fuertes y fronteras.

Pregunta las criaturas

4

Oh, bosques y espesuras,
Plantadas por la mano del Amado!
Oh, prado de verduras,
De flores esmaltado,
Decid si por vosotros ha pasado!

Respuesta de las criaturas

5

Mil gracias derramando,
Pasó por estos sotos con presura
Y yéndolos mirando,
Con sola su figura
Vestidos los dejó de hermosura.

I

Bride

1

Whither hast thou hidden thyself,
And hast left me, O Beloved, to my
sighing?
Thou didst flee like the hart,
Having wounded me:
I went out after thee, calling and
thou wert gone.

2

Shepherds, ye that go
Yonder, through the sheepcotes, to
the hill,
If perchance ye see him
That I most love,
Tell him that I languish, suffer and die.

3

Seeking my loves,
I will go over yonder mountains
and banks
I will neither pluck the flowers
Nor fear the wild beasts;
I will pass by the mighty and cross
the frontiers.

Question to the Creatures

4

O woods and thickets
Planted by the hand of the Beloved!
O meadow of verdure,
Enamelled with flowers,
Say if he has passed by you.

Answer of the Creatures

5

Scattering a thousand graces,
He passed through these groves in
haste
And, looking upon them as he went,
Left them, by his glance alone
Clothed with beauty.

[1] The Roman figures I, II and III have been added only in the second recension.

Esposa	*Bride*
6	**6**
Ay, quién podrá sanarme!	Ah, who will be able to heal me!
Acaba de entregarte ya de vero,	Surrender thou thyself now completely
No quieras enviarme	From today do thou send me now
De hoy más ya mensajero,	No other messenger,
Que no saben decirme lo que quiero.	For they cannot tell me what I wish.
7	**7**
Y todos cuantos vagan,	And all those that serve
De tí me van mil gracias refiriendo,	Relate to me a thousand graces of thee
Y todos más me llagan,	And all wound me the more
Y déjame muriendo	And something that they are stammering
Un no sé qué que quedan balbuciendo.	Leaves me dying.
8	**8**
Mas, cómo perseveras,	But how, O life, dost thou persevere
Oh vida, no viviendo donde vives,	Since thou livest not where thou livest,
Y haciendo porque mueras,	And since the arrows make thee to die
Las flechas que recibes,	Which thou receivest
De lo que del Amado en tí concibes?	From the conceptions of the Beloved which thou formest within thee?
9	**9**
Por qué, pues has llagado	Since thou hast wounded this heart,
Aqueste corazón, no le sanaste?	Wherefore didst thou not heal it?
Y pues me le has robado,	And why, having robbed me of it,
Por qué así le dejaste,	Hast thou left it thus
Y no tomas el robo que robaste?	And takest not the prey that thou hast spoiled?
10	**10**
Apaga mis enojos,	Quench thou my griefs,
Pues que ninguno basta a deshacellos,	Since none suffices to remove them,
Y véante mis ojos,	And let mine eyes behold thee,
Pues eres lumbre dellos	Since thou art their light
Y sólo para tí quiero tenellos.	And for thee alone I wish to have them.

11[1]	11
Descubre tu presencia,	Reveal thy presence
Y máteme tu vista y hermosura;	And let the vision of thee and thy beauty slay me;
Mira que la dolencia	Behold, the affliction of love is not cured
De amor, que no se cura	
Sino con la presencia y la figura.	Save by thy presence and thy form.

11 (12)	11 (12)
Oh cristalina fuente,	O crystalline fount,
Si en esos tus semblantes plateados,	If on that thy silvered surface
Formases de repente	Thou wouldst of a sudden form
Los ojos deseados,	The eyes desired
Que tengo en mis entrañas dibuja-dos!	Which I bear outlined in my inmost parts.

11	11
12 (13)	12 (13)
Apártalos, Amado,	Withdraw them, Beloved,
Que voy de vuelo.	For I fly away.
Esposo	*Spouse*
Vuélvete, paloma,	Return thou, dove,
Que el ciervo vulnerado	For the wounded hart
Por el otero asoma	Appears on the hill
Al aire de tu vuelo, y fresco toma.	At the air of thy flight, and takes refreshment.

Esposa	*Bride*
13 (14)	13 (14)
Mi Amado las montañas,	My Beloved, the mountains,
Los valles solitarios nemorosos,	The solitary, wooded valleys,
Las ínsulas extrañas,	The strange islands,
Los ríos sonorosos,	The sonorous rivers,
El silbo de los aires amorosos.	The whisper of the amorous breezes.

14 (15)	14 (15)
	The tranquil night,
La noche sosegada	At the time of the rising of the dawn,
En par de los levantes de la aurora,	The silent music,
La música callada,	The sounding solitude,
La soledad sonora,	The supper that recreates and en-kindles love.
La cena, que recrea y enamora.	

[1] This stanza has been inserted in the second recension.

TEXT B

15

Nuestro lecho florido
De cuevas de leones enlazado,
En púrpura tendido,
De paz edificado,
De mil escudos de oro coronado.

15

Our flowery bed,
Encompassed with dens of lions,
Hung with purple
And builded in peace,
Crowned with a thousand shields of
gold.

16

A zaga de tu huella
Las jóvenes discurren al camino
Al toque de centella,
Al adobado vino,
Emisiones de bálsamo divino.

16

In the track of thy footprint
The young girls run along by the
way.
At the touch of a spark,
At the spiced wine,
Flows forth the divine balsam.

17

En la interior bodega
De mi Amado bebí, y cuando salía
Por toda aquesta vega,
Ya cosa no sabía,
Y el ganado perdí que antes seguía.

17

In the inner cellar
Of my Beloved have I drunk,
And when I went forth over all this
meadow,
Then knew I naught
And lost the flock which I followed
aforetime.

18

Allí me dió su pecho,
Allí me enseñó ciencia muy sabrosa,
Y yo le dí de hecho
A mí, sin dejar cosa,
Allí le prometí de ser su esposa.

18

There he gave me his breast;
There he taught me a science most
delectable;
And I gave myself to him,
Indeed, reserving nothing;
There I promised him to be his bride.

19

Mi alma se ha empleado,
Y todo mi caudal en su servicio;
Ya no guardo ganado,
Ni ya tengo otro oficio,
Que ya sólo en amar es mi ejercicio.

19

My soul has employed itself
And all my possessions in his service;
Now I guard no flock
Nor have I now other office,
For now my exercise is in loving
alone.

20

Pues ya si en el ejido
De hoy más no fuere vista ni hallada,
Diréis que me he perdido;
Que andando enamorada,
Me hice perdidiza, y fuí ganada.

20

If, then, on the common land,
From henceforth I am neither seen
nor found
You will say that I am lost;
That, wandering love-stricken,
I lost my way and was found.

21

De flores y esmeraldas,
En las frescas mañanas escogidas,
Haremos las guirnaldas
En tu amor florecidas
Y en un cabello mío entretejidas.

21

With flowers and emeralds
Gathered in the cool mornings
We will make the garlands
Flowering in thy love
And interwoven with one hair from
my head.

22

En sólo aquel cabello
Que en mi cuello, volar consideraste,
Mirástele en mi cuello,
Y en él preso quedaste,
Y en uno de mis ojos te llagaste.

22

By that hair alone
Which thou regardest fluttering on
my neck,
Beholding it on my neck,
Thou wert captivated,
And wert wounded by one of mine
eyes.

23

Cuando tú me mirabas,
Su gracia en mí tus ojos imprimían;
Por eso me adamabas,
Y en eso merecían
Los míos adorar lo que en tí vían.

23

When thou didst look on me,
Thine eyes imprinted upon me thy
grace;
For this cause didst thou love me
greatly
Whereby mine eyes deserved
To adore that which they saw in
thee.

24

No quieras despreciarme,
Que si color moreno en mí hallaste,
Ya bien puedes mirarme,
Después que me miraste,
Que gracia y hermosura en mí
dejaste.
7+s.c.

24

Despise me not,
For, if thou didst find me swarthy,
Now canst thou indeed look upon
me,
Since thou didst look upon me
And leave in me grace and beauty.

TEXT J

16

Cogednos las raposas,
Que está ya florecida nuestra viña,
En tanto que de rosas
Hacemos una piña,
Y no parezca nadie en la montiña.

16

Drive us away the foxes,
For our vineyard is now in flower,
While we make a bunch of roses,
And let none appear upon the hill.

17

Detente, Cierzo muerto,
Ven, Austro, que recuerdas los
    amores,
Aspira por mi huerto,
Y corran tus olores,
Y pacerá el Amado entre las flores.

17

Stay thee, dead north wind.
Come, south wind, that awakenest
    love;
Breathe through my garden
And let thy odours flow,
And the Beloved shall pasture among
    the flowers.

18

Oh ninfas de Judea,
En tanto que en las flores y rosales
El ámbar perfumea,
Morá en los arrabales,
Y no queráis tocar nuestros umbrales.

18

O nymphs of Judaea,
While mid the flowers and rose-trees
The amber send forth perfume,
Dwell in the outskirts
And desire not to touch our
    thresholds.

19

Escóndete, Carillo,
Y mira con tu haz a las montañas,
Y no quieras decillo;
Mas mira las campañas
De la que va por ínsulas extrañas.

19

Hide thyself, dearest one,
And look with thy face upon the
    mountains,
And desire not to speak.
But look upon her companions
Who travels mid strange islands.

Esposo

20

A las aves ligeras,
Leones, ciervos, gamos saltadores,
Montes, valles, riberas,
Aguas, aires, ardores
Y miedos de las noches veladores.

The Bridegroom

20

Birds of swift wing,
Lions, harts, leaping does,
Mountains, valleys, banks,
Waters, breezes, heats,
And terrors that keep watch by
    night.

<table>
<tr><td>

21

Por las amenas liras,
Y canto de sirenas os conjuro,
Que cesen vuestras iras,
Y no toquéis al muro,
Porque la Esposa duerma más
   seguro.

</td><td>

21

By the pleasant lyres.
And by the sirens' song, I conjured
   you,
Cease your wrath
And touch not the wall,
That the bride may sleep more
   securely.

</td></tr>
</table>

III

<table>
<tr><td>

22

Entrado se ha la Esposa
En el ameno huerto deseado,
Y a su sabor reposa,
El cuello reclinado
Sobre los dulces brazos del Amado.

</td><td>

III

22

The Bride has entered
Into the pleasant garden of her
   desire,
And at her pleasure rests,
Her neck reclining
On the gentle arms of the Beloved.

</td></tr>
</table>

<table>
<tr><td>

23

Debajo del manzano,
Allí conmigo fuiste desposada,
Allí te dí la mano,
Y fuiste reparada
Donde tu madre fuera violada.[1]

</td><td>

23

Beneath the apple-tree,
There wert thou betrothed to me;
There did I give thee my hand
And thou wert redeemed,
Where thy mother had been cor-
   rupted.

</td></tr>
</table>

---

[1] Here ends the re-arrangement of the verses in the second recension. We have placed both versions side by side so as to preserve the impression of the original poem. Following the most important MSS, we designate the first version B (*Barrameda*), and the second J (*Jaén*). The following table shows their relation to each other:

B: 1–10,   11–14, 15–24, 25–26, 27–28, 29–30, 31–32, 33–39
J: 1–10, 11, 12–15, 24–33, 16–17, 22–23, 20–21, 18–19, 34–40

To realize the meaning of the changes both versions must be read and appreciated as a whole. The question whether the saint himself or another person was responsible for the changes will be discussed here as little as on an earlier occasion, as the material necessary for its solution is not available. But we cannot by-pass the inter-relation of the two versions.

TEXT B. J.

Esposo	*Spouse*
33 (34)	**33 (34)**
La blanca palomica	The little white dove
Al arca con el ramo se ha tornado,	Has returned to the ark with the bough,
Y ya la tortolica	And now the turtle-dove
Al socio deseado	Has found the mate of her desire
En las riberas verdes ha hallado.	On the green banks.
34 (35)	**34 (35)**
En soledad vivía,	In solitude she lived
Y en soledad ha puesto ya su nido,	And in solitude now has built her nest
Y en soledad la guía	And in solitude
A solas su querido,	Her dear one alone guides her,
También en soledad de amor herido.	Who likewise in solitude was wounded by love.
Esposa	*Bride*
35 (36)	**35 (36)**
Gocémonos, Amado,	Let us rejoice, Beloved,
Y vámonos a ver en tu hermosura	And let us go to see ourselves in thy beauty,
Al monte o al collado,	To the mountain or the hill
Do mana el agua pura;	Where flows the pure water;
Entremos más adentro en la espesura.	Let us enter farther into the thicket.
36 (37)	**36 (37)**
Y luego a las subidas	And then we shall go forth
Cavernas de la piedra nos iremos,	To the lofty caverns of the rock
Que están bien escondidas,	Which are well hidden,
Y allí nos entraremos,	And there shall we enter
Y el mosto de granadas gustaremos.	And taste the new wine of the pomegranates.
37 (38)	**37 (38)**
Allí me mostrarías	There wouldst thou show me
Aquello que mi alma pretendía,	That which my soul desired,
Y luego me darías	And there at once, my life,
Allí tú, vida mía,	Wouldst thou give me
Aquello que me diste el otro día.	That which thou gavest me the other day.

38 (39)

El aspirar del aire,	The breathing of the air,
El canto de la dulce filomena,	The song of the sweet philomel,
El soto y su donaire,	The grove and its beauty
En la noche serena	In the serene night,
Con llama que consume y no da pena.	With a flame that consumes and gives no pain.

39 (40)

Que nadie lo miraba,	For none saw it,
Aminadab tampoco parecía,	Neither did Aminadab appear,
Y el cerco sosegaba,	And there was a rest from the siege,
Y la caballería	And the cavalry
A vista de las aguas descendía.	Came down at the sight of the waters.[1]

This song from prison is marvellously rich in images and ideas. In this respect it greatly differs from the verses of the *Dark Night* and the *Flame of Love*. In these two poems a single image dominates the whole, in the one the escape by night, in the other the flaming fire. In the *Canticle*, it is true, there is also a unifying bond—we shall come back to this later—but within it there is a constant change of images. In the former works there was only simplicity and silence, here the soul and the whole of creation are in motion. This is no mere difference in poetic style: it is due to a profound difference in the basic experience. *Night* and *Flame of Love* give, as it were, a cross section of the mystical life at a certain moment of its development, both at a time when the soul has already left all created things behind and is only occupied with God. Its relation to the things of the world is treated merely in retrospect. The *Spiritual Canticle*, on the other hand, describes the whole mystical development, not only in the commentary but in the verses themselves, and is written by a man who was profoundly moved by all the charms of the visible creation. The outside world penetrates to the prisoner in his dark cell, who, a poet and artist, is open also to the magic of music; but he is cut off from this world with its marvellous images and enchanting sounds. True, he does not stop short at images and sounds. They are to him a mysterious script which expresses, and in which he himself can express, what is taking place secretly in his soul. It is truly mysterious. For this script contains such a wealth of meaning that it seems impossible to the saint himself to find the right words to explain what the Holy Spirit was singing in it

[1] The translation is that of Allison Peers, since it conforms more closely to the original, a necessity for this chapter.—Translator.

"with unutterable groanings". For we owe these verses to the Holy
Spirit. They are "inspirations of love and mystical knowledge"; the
Spirit of God gave them to the soul in which he took up his dwelling,
and such things even the mystic himself cannot completely describe
and explain. Therefore the poet affirms from the first that he is not
going to explain everything. He will only "give some general explanations" and leave to the verses "their whole wealth of meaning, so that
everyone may draw from them according to his capacity and the
inclination of his spirit". He is confident that "mystical knowledge
. . . need not be understood distinctly . . . to rouse love and enthusiasm
in the soul".[1] Thus the Spirit who has infused his love in one soul
will give other loving souls access to the mysterious expression of this
love. The saint would not restrain this breathing of the Spirit, and
therefore declares that his own explanations are not binding. When we
have read these explanations we are sincerely grateful for this statement; for the contrast between the poetical and mystical fervour of
the *Canticle* and the totally different style of the commentary is here
far more perceptible than in the *Ascent* and the *Night*. Here we have
the greatest contrast with the *Living Flame*, though both works are
close to each other in time as well as in thought. Here the thinker and
teacher does not only confront his poem as an objective datum that
is almost alien to him, as was the case in the two earlier treatises. (The
interval of time certainly contributed to this: the greater part of the
verses was composed at Toledo in 1578, whereas the first version of
the explanations was written at Granada in 1584.) But over and above
this the reader has the impression that there was another consideration,
beyond the intention of interpreting the image language of the poem.
Apart from his spiritual sons and daughters, for whom he was writing
in the first place, other readers seem to have been envisaged by the
saint, less willing to accept his teaching. While we were trying to
understand the *Ascent* and the *Dark Night* we already expressed the
opinion that St John's treatment of the difference between the properly
mystical and the ordinary life of grace may not have been quite candid;
that it may have been influenced by the thought of the vigilant eye of
the Inquisition and of the suspicion of Illuminism, to which mysticism
was exposed from the start.[2] The *Spiritual Canticle* appears to have
been even more strongly influenced by this consideration, to which the

---

[1] *Spiritual Canticle*, Prologue 1ff, addressed to Anne of Jesus, who had asked for an
explanation of the stanzas.

[2] Cf. the pleasantly objective presentation of the Inquisition in J. Brouwer, *De
Achtergrond der Spaanse Mystiek*, Zutphen 1935, p. 79f.

second version seems to owe its very existence.[1] For the changes of this version are not restricted to explanations but have cut deep into the *Canticle* itself.

We would here first point out four facts which are evidently closely connected with each other: 1. The second version contains a verse that had not been in it before. (This verse, it is true, appears already in several printed editions that otherwise follow the first version, but it was probably taken over from a manuscript of the second version.[2]) 2. The second version divides the *Canticle* into three parts, I, II and III. 3. It re-arranges the stanzas and thus cuts through the original structure. 4. Before the explanation of the first verse of the *Canticle* it inserts an *argumentum*, i.e. a brief statement of the leading thoughts. According to this the verses treat of the way of a soul from the moment when it began to devote itself to the service of God to the highest stage of perfection, the spiritual marriage; hence the three ways leading to the goal are also touched upon: these are the purgative, illuminative and unitive ways (or the way of beginners, proficients—up to the spiritual betrothal—and perfect: state of mystical marriage). The last stanzas treat also the state of the blessed to which the perfect aspire.

The later division of the *Canticle* into three sections corresponds to the inserted Argument stressing the traditional distinction of the three ways. "Accordingly, looking back on the way that has been traversed, an allusion to the three ways is inserted at the beginning of the second version."[3]

The inserted stanza, n. 11, expresses the longing of the soul for the unveiled vision of God in eternal life and prepares the re-interpretation of stanzas 36–39 (35–38): in the first version these stanzas refer unmistakably to the state of the mystical marriage, but in the second version they are changed by certain alterations and additions into an anticipating description of the life to come.

All this points to an underlying intention in the second version, namely, to present the mystical development of the soul as far as possible in a traditional and unsuspicious form and to draw a sharp distinction between the highest stage, the mystical marriage, and the perfection of the soul in eternal life. We shall soon examine whether the re-arrangement of the verses serves the same purpose.

If the first explanations have evidently been worked over with

---

[1] Cf. the diametrically opposed view of Allison Peers, II, 11ff.
[2] Cf. P. Silverio in his appendix to the *Spiritual Canticle*, Obras, III, p. 456.
[3] Compare the explanation of stanza 27 with that of stanza 22.

the purpose of correcting anything that might give rise to suspicion and misinterpretation, this fear may have influenced even the first version. At the beginning of the *Ascent* and of the *Living Flame* the saint also gave the customary assurance that he submitted in all things to the judgement of the Church, besides adducing the teaching of Scripture in his support. Here he does so even more emphatically. At the end of the Prologue[1] he gives the assurance that he affirms nothing on his own authority, as if trusting in his own experience and in his knowledge of other souls; but that he wants to prove and expound everything on the basis of Scripture, at least whatever is not easily understandable. In fact, in the *Spiritual Canticle* the Biblical citations do not always appear so natural as in the *Living Flame*, especially in the case of the many parallel passages from the Canticle. They often give the impression of wanting to prove that certain daring expressions are based on Scriptural usage and employed in the same sense. Finally, the external purpose may also explain the undeniable difference between the poem and its interpretation, though other circumstances probably also contributed to this. As has already been pointed out, this poem differs from the others explained by treatises in the abundance and variety of its images. The commentary looks almost like a dictionary of this image language. In a way this is suggested by the peculiarity of its many images. There is no original unity between them and what they are intended to represent, as in the case of the symbol in the narrower and proper sense, for example that of the night or the flame. There is, indeed, some kind of similarity between the image and that which it is meant to signify, and thus an objective foundation of the sign-relation. But this basis is not sufficient for an immediate understanding of the meaning of the images. Their language must be learned; moreover, it seems far more arbitrary in the choice of its expressions than a natural language of words, even though not as arbitrary as an artificial language or a sign system invented entirely according to one's own ideas. As a result of this freedom of choice and of the loose objective connexion, these images have not only one meaning but admit of several interpretations; on the other hand, that which they signify can also be represented in a different way, because it is not a necessary expression. All these are characteristics of what we call allegory. This was in the taste of the time and characteristic of the poetry of the Baroque. John knew the

---

[1] Prologue 4, Allison Peers, III, p. 25.

poetry of his time very well and had been formed by it. Thus the use of this artistic form was quite natural to him, and he employed it in his poems in masterly fashion.[1] But in his interpretation he strings one explanation of a term to the other and sometimes gives several quite different expositions of the same image, e.g. in the second verse the shepherds are interpreted as the desires and affections of the soul or, again, as angels; this, surely, goes beyond what is required by the allegory as such and mars the impression of the poem by dissolving its unity into a multitude of details and emphasizing what is abstruse and arbitrary in the images. But this multitude of explanations may also be caused by his intention to prevent doubtful and dangerous interpretations. The heart of the poet may sometimes have rebelled against the method of the commentator. If St John tells his readers that his own interpretations are not meant to prevent the Spirit from breathing in their souls, this may certainly be taken as an invitation to consider above all the poem itself.

(b) The Key Idea according to the Presentation of the Saint

If we approach the *Canticle* in its first version without any preconceived ideas it will appear to us as the faithful expression of the whole *mystical* way. We emphasize *mystical*, because in the aforementioned retrospect when explaining stanza 27 (22)[2] the saint says that the first five stanzas are devoted to the beginnings of the spiritual life, that is to the time when the soul practises meditation and mortification. The second version adds that the description of the contemplative life begins only with the sixth verse. But even the longing cry *A dónde te escondiste?* (Where hast thou hidden thyself?) with which the *Canticle* opens expresses the complaint of a soul deeply wounded by the love of God. Surely it does not only know its Master from "hearsay" but has met him personally, has experienced his touch in its inmost being. Its sorrow is the sorrow of a lover who has been allowed to taste the blissful presence of the Beloved and must now be without him. He has left her sighing, for the absence of the Beloved causes a constant "sighing in the heart of the love", "especially when it has already enjoyed something of His sweet, refreshing presence and is then left alone in dryness and solitude . . .".[3] Surely, we must think

---

[1] It cannot be ascertained how far he here creates quite naturally as an artist and how far he does so under the special inspiration of the Holy Spirit. We shall later revert to this question.

[2] *Spiritual Canticle*, 22. 3. [3] *Ibid.*, 1. 14.

7*

of high mystical graces when he speaks of "burning touches of love"
that "wound and pierce the soul like a fiery arrow and leave it altogether
burnt out by the fire of love". Here the will is so inflamed that it seems
to the soul "as if it were consumed in this flame, went out of itself
and were wholly renewed like the phoenix that is burned and re-
born".[1] We recognize in this description the union of love which,
according to St Teresa and to St John himself, is the preparation for
the mystical betrothal and marriage.[2] It is an entirely new state which
the soul itself does not yet understand. Hence it seeks its lost Lover
by meditating on creatures, but finds no satisfaction in that. This
distinguishes it clearly from the beginners in the spiritual life who
enjoy the ordinary practices of piety because they have not yet entered
the night of contemplation. The soul that has been inwardly touched
by God can no longer find peace in anything that is not God: "There
is nowhere a medicine for the wounds of love save with Him who has
inflicted them." Therefore the wounded soul goes out hurriedly and
calls after the Beloved. "This going out . . . means the going out from
all things . . . and the going out from oneself through forgetting oneself and loving God."[3] Now the soul can do nothing else but love
God and is consumed by the longing for his vision. The Lord cannot
resist this desire for long. The love he has enkindled moves him to
new, unheard-of proofs of love. He appears suddenly and, in a steep
flight, lifts it up to himself.[4]

   This is a description of the spiritual betrothal which involves the
breaking of all natural conditions of its being that is so terrifying to
the soul; it definitely corresponds to what St Teresa describes in the
sixth mansion of her *Interior Castle*. Weak nature fears to give way
and breaks into the cry: "Withdraw them, Beloved" (i.e. the eyes for
which it has been longing). But this request is not meant seriously.
Rather, the soul hopes to be freed from the fetters of this life in order
to be able to bear the blissful presence. But this time is not yet. The
vuélvete, paloma (Return thou, dove) calls the soul back to its earthly
existence. For the present it must be content with what it can receive
in this life. And this is a great deal. Now begins the play of love
between the divine Lover and the beloved soul. It no longer needs
creatures to find a way to the Beloved. He himself visits it again and
again and increasingly discovers his beauty to the soul. All the charms
of creatures must now help it to sing the praises of the divine beauty.

[1] *Ibid.*, 1. 17.   [2] Cf. the various kinds of union discussed above.
[3] *Spiritual Canticle*, 1. 20.   [4] Exposition of stanza 13.

In its union with the heavenly Spouse the soul itself is overwhelmed with gifts, adorned with marvellous grace and strength, wholly plunged into love and peace. Sharing in the life of God, it also rejoices in the fire of love which he enkindles in other souls. The bride herself is now introduced into the "innermost wine cellar", the most hidden sanctuary of love where God communicates himself to it and transforms it into himself. Full of the overwhelming beatitude of this new divine life the soul forgets all the things of this world; all desire for them vanishes. And as the Beloved surrounds it with incomparable tenderness, it gives itself entirely to him, it now lives only for him and is dead to the world. In this loving union all the virtues blossom forth. The soul is happy to know the heavenly beauty with which it is now adorned. But it knows that all this abundance is due solely to God's gracious glance, hence it will use it only to give delight to the Giver himself. All disturbances are to be removed from the blissful life of love, the Lord himself takes away everything that may hinder the permanent union. Thus he can lead the soul into the desired garden, there to rest with him in undisturbed peace. In the deepest solitude he will introduce it into the hidden mysteries of his wisdom, make it burn in the flames of love, and no creature will see anything of what God has prepared for the soul he has for ever hidden in himself.

Thus we would understand the original structure of the *Canticle* as an ascent from one step of the union of love to another, or as a descent in which the soul is drawn ever more deeply into God. First there is a brief meeting, then, after the longing torment of seeking, the soul is caught up into the most intimate union; after that follows a period of preparation for the permanent union, and finally the indestructible peace of the spiritual marriage. There can hardly be a question of the work being divided into the three ways or states of purification, illumination and union. These are rather three effects linked to one another throughout the whole life of grace and during the whole mystical way,[1] even though one or the other is more emphasized at the different stages. In the description of the *Spiritual Canticle* the union comes at the beginning and at the end, governing the whole. The purgation is mentioned most frequently at the transition from betrothal to marriage. The illumination accompanies the union.

It is remarkable that in the first version the stanzas are so arranged

---

[1] This agrees also with the intention of the Areopagite, to whom the threefold division is due.

that the transition from betrothal to marriage is fluctuating and begins very early. In stanza 15 (24) the perfect intimacy of union is already reached. The only difference between it and the mystical marriage is that disturbances are still possible, which must disappear so that the union can become permanent. In the re-arrangement of the stanzas in the second version the limits are more clearly defined. The exclusion of all disturbances is placed first, being followed by the description of the complete union that begins with entering the desired garden (stanza 22). This is an advantage of the second version, which balances the slight drawback that the beautiful stanza 15 with its nocturnal magic is followed immediately by the mention of the "foxes in the vineyard" in stanza 16. It is quite understandable that, when the poem was first written down, the stanzas were not yet in the most suitable order. Nor were all of them composed at the same time. Even those written during his imprisonment evidently came into existence only gradually, following the inner experiences. As has been mentioned before, the witnesses differ on the point whether the poems could be written down in prison at all or only after his escape. The former is more probable, but does not exclude the possibility that the prisoner had first to memorize them before he obtained writing materials. He may have sung to himself now one stanza, now another, according to his mood. He probably wrote them down as soon as he had the opportunity, without considering the best order as carefully as he did in the last recension. Hence we prefer to follow the order of the second version when considering the thought and artistic form of the poem in greater detail.[1] We shall not, however, overlook what has been said about the leading intention of the second version and will therefore also take into account the original interpretation of the stanzas.

(c) The Principal Image and its Importance for the Canticle

Our first summary was intended only to realize the meaning of the whole; it could hardly give an indication of the wealth of individual traits. If this is to be done we must try to penetrate into the image language of the poem to which the "dictionary" of the saint is the obvious guide, even though it need not be followed slavishly.

The fundamental mood of the *Canticle* is one of tension: the loving soul hovers between painful longing and blissful finding. This mood

---

[1] In the following discussions the verses are therefore counted according to the second version.

is expressed in the image that governs the whole despite the wealth of particular images included in and subordinated to it; this is the image of the bride who longs for her Beloved, goes to seek him and in the end happily finds him. This is nothing new to us. In the *Canticle of the Dark Night*, too, the bride leaves her house to hasten to her Beloved; in the *Living Flame* she also addresses the Spouse. But there the bridal relationship is not at the centre but rather presupposed as the background. In the *Canticle*, on the other hand, it is the focal point on which all else converges. This image is not an allegory. If the soul is called the bride of God this involves more than a mere similarity between two things permitting one to be signified by the other. Rather, there is such an intimate union between the image and what it signifies that we can hardly still speak of a duality. This is characteristic of a symbolic relationship in the narrower and proper sense. The eternal purpose for which God has created the soul is a relationship with him that could not be described more accurately than by a bridal union. Conversely, the true meaning of a bride relationship is nowhere so truly and perfectly fulfilled as in the loving union of God with the soul. Once this has been grasped, the image and what it signifies actually exchange their rôles: the bridal union with God is seen to be the original and true bridal state, while the corresponding human relationships appear as imperfect images of this original, just as the Fatherhood of God is the archetype of all earthly paternity. Because of its image relationship, the human bridal relation becomes a fitting expression of the divine union. Compared with this, the purely human relation in ordinary life takes the second place; indeed, its highest meaning is its capacity to express a divine mystery.[1]

(d) *Bridal Symbol and Particular Images*

How is this principal image, the bridal symbol, related to the variety of allegorical presentations? To answer this question we must discuss another that had been posed earlier: Are these images arbitrary inventions or inspirations of the Holy Spirit? This question had been put to the saint himself by Sister Magdalen of the Holy Ghost. She writes in her testimony that John had left his book, containing the poems written in prison, at the convent at Beas and that she had been told to make some copies of it. She greatly admired the vivid language and the beauty and exactness of expression. So she once asked the poet whether

---

[1] Cf. Eph. 5. 23ff.

God had inspired those words that contained so much and were so beautiful. He replied: "My daughter, sometimes God gave them to me, at others I sought them." [1] The work itself gives a similar answer. In the Foreword St John stresses that the verses were inspired by the spirit of love and that it is therefore impossible to find the right words to explain them. This evidently refers in the first place to the difficulties of a later interpretation. The poetic expression seems to have been received from the Holy Spirit together with the contents. But later we are told that even the immediate expression cannot reproduce what the Spirit of God caused the soul to feel and understand interiorly. Therefore it uses images and parables to indicate some of it. Hence we have to distinguish what is purely spiritual and interior in the experience of the mystic from its linguistic expression. This formless and modeless fullness of the spirit can never be wholly enshrined in words. If the mystic gropes for images and parables this may be interpreted as his own seeking for the right expression. But it can also be a grasping of what the Spirit of God offers. If John refers to Scriptural images that often sound strange and are open to misinterpretation, we may well suppose that he received supernatural assistance for expressing his experience. Now, it is true, the concept of inspiration (*Inspiration*) cannot be understood in such a way that everything the sacred authors say, including their images and terms, should be attributed to divine suggestion (*Eingebung*), but in many places the external word, too, must be understood as the Word of God in the literal sense. [2] According to his own evidence this has also sometimes happened in the case of St John. But even when he himself was searching for expression, the assistance of the Holy Spirit need not be excluded. During his imprisonment the activity of his lively artistic imagination must have been increased by being unnaturally deprived of all that could satisfy the outer senses, and this might well have conjured up a wealth of gorgeous images before his soul. But the fact that all these are in harmony with his inner experience cannot be attributed to the imagination nor to an arbitrary interpretation: he *finds* in the images the wanted expression for the ineffable; the Holy Spirit opens to him the spiritual meaning of this wealth of imaginary pictures and guides him in his choice. Thus we can understand the harmony of the whole and the inner conviction produced by this

---

[1] Allison Peers I, xxxiii.
[2] This equation of Scriptural with poetic-mystical inspiration is not due to St John of the Cross.—Translator.

imagery. Nevertheless, this does not apply to all of them; some images have certainly been chosen in the natural way and are even far-fetched. This is probably so even more frequently in the case of the later interpretations.

The *Canticle* introduces us to the world such as it appears to the longing soul intoxicated with love. It only goes out to seek its Beloved. It is anxious to find traces of him everywhere; everything reminds it of him and is important only insofar as it gives news of him or contains a message from him. As the hart appears for a second at the edge of the forest and vanishes as soon as it is seen by man, so did the Lord at the first meetings: he showed himself to the soul but had disappeared before it could take hold of him. The crystal fount that refreshes the wanderer is the faith: for the truth it gives is pure, not darkened by error, and from it springs the water of life that flows on to eternal life (John 4. 14). Longingly the soul bends over it: may not the eyes of its Beloved shine from its clear mirror? His eyes—this means the divine rays that have wounded, enlightened and inflamed its inmost parts. The soul always feels that these eyes see it, they are imprinted in its ground. All this can be understood directly from the general situation. But over and above this the interpretation says that the face is the articles of faith which present the divine truths (the rays) veiled and imperfectly, and that it is called "silvery" because the pure gold of truth is presented to us in the faith overlaid by silver.[1] Here we can no longer follow nor discover any connexion with the dominant symbol. We are faced with a purely rational, artificial interpretation, which we may or may not accept on the authority of the poet and commentator, since he himself has left us free to reject it.

The poem then describes the long desired event. Suddenly and unexpectedly the bride meets the glance of the divine eyes. Her passionate desire has caused the Beloved to "visit her sublimely, tenderly, interiorly and with great power of love".[2] He has appeared again like the hart, on the hill, that is in the height of contemplation. He only grants the soul a glance, for "however sublime the experiences God grants to the soul in this life, they are yet only brief, sudden appearances from afar". But he, too, is wounded. "For between lovers the wound of one is common to both, and both have one and the same feeling." The air of its flight brings refreshment to him. He calls it a dove, because it rises high and light in the flight of contemplation,

---

[1] Exposition of stanza 12 (11). 2f.   [2] *Ibid.*, 13. 2 (12. 1).

since its heart is simple and aglow with love. The air of its flight is the spirit of love which it breathes in this sublime contemplation and knowledge of God as the Father and the Son breathe the Holy Spirit. The flight signifies the infused knowledge of God, the air of the flight is the love springing from it. This love allures the Spouse and refreshes him like a fountain: "As the breath of wind refreshes and restores the man who is fatigued by the heat, so the breath of love refreshes him who burns with the fire of love. For in the lover love is a flame burning with the desire to burn more." And because the love of the bride feeds this flame it is a refreshing breath.[1]

Since the soul now enjoys the presence of the Beloved it no more cries out in longing; but it now begins to praise the glories it experiences in its union with him. For, as we have seen, in the flight of the spirit its betrothal with the Son of God is accomplished. Here "God communicates to the soul marvellous illuminations concerning His Godhead, He adorns it with greatness and majesty, enriches it with gifts and virtues, clothes it with divine knowledge and glory, just like a bride on the day of her betrothal".[2] It enters upon "a state of peace, delight and sweetness of love" and can do nothing else but "relate and sing the great deeds of its Beloved". In the ecstasies of love the soul experiences what St Francis meant by the words: "My God and my all." Now God is truly its all, the good of all spirits, and thus it finds an image of his perfections in the creatures. Each of these is God and all together are God. "And as the soul is united to God in this ecstasy it has the feeling as if all things were God", as St John experienced when he said: "That which was made in him was life."[3] This does not mean that the soul sees the creatures in God "as things are seen in the light, it only meant that, possessing God, it has the feeling as if all things were God". Nor is this the clear and substantial vision of God. True, it is "a powerful and abundant communication", but it is only "a weak reflexion of what He is in Himself",[4] though by this the perfections of the creatures are revealed to the soul.

The mountains with their summits and the charms of their scented flowers have something of the grandeur and beauty of the Beloved. The soul rests in his peace as in the silence of a cool, solitary wooded valley. In the knowledge of God it discovers a marvellous new world, like a seafarer in distant islands. Like a swollen river that floods everything, filling all the low places and drowning every other sound with

---

[1] Stanza 13. 12 (12. 11).   [2] *Ibid.*, 14. 2 (13. 1).
[3] John. 1. 4 according to a reading formerly in use.   [4] Stanza 14. 5 (13. 5).

its noise, thus the soul "is forcefully seized . . . by the torrent of the Spirit of God and overwhelmed so that the waters of all the rivers of the world seem to break upon it". But this does not give it pain, for these are rivers of peace, and their overflowing "wholly fills it with peace and glory". Their waters fill the depths of its humility and the emptiness of its desire, and in the roaring of the torrents it hears "a spiritual voice that . . . drowns all other voices and exceeds all the sounds in the world. . . . It is an interior voice of immense sound and fills the soul with power and strength, as happened when the Holy Spirit descended on the apostles. The vehement sound that was heard by the inhabitants of Jerusalem was only an indication of what the apostles heard inwardly. Despite its great power this spiritual voice is very pleasing to the ear. St John heard it 'as the noise of many waters and as the voice of great thunder', yet at the same time 'as the voice of harpers, harping on their harps' (Apoc. 14. 2)."[1]

The virtues and graces of the Beloved are infused into the soul like gentle breezes playing on man's face: "A most sublime and sweet knowledge of God and His perfections that flows into the understanding through the touch of these perfections in the substance of the soul."

"As the touch of the air is perceived by the sense of touch and its whisper by the sense of hearing, thus the touch of the perfections of the Beloved is felt and enjoyed with the sense of touch of the soul, i.e. in its substance (by means of the will); and the knowledge is gained through the soul's sense of hearing, the understanding." This communication is extremely lovely and beneficial. "As the whisper of the air is very freely communicated to the ear, so this extremely tender and delicate knowledge penetrates the interior of the substance of the soul with marvellous delight and enjoyment; and this delight . . . surpasses every other . . ., because the soul is given a substantial knowledge that is free from all accidental images and forms." "This divine whispering that penetrates the hearing of the soul is not only a substantial knowledge, but also a revelation of divine truths in the understanding or a revelation of divine secrets. . . . Whenever Holy Scripture mentions a communication from God . . . through the hearing, we may normally suppose a revelation of these pure truths in the understanding. These are purely spiritual revelations or visions given only to the soul, without the mediation or help of the senses. For this reason the communications of God . . . by means of the

[1] Stanza 14 (13). 9–11.

hearing . . . are altogether sublime and sure." So it is supposed that
Elias saw God "in a gentle air" (3 Kings 19. 12) and also St Paul,
when he "heard secret words which it is not granted to man to utter"
(2 Cor. 12. 4). For the "hearing of the soul is a seeing with the understanding". It is not, however, the perfect and clear vision of God in
glory, but still only "a ray of darkness".[1]

Since the soul receives such dark and unfathomable knowledge,
enjoying refreshing repose on the breast of the Beloved, it compares
him with the silent night; but it is a night already illumined by the
morning light, for it is "a rest and silence in the divine light and in a
new knowledge of God, wherein the spirit . . . tastes the sweetest
rest". It rises "calmed and satisfied in God, from the darkness of
natural knowledge to the morning light of the supernatural knowledge
of God. . . . When this morning light begins to shine in the soul
there is neither complete night nor full day, but rather . . . twilight." [2]

In the calm and silence of this luminous night "the soul is allowed
to see the wonderful harmony and order of the divine wisdom in the
diversities of all its creatures and works. . . . They all and each one
of them are in a certain relation to God, and each individual creature
raises its voice in its own proper way to announce how far God is
within it, so that it seems like a harmony of the sublimest music far
surpassing all the serenades and melodies of the world." But it is a
soundless music, for this quiet and silent knowledge communicates
itself without the noise of words "and in it are enjoyed both the loveliness of music and the quiet of silence".[3] This beautiful music is heard
only in solitude and withdrawal from all external things. Therefore
the solitude itself is called sounding.

As the vision of God is the food of angels and saints, the soul is
refreshed by this calming knowledge as by a supper. It enjoys it with
the happy feeling that all the labours and sufferings of the day are over.
The Beloved himself "sups with it" (Apoc. 3. 20); he gives it a share
in the enjoyment of all his goods and by his liberality inflames it to
new love.

Adorned with the virtues given her by God's abounding mercy,
the bride sees her own inner being as a garden full of sweet-smelling
flowers or as a vineyard in blossom. She feels the presence of the
Beloved in her heart as if he were there reposing on his own bed.
She would surrender herself to him with all these blossoms to offer

---

[1] Dionysius the Areopagite, *Mystical Theology*, ch. 1.
[2] Stanza 15 (14). 12–18.   [3] Stanza 15 (14). 25.

him the most sublime homage and to give him joy, and she would keep every disturbance away from him. But the sensual desires that have long been at rest, like foxes pretending to sleep, suddenly break forth, incited by the evil spirits, to destroy the peaceful flowery kingdom of the soul. For the devil "is far more concerned to keep back from this soul even one ounce of its wealth and blissful delight than to cause others to fall into many and grave sins. For others have to lose little or nothing, but this soul much, since it has already gained so many and precious things".[1] Thus the evil spirits greatly excite the desires in order to disturb the soul; if they can do nothing in this way they attack it with bodily torments and shrieks. The pain becomes intolerable if they torture it with spiritual terrors and fears. "And this they can easily do at this time if they are given permission. For if the soul begins its spiritual exercises in the greatest detachment of spirit the devil, being also a spirit, can easily appear to it. Sometimes he attacks it with other terrors, . . . just when God is beginning to lead it to some extent out of the house of its senses in order . . . to let it enter into the garden of the Spouse. For the enemy knows that once the soul is in that recollection it is so well protected that he can no more harm it despite all his efforts. Frequently, when the devil is about to cause it to fall, the soul quickly withdraws into the hiding place of its inmost being where it finds great delight and safe protection; there it feels these terrors as something quite external and distant, so that they do not terrify it but rather give it joy and delight."[2] But if it is troubled, it implores the angels to "catch the foxes", for it is their task to drive away the evil spirits.

When all that causes it harm has been removed the soul, united to the Beloved, is able to rejoice in all the blossoms of virtue that open under his glance and breathe forth their perfume. It gathers them into a bunch "and offers them all united and each one singly to the Beloved in the most tender and intimate love". But it needs his help to do this; without him it would be unable to make a bouquet. They bind it firmly, so that it resembles a pine cone in which all parts are tightly held together: thus the perfection of the soul, too, is a complete whole: it comprises an abundance of shining virtues firmly bound and beautifully arranged. While the soul is making this bouquet by practising the virtues no intruder ought to appear on the hill, i.e. no particular kinds of knowledge or memories should present themselves

[1] Annotation 2 to stanza 16 (addition of the second version).
[2] Stanza 16. 6.

to its faculties so that nothing may distract it from its loving sojourn with God.

But the soul's happiness may be disturbed also in another way. At the time of its betrothal the Beloved is not yet permanently united to it. And as its love is very intense the soul is greatly tormented when he withdraws. Hence it fears the dryness like the cold north wind that kills all blossoms. It seeks refuge in prayer and spiritual exercises so as to master the aridity. But at the exalted stage of the spiritual life which it has now reached all spiritual communications are so interior that they cannot be attained by any activity of its own faculties. Therefore it invokes the aid of the warm, humid south wind, which causes the flowers to open and breathe forth their scent, that is the Holy Spirit "that awakens love in it". When he seizes the soul, "He wholly enkindles, refreshes and revives it and excites its will and desires . . . to the love of God". It asks him to breathe through its garden, not in it. "For there is a great difference between the breathing of God in the soul and His breathing through it. The breathing in the soul signifies the infusion of grace, of the gifts and virtues, whereas the breathing through the soul is a touch and activity of God, whereby the virtues and perfections that have already been given are renewed and set in motion so that they diffuse a marvellously sweet perfume. It is just as if fragrant spices were shaken"; they then diffuse "a wealth of scent that was not there before". Thus the soul, too, has not always the actual sensation and enjoyment of its virtues. In this life they rather resemble flowers that are still in bud, or spices that are covered up. Sometimes, however, when the divine Spirit breathes through the garden of the soul, he opens all the buds of the virtues and uncovers the aromatic spices of the gifts, perfections and riches of the soul. "Thus, by revealing its interior treasures and riches He manifests the whole beauty of the soul. These perfumes of the blossoms of virtue are sometimes in the soul in such abundance that it is wholly clothed in delight and plunged in inestimable glory. Something of this will also "penetrate to the outside so that men who have a sense for it perceive it. To them such a soul appears as a pleasure garden full of the delights and riches of God.

"Even when the blossoms are not open . . . such holy souls have a certain mysterious greatness and dignity that imbues others with reverence and respect." But in the breathing of the Holy Spirit the Son of God communicates himself to the soul in an exalted manner. He more than anyone delights in the fully opened flowers and their perfumes, and the soul itself desires then only to delight him. He has nourished and transformed it into himself, hence it is now "ripened, prepared and seasoned by the blossoms of virtues, gifts and perfections". The lovers delight both together in their taste and sweetness, "for it is proper to the Spouse to unite Himself to the soul in the fragrance of these blossoms".[1]

In the midst of this happiness the soul yet suffers, because even now it has not yet gained full control of its inferior powers; the desires still rebel and harm the life of grace. The soul turns to these lower motions asking them not to transgress their limits. It calls them nymphs, because they seek to seduce the will by insistent flattery. It calls the sensual part of the soul Judaea "because it is by nature weak, carnal and blind like the people of the Jews".[2] While the rose bushes of the higher powers bring forth blossoms of virtue and exhale the amber perfume of the Holy Spirit, those nymphs are to remain in the ante-room or outskirts of the interior senses and not to touch the threshold leading to the interior, i.e. the first movements of the higher part of the soul. (In this passage not only the interpretation but the verse itself seems artificial and too much influenced by contemporary taste. The next, however, is in harmony with the framework of the whole.)

The soul desires to see God face to face. It has found him in its inmost being where it would like to remain hidden with him. If he reveals the glory of his Godhead in the secret chamber of its heart nothing is to penetrate outside so that no disturbance may come from there. The soul knows that the weakness of its sensual nature would faint under the grandeur of what happens on the mountains, and this would hinder the spirit in its contemplation of the face of God. Hence it wants to be wholly free from any interference by the body, to experience the touch of the divine essence and rejoice in the marvellous jewels with which he himself has adorned it, that is with a knowledge of his Godhead far above the ordinary ways of knowledge.

The Spouse himself, too, desires the marriage. He wants to give the bride the extraordinary strength of soul, purity and unique love needed to endure the powerful and intimate embrace of God. He establishes a perfect harmony in her soul. All the fickle play of the imagination, all violent outbreaks of passion, all cowardly fear are now done away with. Mountains and valleys are levelled, whatever is above or below the right measure. The waters of sorrow must recede, the winds of hope be silent, the fire of joy may no longer make them flare

---

[1] Stanza 17 (26).   [2] Stanza 18 (31) 4.

up. Banished are all the terrors by which the enemy seeks to spread darkness in the soul and to obscure the divine light. Thus the bride can rest quite undisturbed in the arms of her Beloved. She has attained a greatness of spirit and a constancy that nothing can shake. Though she is most sensitive to her own as to others' faults they no longer cause her pain. For in this state the soul has lost whatever "the virtues had of weakness. There only remains what is strong, constant and perfect. Like the angels who are perfectly aware of all that causes pain yet feel no pain and practise the works of mercy without any feeling of compassion, so is the soul in the transformation by love".[1] If God still causes the soul to feel some things as painful he does so to give it more merit; it has nothing to do with the mystical marriage. Its hope for union with God is also satisfied in so far as this is possible in this life and it no longer expects anything from this world. "Its joy is habitually so great that it resembles an ocean: it is not diminished by rivers that flow out nor enlarged by those that enter." It is true, the soul still receives accidental joys in abundance, but "the substantial spiritual communication is not increased thereby. For the soul already possesses all that is capable of coming to it anew. . . . In this the soul seems in a certain sense to participate in a divine attribute. For even though God has joy in all things, nevertheless He does not rejoice in them as much as in Himself, for He possesses them all in Himself in a far higher, eminent manner." Thus in the case of the soul, too, all new joys serve only to encourage her to surrender to the bliss of union. If it finds satisfaction in anything else it at once remembers the far higher Good present in itself and turns to him to seek its delight in him. In comparison with this the gain of that which is added is "so insignificant that it may be regarded as nothing". At the same time the soul has the feeling of constantly tasting new delights, because the Good it enjoys always is always new to it.

"If we would now speak of the light of glory which God sometimes grants to the soul in this constant embrace, there are no words to give any idea of it. In a certain sense this is a spiritual transformation in which He lets the soul see and at the same time taste the whole sea of delight and riches which He has given it. As the sun when it casts its fiery rays from the zenith on to the sea lights it up even to its deep caverns and abysses and causes the richest veins of gold and other precious minerals to shine forth, so also does the divine Sun . . . reveal

[1] Stanza 20 (29)10.

to the bride all the riches of her soul. . . . Yet despite these sublime illuminations the soul receives no increase, only what it possessed already is then brought to light and enjoyed."

Thus enlightened, strong and firmly grounded in God, the bride is no longer frightened of the terrors of evil spirits. "Nothing can now touch and trouble her." She has entered into God and enjoys a perfect peace that passes all understanding and cannot be expressed in human words.[1]

"The bride has entered the pleasant garden of her desire." The whole way lies now behind her, the preparation is finished, in the time of her engagement she has remained faithful. Now God calls her to the marriage in the blossoming garden: this is he himself, whom she has desired, into whom she is now being completely transformed. "Thus is effected such an intimate union of both natures and such a communication of the divine with the human nature that both, without any change in their being, appear as God. It is true, this union cannot be perfect in this life, but it surpasses all one could say or think."[2] Here, at the goal, the soul possesses a marvellous, divine fullness of grace that cannot be compared with that of the spiritual betrothal. It feels itself united to God in a real, intimate spiritual embrace and thus lives the life of God. Its neck reclines on the arm of the Beloved; he lends it his strength to transform its weakness into divine power.

The soul has entered a new paradise; the marriage is consummated under the apple tree. The faithful soul is introduced into the marvellous secrets of God, above all into the sweet mysteries of the Incarnation and Redemption. As in paradise human nature was destroyed and delivered to perdition through the fruit of the forbidden tree, so it was redeemed and restored by God under the Tree of the Cross. From the height of the Cross the Spouse gave the bride his hand of grace and mercy and through the merit of his Passion and Death put an end to the enmity caused by Original Sin, that separated man from God. Under the tree of paradise the Mother (human nature) had been corrupted by sin in the person of the first Parents; under the tree of the Cross the human soul was restored to life. The betrothal under the Cross cannot be simply identified with the mystical betrothal: for the former is accomplished once and for all in baptism, whereas the mystical betrothal is linked to personal perfection, hence

---

[1] Stanza 21 (30).   [2] Stanza 22 (27).

it is brought about gradually and depends on the generosity of the soul. But fundamentally it is the same union.[1]

(e) Bridal Symbol and Cross

(Mystical Marriage—Creation, Incarnation and Redemption)

We have now reached an essential point and must attempt to understand the meaning of the work even more deeply than the explicit explanations of the saint himself allow us to do. We have seen in the Cross the symbol of the suffering and death of Christ and of all that is connected with them as regards both their cause and their meaning. Here we have first to think of the fruit of the death on the Cross, i.e. of the Redemption. This is intimately connected with the Incarnation as the condition of the redemptive Passion and Death with the Fall as the motive of both. We have said earlier that the sufferings of the Dark Night are a share in the sufferings of Christ, especially in his abandonment by the Father. This is emphatically confirmed in the *Spiritual Canticle*, since here the longing desire for the hidden God is *the* suffering that governs the whole mystical way. It does not even cease in the bliss of the bridal union; in fact in a certain sense it still increases with the growing knowledge and love of God, because thus is realized ever more clearly what the beatific vision is to give us. (This is elaborated especially in the second version.) But no human pain of desire can be compared with the suffering of the God-man who possessed the beatific vision throughout his life until he gave up this happiness of his own free will in the night of the Mount of Olives. A human mind and heart can penetrate into the unfathomable mystery of such deprivation as little as they can realize the meaning of eternal beatitude. He alone, the only One who has experienced it, can give his chosen ones a taste of it in the intimacy of the bridal union. It was his unique prerogative to feel utterly abandoned by God, and he could suffer this only because he was both God and man; for as God he could not have suffered, and as a mere man he could not have grasped the good of which he deprived himself. Thus the Incarnation is the condition of this suffering; and Christ's human nature is the instrument of Redemption because it is both capable of suffering and actually suffered.

[1] This explanation of stanza 23 (28) was greatly enlarged in the second version. The comparison of the betrothal by baptism with the mystical betrothal has been added. It corresponds to the desire to bring union by grace into close connexion with the mystical union.

The motive cause of this redemptive suffering, hence also of the Incarnation, is human nature as capable of falling and actually fallen.[1] Through the fall of the first men this nature has lost its honour, that is its original perfection and elevation by grace. It is elevated anew in every human soul which by the grace of baptism is reborn as a child of God, and it is crowned in the chosen souls that attain to the bridal union with the Saviour. This happens "under the tree of the Cross", as the ripe fruit of Christ's death on the Cross and the soul's own share in it. Now why is the place of the lifting-up the same as that of the Fall, why is the tree of the Cross the same as the tree in paradise? It seems to me the solution lies in the mystery of sin. The tree in paradise, the fruits of which were forbidden to men, was the tree of the knowledge of good and evil. Men could gain a genuine experimental knowledge of evil and its radical opposition to the good only by doing evil. Thus we may take the tree in paradise to be a symbol of human nature in that it is accessible to sin, and real sin (the first one as well as all later ones) with all its consequences as its fruit. Now the most frightful effect of sin and thus the revelation of its fearful gravity is the suffering and death of Christ. Hence the Redemption is the fruit of the tree of paradise in more than one sense: because sin caused Christ to take upon himself suffering and death, because he was crucified by sin in all its forms, and because in this way it was turned into an instrument of redemption. The soul that is united to Christ gains the "knowledge of good and evil" through suffering with the crucified Saviour (i.e. in the Dark Night of contemplation) and experiences this knowledge as a redeeming power: for it is stressed again and again that the soul achieves purification through the sharp pain of its self-knowledge (as knowledge of its own sinfulness).

Moreover, the mystical union is to be considered also as a share in the Incarnation. This is already suggested by the close connexion of the two mysteries. It is further indicated by the terms in which the saint speaks about the mystical marriage. He writes of "such an intimate union of the two natures and such a communication of the divine with the human nature" that the soul in the state of the mystical marriage appears as God himself,[2] an expression that recalls the relation of the two natures of Christ in the hypostatic union.

[1] We do not consider sin and the need for redemption the *only* reason for the Incarnation. This seems to us sufficiently motivated by the fact that Creation is ordered towards Christ. John of the Cross, too, knows a motivation of the Incarnation independent of the Fall. Cf. his *Romance*.

[2] Exposition of stanza 22.

Theologians, too, call the assumption of the human nature by the divine Word a marriage with humanity, [1] which gave him access to the individual souls. And each time a soul surrenders to him so completely that he can raise it to the mystical marriage he once more becomes man, as it were. There is, however, this essential difference, that in Jesus Christ both natures are united in one Person, whereas in the mystical marriage two persons come in contact with each other but remain two. Yet the union that is effected by the mutual surrender of both comes close to the hypostatic union. It opens the souls to the divine life and completely subjects the human to the divine will, so that God can dispose of such men as of members of his Body. They no longer live their own life but the life of Christ, they endure not their own sufferings but the Passion of Christ. Therefore they also rejoice in the life of grace which the Lord enkindles in other souls when the spark of divine love touches them and the wine of his love inebriates them. [2]

The soul that has attained to the mystical marriage is in the inner wine cellar, i.e. the highest stage of love. The saint here distinguishes seven steps of love, corresponding to the seven gifts of the Holy Spirit, the last of which is fear, which perfects the others: "If . . . the soul has . . . attained to perfect possession of the spirit of fear it also possesses the spirit of love in its perfection; for this fear, the last of the seven gifts, is wholly filial, and the perfect fear of the child proceeds from the perfect love of the Father." [3] In this most intimate union the soul *drinks* of the Beloved. As a draught "is diffused and spread through all the members and veins of the body, so this substantial communication of God is also diffused through the whole soul . . . as far as its substance and spiritual faculties permit. With the understanding it drinks wisdom and knowledge, with the will sweetest love and with the memory the recreation and delight caused by the remembrance and sense of glory." [4] When the soul emerges from its deep absorption, which does not mean an interruption of the substantial union itself but only of its effect in the faculties, it has "lost all knowledge": "In this union it has drunk the sublimest wisdom of God which has made it forget all the things of this world. It seems to the soul that, compared with that knowledge all it has known before,

---

[1] St John of the Cross has treated the Incarnation as the marriage of the Word with humanity in the *Romances* on creation. Here this marriage appears even as a motive of creation. Surprisingly, he has passed over the Fall in the *Romances*; the Redemption appears as deliverance from the yoke of the Law.

[2] Cf. exposition of stanza 25 (16).   [3] Stanza 26 (17). 3.   [4] Stanza 26 (17). 5.

indeed all that the whole world knows, is sheer ignorance. . . . Besides
the deification and elevation of the spirit to God do not allow . . . any
remembrance of earthly things; the soul is estranged not only from
all creaturely things but from itself, it is annihilated and as it were
consumed and dissolved in love. . . . In a sense the state of such a soul
is like that of Adam in his first innocence, when he did not yet know
evil. It is so innocent that it neither understands evil nor thinks anything to be evil. Even though it may hear very evil things and see them
with its own eyes, it nevertheless cannot understand anything of
them." (This does not contradict what has just been said, namely that
contemplation gives the knowledge of good and evil. That knowledge
belongs to the beginning of the mystical way, whereas the ignorance
of evil belongs to the innocence that has been recovered at the summit
of perfection.) Besides, the ignorance of the soul at this stage "is not
to be understood so as if it had lost the habits of knowledge it had
acquired; on the contrary, they receive a higher degree of perfection
from the supernatural knowledge that God had infused into them.
But even though the acquired habits of knowledge do not dominate
the soul in such a way that it needs them to know anything, it can yet
sometimes make use of them. For in this union with divine Wisdom
these acquired forms of knowledge unite with the higher wisdom . . .
as a weak light combines with a stronger. The strong light predominates
and shines, nevertheless the weaker one does not disappear but gains in
perfection. . . . But when the soul is absorbed in this love it completely loses all particular kinds of knowledge and forms of things
. . . and knows no more about them. . . . First, because by that draught
of love it is so absorbed in God . . . that it cannot actually occupy
itself with anything; secondly, and this is the main reason, this transformation in God makes the soul conform to the simplicity and purity
of God, in whom there is neither form nor imaginary shape, so that it
becomes quite clean and pure and free from all previous forms and
shapes."[1] But this unknowing lasts only till the particular effect of
love is past.

The drinking in the cellar has yet another effect: the old man is
transformed into a new man. Before the soul entered the state of
perfection a small flock of desires, joys and imperfections still remained
in it despite its high spirituality. "It goes after this flock to give it
pasture and thus to satisfy it." The understanding mostly retains

---

[1] Stanza 26 (17). 13ff.

something of its former thirst for knowledge, the will is still attracted by personal desires and enjoyments. Man still longs to possess some trifles and cultivates certain inclinations; he wants to be esteemed and easily thinks himself slighted; he still follows his taste in food and drink and is agitated by unnecessary worries, joys, sufferings and fears. This is the flock of imperfections followed by such souls "until they enter the inner cellar to drink; then they lose them altogether through the perfection of love".[1]

In the bridal union God surrounds the soul with a love that cannot be compared even with the tenderest love of a mother. He "gives it His breast", i.e. he reveals his secrets to it and gives it the sweet knowledge of mystical theology, the secret science of God. In return the soul, too, gives itself to him unreservedly: "It has only the one desire to belong to Him for ever and to retain nothing that is different from Him." And since God has removed from it all else to which it had been attached, the soul can give itself to him not only with its will but indeed wholly and completely. The will of both is utterly one, for ever united in faithful constancy. Even the first movements of the soul no longer turn against what it recognizes to be God's will. It knows nothing but love and communion with its divine Spouse. It has reached "that state of perfection whose essence and form . . . is love". It is "so to speak wholly love. It acts only under the inspiration of love and uses all its faculties and wealth only for love. . . . It has realized that its Beloved esteems nothing but love and that He is pleased with nothing else. And because it wants to serve Him perfectly it employs everything in pure love of God. . . . As the bee . . . sucks honey from all flowers and seeks nothing else in them, so the soul also extracts with surprising ease the sweetness of love from all events of life."[2]

The reason why God is pleased only with love and all its manifestations is that all our works and efforts are pure nothingness in his eyes. We can give him nothing, he needs nothing and asks for nothing: "He wants only one thing: to exalt the dignity of our soul . . .; He is pleased only with the enrichment of the soul. Since there is no way in which it can be honoured more than if He makes it equal to Himself, therefore He wants only that it should love Him. For it is proper to love to make the lover equal to the object of his love. And since the soul here possesses perfect love it is called the bride of the Son of God and this means equality with Him, equality through

[1] Stanza 26 (17). 18f.   [2] Stanza 27 (19). 7f.

the love of friendship in virtue of which all things are common to both."[1]

The soul now serves God with all it possesses. It is so natural to it to work for him and his honour that it often does so without thinking and being conscious of the fact that it is working for God. Formerly it indulged in "many useless occupations. . . . For all its habitual imperfections may be called so many occupations . . .: the inclination to speak, think and do useless things by doing all this without regard to the perfection of the soul." It now no longer knows any of these occupations; for "all its thoughts, words and works are now from God and directed to God".[2] It now has no other office than love. All its faculties are active only through and in love. This is true of its life of prayer as well as of its occupation with temporal things. "Before the union of love it had to practise love in the active as well as in the contemplative life. But in this state it is no longer fitting to occupy oneself with any other works and external practices that might hinder its life of love in God be it ever so little. And this is true even if it is a question of works that would greatly increase His honour. For one spark of pure love is more precious before God, more useful for the soul and of greater profit to the Church than all other works together, even though it might seem as if the soul did nothing."[3]

If the world thinks that such a person who is no longer interested in its affairs and distractions is necessarily lost, the soul gladly accepts this reproach. It bravely confesses: Yes, I have lost myself. For this being lost is really gain: "The soul wants no gain and no reward but has only the one desire to lose all and even itself so as to belong to God." Spiritually understood this means that in its communion with God the soul has given up all natural ways and means and approaches God only in faith and love. Then it is gained for God, because "it is in truth lost to all that is not God".[4]

But then all is gained for the soul. It is adorned with choice virtues and gifts as with flowers and emeralds. Made into a crown they are a perfect bridal ornament. And all holy souls together in their turn form another crown which the Bride-Church makes for its Bridegroom. All the blossoms with which the soul is adorned are gifts of the Beloved. The hair that binds together the virtues is the will and its love is the bond of perfection (Col. 3. 14). Without this bond the blossoms of the virtues are scattered and destroyed. Love must be strong to hold

[1] Annotation to stanza 28.   [2] Stanza 28. 5–7.   [3] Stanza 29, annotation 2.
[4] Stanza 29. 11.

the crown of virtues together. If it is so and faith is true and simple, God looks upon it graciously and makes himself its prisoner. "Great is the power and vehemence of love since it knows how to take captive and wound God Himself. . . . If a man possesses Him in such unselfish love he will obtain all he desires. But he who does not know this love speaks to Him in vain and has no power over Him, not even if he accomplishes extraordinary works. . . . The soul recognizes this truth and it also understands that He has given it such great graces without its merit."[1] It attributes nothing to itself but all to God. If it is lovable in his eyes, this is due to his loving glance. He has made it so beautiful by his grace that he can now love it deeply. For God cannot love anything outside himself. If he "loves a soul He receives it in a certain sense into Himself and exalts it to equal height with Himself, and so He loves the soul in Himself, with Himself and with the same love with which He loves Himself. Hence, with every work the soul does in God it merits an increase of love. Raised to this grace and dignity, it merits God Himself by every work." To work in God's grace means for the soul to see God. Enlightened by grace, the eyes of its spirit are capable of seeing what was formerly hidden to its blindness: "The glory of the virtues, the ineffable delight, immense love, goodness and mercy of God, innumerable benefits it has received from God." Formerly the soul could neither see nor adore all this. "For great is the dullness and blindness of the soul that is deprived of grace." It does not remember its duty to recognize and adore God's favour, this never enters its mind. "So great is the misery of those that live in sin, or, better, that are dead through sin."[2]

But if God has freed the soul from its "sins and faults He no longer blames it for them nor do they prevent Him from granting it greater graces. But the soul, for its part, should not forget its former trespasses; for thus it will not become arrogant but remain always grateful and its confidence will grow so that it can receive still greater gifts. Indeed, the remembrance of its former ignominious state will even increase its bliss at the side of its heavenly Spouse. If it once was swarthy on account of its sin it is now adorned with beauty by the grace of God and thus has become worthy of new grace, for he gives "grace for grace" (John 1. 16). "If He finds a soul worthy of His benevolence He feels urged to increase its measure of grace, because He has found a pleasant dwelling in it. . . . If He has loved it even before this elevation to

---

[1] Stanza 32, annotation.   [2] Stanza 32. 6ff.

grace for His sake, He now loves it for His sake as well for its own. Delighted by the beauty of the soul . . . the Lord grants it ever new love and graces, and while He honours and glorifies it unceasingly, His love for it becomes ever more intimate and tender. . . . Who can describe the dignity to which God raises a soul that has found favour with Him? This cannot be expressed or imagined; for there God acts in every way as God in order to show what He is." [1]

For the sake of its Beloved the soul has voluntarily sought solitude, that means it has renounced all earthly things. But in this solitude it lived in pain and fear. Now, however, God has led it into a new and perfect solitude where it finds rest and refreshment. "In this solitude, in which the soul, separated from all creatures, lives alone with God, it is He who leads, inspires and raises it to divine things." And "it is only He who works in it without any co-operation. . . . God works in it and communicates Himself to it without any mediation from the heavenly spirits or a natural power. All inner and outer senses, the created things, even the soul itself can contribute practically nothing to the reception of these wholly supernatural graces which God grants in this state . . .; He will not give it any other company and entrusts it to no one but Himself." [2]

From the highest summit of this life the desire of the soul then rises to the eternal vision: to the mountain of the essential knowledge of God in the Eternal Word and to the hill of a "wisdom of lower rank, which reveals itself in the creatures and marvellous works". This divine wisdom is to free it like pure water from all stains of ignorance. The more love grows the greater will be the desire to know the divine truths purely and clearly and to penetrate ever more deeply into the abysses of the inscrutable counsels and secrets of God. "To attain this, it would be a comfort and joy to it to take upon itself all the trials and sufferings of the world and it would agree to all that might aid it to this end, however difficult and painful it might be. . . . The unfathomable depth which the soul . . . desires to penetrate . . . can . . . also be regarded as a symbol . . . of the sufferings and distress which the soul wants to take upon itself. For in suffering it finds its greatest delight and its highest gain, because it is a means to penetrate more deeply into the delights and depths of the wisdom of God. Suffering purifies, and the more . . . purity increases, the deeper and clearer becomes also the knowledge, and the more perfect and sublime is the

[1] Stanza 33.   [2] Stanza 35.

enjoyment which derives from deeper knowledge. For this reason the soul is not content with some kind of ordinary suffering but wants to take upon itself even agonies of death . . . as a means . . . to see God. . . . When will men realize that the depths of the wisdom and the infinite riches of God are inaccessible to the soul unless it takes upon itself the fullness of suffering, unless it longs for this and finds its consolation in it? When will men be convinced that the soul which truly desires divine wisdom must first begin to penetrate into the depths of the sufferings of the Cross? For the Cross is the entrance gate to the riches of the wisdom of God, and this is narrow." [1] It leads into the deep caverns of the rock, that is into "the lofty, deep and inscrutable secrets of the divine wisdom which are hidden in the Person of Christ by virtue of the hypostatic union . . . of the human nature with the Word of God which is the condition of the union of the humanity with God. . . . Each one of the mysteries that are united in Christ . . . is in itself an abyss of wisdom and includes innumerable hidden counsels of the predestination and foreknowledge of the children of men. . . . However many mysteries and marvels have been discovered by the holy doctors, and however deeply souls have penetrated them in this life, in truth they have explained and known scarcely anything. Christ is and remains an unfathomable abyss . . ." filled with "all the treasures of wisdom and knowledge" (Col. 2. 3). The soul can attain to these treasures only "if it has first been purified by the outer and inner fire of suffering according to the plans of divine wisdom. Even a limited knowledge of these secrets can be gained in this life only through many sufferings, through innumerable graces of God both in the spirit and the senses and through the faithful practice of the spiritual life. For all these graces are of an inferior nature compared with the wisdom of the mysteries of Christ, being only preparations for these." [2] The enjoyment of these divine forms of knowledge is the new wine the lovers taste together.

"The greatest desire of the soul is equality with the divine love. It wishes to love God in the same way as it is loved by Him. But it cannot achieve this in this life, not even in the highest stage, since this needs the transformation of glory. There it will love God with the will and power of God Himself, because it is united with the power of divine love, or with the strength of the Holy Spirit into which the soul sees itself transformed in the state of glory. The Holy Spirit is given to the soul so that it should possess the strength of this love, and He supplies all that is lacking to it for the powerful transformation in eternal glory." [1]

Together with the perfection of love the soul awaits the eternal glory, i.e. the vision of the divine Essence for which God has predestined it from all eternity. The soul names this only in the second place, because love has its seat in the will and is the first goal; for it is the property of love to give, not to receive, but of the understanding, which is the seat of glory, to receive rather than to give. "Overwhelmed by love, the soul is not occupied with the essential glory which God is to give it but thinks only how it can give itself to Him by true love, regardless of its own gain." Besides, the first request includes the second: "For it is impossible to attain to the perfect love of God without enjoying the perfect vision of God." This is what God has prepared for it from all eternity. Now this is also what "eye hath not seen nor ear heard: neither hath it entered into the heart of man" (1 Cor. 2. 9; Is. 64. 4). What the soul realizes of it is so overwhelming that it finds no other word for it than "what". It is impossible to give an explanation of this mysterious word. The Lord himself has indicated it through St John in the Apocalypse by seven different terms and comparisons: "To him that overcometh I will give to eat of the tree of life which is in the paradise of my God" (Apoc. 2. 7). "Be thou faithful unto death: and I will give thee the crown of life" (2. 10). "To him that overcometh I will give the hidden manna and will give him a white counter, and in the counter a new name written, which no man knoweth but he that receiveth it" (2. 17). "And he that shall overcome and keep my works unto the end, I will give him power over the nations. And he shall rule them with a rod of iron: and as the vessel of a potter they shall be broken. As I also have received of my Father. And I will give him the morning star" (2. 26–8). "He that shall overcome shall thus be clothed in white garments: and I will not blot out his name out of the book of life. And I will confess his name before my Father" (3. 5). "He that shall overcome, I will make him a pillar in the temple of my God; and he shall go out no more; and I will write upon him the name of my God, and the name of the city of my God, the new Jerusalem, which cometh down out of heaven from my God, and my new name" (3. 12). "To him that shall overcome, I will give to sit with me in my throne: as I also have overcome and am set down with my Father in his throne" (3. 21). "All these are words

[1] Stanza 38. 3.

of the Son of God intended to make us understand that 'what'. Each one of them corresponds to it perfectly, but they do not explain it. For the infinite cannot be expressed in words."[1]

The soul in the state of the mystical marriage is not altogether ignorant of this ineffable immensity of which the transformation in God has given it pledges: the breathing of the air that has been given it by the Holy Spirit, which is an exhalation of this same Spirit, the Spirit of life that Father and Son breathe together. "In this transformation He breathes into the soul in the Father and the Son so as to unite it with Himself. For this transformation of the soul would not be real and perfect if it were not clearly manifested in the soul in the three Persons of the Most Holy Trinity. And this breathing of the Holy Spirit in the soul, whereby God transforms it into Himself, overwhelms it with such a sublime, delicate and profound delight that no human tongue can express it and no human understanding conceive it in any way. . . . If the soul is granted this transformation here on earth this mutual breathing between God and the soul is very frequent . . . giving the soul the greatest delight of love. But this delight never attains the same clear and definite character as in the next life. . . . Such a sublime activity ought not to appear impossible to us. . . . If God grants the soul the grace to unite it with the Most Holy Trinity so that it is deified and becomes God by participation—how should it then be incredible that it should perform its work of understanding, willing and loving in the Most Holy Trinity, united to It and like the Triune God Himself? . . . This is meant by being transformed into the three Persons according to power, wisdom and love, and thus the soul is like God. For He created it in His image and likeness so that it might attain to this sublime way of life."[2]

In the movement of this gentle breeze the soul hears inwardly the sweet voice of the Spouse and unites its own voice with it in jubilant bliss. As in spring the nightingale sings when the cold, rain and uncertainty of winter are over, so the canticle of love sounds in a new spring of the soul. Then, "after all the storms and vicissitudes of life, purged and cleansed from the imperfections, pains and obscurities of senses and spirit, it feels itself in liberty, enlargement and joy of spirit. . . . Refreshed, protected and penetrated by the feeling of joy it . . . begins a new hymn of joy, united with God. . . . He lends the soul His voice that it may unite with Him in the praise of God." For God

[1] Stanza 38. 7f.   [2] Stanza 39. 3f.

longs "to hear the soul's voice express the perfect jubilee of joy". It is part of the perfection of the song of praise that it is grounded in the knowledge of the mysteries of the Incarnation, Now, all the soul does in the state of perfection is perfect. There its jubilant joy is sweet for God and sweet for itself, even though it does not yet attain to the new song in eternal glory.[1]

God will also reveal himself to the soul as the Creator who keeps all creatures in being (like a grove with its multitude of animals and plants) so that it will come to the knowledge of the grace, wisdom and beauty of God in every creature of heaven and earth as well as in their mutual relations and harmonious order. This it now receives in the Dark Night of contemplation, in a mysterious way which the soul cannot explain itself. Later it will take place in the "serene night" of the clear vision of God.[2]

Finally, the flame of divine love will transform the soul into the perfection of love without causing it pain. This is "possible only in the state of eternal beatitude, where the flame is only delightful love. . . . Though the strength of love may vary more or less, the soul feels no pain as it did formerly, when it was not yet capable of perfect love." In this life, however, the transformation is never free from pain, not even at the highest stage of love, and nature is still subject to agitation. "The pain arises from the violent longing for the beatifying transformation. . . . The agitation of nature is caused by the fact that weak, corruptible sense is affected by the strength and greatness of such a sublime love; for all that is sublime depresses weak nature and causes it pain. . . . In that beatifying life, however, the soul will no longer suffer pain and detriment, even though its knowledge will be unfathomable and its love immeasurable; God will then give it the necessary capacity for knowledge and the strength for love. He will perfect its understanding by divine wisdom and its will by divine love."[3]

The soul awaits this beatific perfection in profound peace, certain of being completely prepared for it and having nothing to fear from anywhere. The devil has been put to flight so completely that he does not dare to show himself. No creature suspects anything of what the soul enjoys, hidden in God. It is no longer besieged by passions and desires that threaten its calm. The sensual powers are so purified and spiritualized that they are capable of sharing in the favours God grants

---

[1] Stanza 39. 8f.   [2] Stanza 39. 11–13.   [3] Stanza 39. 14.

to the inmost spirit. It is true, however, that they cannot taste the waters of the spiritual good things but only see them. "For the sensual part . . . has no real capacity to enjoy the essence of the spiritual goods, neither in this life nor in the next. But it receives sensible refreshment and delight from a certain overflowing of the spirit, and through this enjoyment the bodily senses and faculties are drawn into interior recollection, where the soul drinks the water of the spiritual good things. They dismount, like riders from their horses, since they "give up their natural activity . . . and give themselves to spiritual recollection".[1]

The whole way of the soul has been laid open before us in this varied sequence of images. At the same time we were allowed to look into the secret counsels of God in which this way had been traced from the morning of creation. We realize how the hidden way of the soul is intertwined with the mysteries of the faith. From all eternity it has been destined to share the Triune life of the Godhead as the bride of the Son of God. To bring home his bride the Eternal Word puts on a human nature. God and the soul are to be two in one flesh. But the flesh of sinful man rebels against the spirit, therefore all life in the flesh is struggle and suffering: for the Son of Man even more than for any other man, and for the others the more so, the more closely they are united to him. Jesus Christ woos the soul by giving his life for it in his struggle against the enemies of them both. He puts Satan and all bad spirits to flight wherever he meets them in person and frees the souls from their tyranny. He mercilessly castigates human wickedness where it opposes him deceitfully and obstinately. But to those who recognize their sinfulness, confess it with contrition and earnestly long to be delivered he gives his hand, but he demands that they should follow him unconditionally and renounce whatever is opposed to his Spirit. Thus he rouses the fury of hell itself and the hatred of human wickedness and weakness until they break out and prepare for him the death on the Cross. In extreme torment of body and soul, above all in the night of being forsaken by God, he pays the debt of sin to the divine Justice. Thus he opens the gates of the Father's mercy to all who are brave enough to embrace him and his Cross. His divine light and life will then pour into them, but because they inexorably destroy all that bars his way, this light and life are first experienced as night and death. This is the Dark Night of con-

[1] Stanza 40. 6.

templation, the crucifixion of the old man. The more powerfully God woos the soul and the more completely it surrenders to him, the darker will be the night and the more painful the death. As nature is progressively crushed the supernatural light and the divine life are given more space. These seize the natural powers which they deify and spiritualize. Thus Christ becomes once more incarnate in the Christian, which means another resurrection from death on the Cross. The new man bears the marks of Christ's wounds in his body: the remembrance of the misery of sin from which he has been raised to a life of bliss and of the price he had to pay for it. There remains in him the pain of longing for the fullness of life until he is allowed to enter the shadeless light by the gate of the real death of the body.

Thus the bridal union of the soul with God is the end for which the soul was created, bought by the Cross, accomplished on the Cross, and sealed with the Cross for all eternity.

III. THE IMITATION OF THE CROSS
(FRAGMENT)

ST JOHN's doctrine of the Cross could not be called a science of the Cross in our sense if it rested on a merely intellectual understanding. But it bears the genuine stamp of the Cross; it is the splendid top of a tree whose roots are in the depths of his soul, nourished by his heart's blood, and whose fruits are evident in his life.

His love of the image of the Cross shows how deeply he loved Christ Crucified, whose picture gave his small house at Duruelo its characteristic atmosphere. The impression it made on St Teresa is well known: "When I entered the chapel I was surprised by the spirit which the Lord caused to breathe there. Not only I had this impression, but also two merchants who were friends of mine and had accompanied me from Medina to Duruelo could do nothing but weep. There were so many Crosses and skulls there. I have never forgotten a small wooden Cross that hung over the holy water stoup, on which was stuck an image of Christ. This seemed to inspire more devotion than the most beautiful work of art."[1] It may be assumed that the first Discalced Carmelite who had once been an apprentice of image carvers and painters had himself made these Crosses to adorn his tiny monastery. They were quite in keeping with what he later wrote about the veneration of images: that precious materials and clever execution can be a danger, because they easily distract from the essentials, the spirit of prayer and the way to union with God.[2] But he wanted to lead himself and others to union by the image of the Cross as well as by all other means; therefore he liked also in later life to carve and give away Crosses. For the friendly warden of his prison, Father John of St Mary, he could find no better gift than a Cross to express his gratitude for having secretly relieved his sufferings. This gift must also have been humanly dear both to the giver and the recipient, for John had received it at Duruelo from St Teresa. For him this was probably another reason for parting with it.

This love for the image of the Cross and the zeal with which John

---

[1] Teresa of Jesus, *Foundations*, 14.   [2] Cf. *Ascent*, 3. 37.

promoted its veneration must have been very pleasing to the Lord, as is proved by the visions of the Cross mentioned before.[1] They must certainly have contributed to impress the sacred sign ever more deeply on his heart. During the last night of his life he held his Cross in his hands. Shortly before midnight, when death was approaching as he had foretold, he gave it to one of those present to hold, so as to have both hands free to arrange the position of his body. But then he took back the "holy Christ", spoke tenderly to him and kissed him for the last time before expiring almost imperceptibly.[2]

It is good to venerate the image of Christ Crucified and to make pictures to induce devotion to him. But living images are even better than those of wood or stone. It was the great, life-long task of the reformer of the Carmelite Order and the director of souls to form human beings after the image of Christ and to implant the Cross in their hearts. All his writings served this end, which is expressed in even more personal form in his letters and the declarations of witnesses.

In the Carmel of Granada he gave his spiritual daughter Maria Machuca the habit and the name of Mary of the Cross. When she was afterwards taken to the parlour someone suggested that she would probably be particularly dear to him because she was called "of the Cross". He replied: Certainly, she would be dear to him if she loved the Cross.[3] He used to impress on those with whom he came into contact that they "should have a great love for suffering solely for the love of Christ, without asking for earthly consolation; he would frequently say . . .: 'My daughter, ask for nothing save the Cross and this without consolation; for this is perfect.'"[4]

To his penitent Juana de Pedraza at Granada he wrote in answer to complaints about her sufferings: "All these terrors and blows . . . increase love and have the effect that one prays more eagerly and raises one's spirit to God. . . . O Lord, You great God of love, what riches do You not give to him who loves nothing and finds satisfaction in nothing save only in You! You give Yourself to him and unite Yourself with him in love. And thus You let the soul taste in love what it most ardently desires in You and what is most profitable to itself. For this reason we ourselves may no more be without the Cross than our Beloved, even to the death of love. He gives us sufferings according to the measure of our love so that we may give Him greater sacrifices and gather more merit. But all this does not continue long,

---

[1] Cf. I, 4.   [2] Cf. Bruno, *Vie d'Amour*, p. 264.   [3] Bruno, *Saint Jean*, p. 307.
[4] *Other Maxims of the Spiritual Life*, 10, *Ed. Crit.*, III, 70 (not in Allison Peers).

since it only lasts till the knife is raised; then Isaac remains alive and receives the promise of his merits." [1]

St John was especially friendly with the Carmelite nuns at Beas. As superior at Calvario (soon after his escape from prison) and as rector of the College at Baëza he lived in their neighbourhood and met them personally, instructing them by sermons, spiritual conversations and exhortations in the confessional. Later, too, he was sometimes their guest. Letters supplemented the oral teaching; in one dated 18 November 1586 he writes: "He who . . . seeks pleasure in anything is not an empty vessel which God can fill with His ineffable bliss. In this way one turns away from God instead of meeting Him, and your hands cannot receive what God wants to give. . . . Serve God, my beloved daughters in Christ, follow in His footsteps by denying yourselves in all patience, in silence and true love of suffering; attack mercilessly all self-satisfaction, mortify all that must die in you and that hinders the inner resurrection of the spirit." [2] To Mother Eleonora Baptista, Prioress at Beas, he writes on 8 February 1588: "When I consider that God has called you to an apostolic life, i.e. to a life of contempt and leads you in this way this is a consolation to me. For it is God's will that the mind of true religious should be that they have finished with everything and that everything has lost its importance for them. God alone wants to be their wealth, their comfort and their blissful glory. God has granted Your Reverence a great favour that now, forgotten by all, you can find your joy only in Him. Be quite undisturbed if now is done to you whatever men will do to you for the love of God. You no longer belong to yourself but to God." [3]

He gives this advice to a postulant: "As regards the Passion of our Lord: treat your body with wise severity, through hatred of yourself and prudent self-denial, and seek never to follow your own will and taste. For this self-will was the cause of His suffering and death." [4]

To the Prioress of the newly founded convent at Cordova he writes: "That you should have had to go into such poor houses in scorching heat has been ordained by God. You are to set a good example and show that you confess the poverty of Christ by your profession. Those who apply for acceptance will see from this what spirit ought to move them when they enter. . . . Preserve most carefully the spirit of poverty and of contempt of all earthly things and be occupied with God alone; else, as you know, a thousand spiritual

[1] Letter 10 of 28 January 1589.   [2] Letter 5.   [3] Letter 7.   [4] Letter 11.

and temporal needs will arise in you, whereas you ought to have and
feel only those needs that you want to arise in your heart. For he who
is poor in spirit is more content and happy in want, because he has
made complete nothingness his all, and thus preserves freedom of heart
in all things. Blessed is the nothingness and the solitude of heart that
have such strength that they subject all things, while being themselves
subject to nothing, ridding themselves of all cares so as to burn more
ardently in love." The sisters should "profit by the first-fruits of the
spirit that God gives in such new foundations, so that they may enter
the way of perfection with completely renewed spirit in all humility
and detachment, both inwardly and outwardly, not with a childish
mind but with a strong will. They are to practise mortification and
penance, desiring Christ to cost them something, and not to be like
those that seek their own convenience and comfort, whether in God
or apart from Him, but suffering for God, in God and apart from God,
in silence and hope and loving remembrance." [1]

The darkest is also the surest way. This doctrine of the Dark Night
is also emphasized in the direction of souls: "Because your soul is
in this darkness and emptiness of spiritual poverty you believe that
all is lacking to you and that all men have abandoned you. This is not
surprising, since you even think that God has abandoned you; yet
nothing is lacking. . . . If a man seeks nothing but God he does not
walk in darkness, however much darkness and poverty he may see in
himself. He who does not walk in presumption nor follow his own
taste whether with regard to God or to creatures, and who does not
insist on his own will whether inwardly or outwardly will not stumble.
. . . You have never been in a better state than now, for you have
never been so humble and submissive and have never thought so
little of yourself and of everything in the world. You have never
known yourself to be so evil and God so good, you have never served
God so purely and unselfishly as now. . . . What more do you want?
. . . What do you think—is the service of God anything else but
fleeing evil, observing His commandments and going about our
business as well as we can? If you do this, what need is there of other
apprehensions, illuminations and enjoyments, since the soul normally
only meets deceptions and dangers in them? . . . Therefore it is a
great grace when God leads the soul in darkness and detachment, so
that it can no longer be deceived by its faculties. . . . Let us live here

[1] Letter 15.

on earth as pilgrims and poor men, as exiles and orphans, in dryness, without a road or anything else, but hoping all things." [1]

The saint writes to his spiritual daughters very lovingly; but it is a love that seeks only their eternal salvation. "As long as God does not give us this in heaven, persevere in . . . self-denial and patience, with the desire by your suffering to become in some way like this great God in His humility and love of the Cross. Unless our life consists in the imitation (of Christ crucified) it is worthless." [2]

St John of the Cross, therefore, could not believe that alleged great graces of prayer were genuine if the person who received them was lacking in humility. When Nicholas Doria, the Vicar General of the Discalced Carmelites, asked him to examine the spirit of a nun who was supposed to have received great graces he expressed his conviction in the following opinion: "The main fault . . . consists in this that her behaviour does not seem to express humility; for these favours of which she speaks, if they are such at all, are generally given to the soul only when it has first completely stripped and as it were annihilated itself in perfect interior humility." Even though the effects of humility "are not perceived in such a high degree in all divine apprehensions, yet those favours which are granted in the state of union—and of these she speaks—produce a humble mind. . . . She should be tested in the practice of virtues that give no satisfaction, especially in self-contempt, humility and obedience. In her reactions to this blow the purity of the soul that is supposed to have received such sublime favours will be revealed. But these tests must be searching, for there is no devil that would not suffer something for his honour." [3]

The counsels to religious written by the saint on various occasions breathe the same spirit. Among those probably written for the Carmelite nuns at Beas are the following three against the flesh:

"1. In the first place, you should consider that you have entered the convent only in order that all may fashion and train you. To be free from all imperfections and disturbances that might come to you from the character and behaviour of the religious, and to derive profit from all that happens, you should think that they are all instruments (as they really are) which are in the convent to fashion you. One has to fashion you by words, the others by works, the third by thoughts

[1] Letter 18, to Juana de Pedraza.
[2] Letter 21, to Anne of Jesus, of 6 July 1591.
[3] Allison Peers, Sundry Documents 1, vol. III, p. 299f.

that are directed against you; be subject to them all like an image that is being carved by one, painted by another and gilded by the third. If you do not practise this you will neither be able to conquer your sensuality and feelings nor be on good terms with the religious in the convent, nor will you enjoy holy peace and keep free from many failings.

2. . . . Never leave a work undone because you do not like it and find no taste in it, if it concerns the service of God; nor do anything solely because it affords you enjoyment and satisfaction . . . but rather as if it were distasteful to you; else you will never attain to constancy and overcome your weakness.

3. . . . A spiritual soul should never in its exercises be absorbed by what is pleasant in them and perform them only for this reason; even less must it revolt against them because they seem disagreeable to it, but it should rather prefer what is hard. . . . Thus one bridles one's sensuality. You will not rid yourself of self-love and attain to the love of God in any other way." [1]

God calls souls to the cloister "to test and purify them like gold by fire and hammer; therefore they must also be tested and tempted by men and evil spirits and by the fire of anxiety and desolation. . . . The religious must seek to bear these things in patience and conformity with the will of God and not in such a way that God would be compelled to reject him because he refused to bear the Cross of Christ with patience." [2] "Do not seek to choose the Cross that seems lighter to you, for . . . the heavier the burden the lighter it is if it be borne for the love of God." [3] "If you are heavy-laden, you live in union with God who is your strength; for God sustains the afflicted. If you are rid of the burden, you find support only in yourself who is weakness itself. For the strength and vigour of the soul grows and is established if trials are patiently borne." [4] "God esteems more highly in you an inclination for aridity and suffering for love of Him than all consolations and spiritual visions and all meditations you may make." [5] "Perfection cannot be attained if a man does not succeed in being satisfied with nothing, so that his natural and spiritual concupiscence are content in emptiness; for this is necessary to reach the highest tranquillity and peace of spirit; and in this way the love of God is constantly active in the pure and simple soul." [6]

---

[1] *Cautions*, 15–17, *ibid.*, p. 225f.   [2] *Counsels to a Religious*, 3, *ibid.*, p. 229.
[3] *Ibid.*, 6, p. 230.   [4] *Maxims and Sentences from the MS of Andujar*, 4, *ibid.*, p. 241.
[5] *Ibid.*, n. 14, p. 242.   [6] *Ibid.*, n. 51, p. 246f.

A whole group of maxims is directly concerned with the imitation of Christ: "Progress in the spiritual life is impossible unless one follows Christ. He is the way, the truth and the life and the door by which one must enter to be saved."[1] Let your first care be to acquire an ardent longing . . . to imitate Christ in all your works; strive to perform each one of them in such a way as the Lord Himself would do it."[2] "If your senses are offered an enjoyment that does not serve solely the honour and glory of God you should renounce it and keep yourself free from it for love of Jesus Christ, who sought no other enjoyment in this life . . . than to do the will of His Father: this He called His food and meat."[3] "Let yourself be inwardly and outwardly crucified with Christ and you will live in this life in the calm and peace of His soul and preserve yourself in His patience."[4] "Let Christ crucified be sufficient for you. Suffer and rest with Him, without Him neither suffer nor rest; but free yourself from all external things and interior idiosyncracies."[5] "If you desire to possess Christ never seek Him without the Cross."[6] "He who seeks not the Cross of Christ seeks not the glory of Christ either."[7] "What does he know who does not know how to suffer for the sake of Christ? The greater and heavier the burdens, the better the lot of him who bears them."[8] "Always rejoice in your God, your salvation, and consider how sweet it is to suffer in every way for Him who is truly good."[9] "If you would be perfect, sell your will, give it to the poor in spirit, come to Christ in meekness and humility and follow Him to Calvary and to the tomb."[10]

"The trials and sufferings that are borne for the love of God are like precious pearls; the larger they are the more valuable are they, calling forth in him who receives them a greater love for their Giver. So also are the sufferings caused by a creature if they be accepted for God; they are the more precious the greater they are, and they will induce a greater love of God. And as a reward for having endured for the love of God sufferings on earth that last but a moment, His Majesty will give infinite and eternal things in heaven, namely Himself, His beauty and glory. . . ."[11]

One day a Sister made a derogatory remark about a layman hostile to the convent. The saint, who was present, admonished her: "Then

---

[1] *Other Counsels and Maxims*, n. 76, cited from *Ed. Crit.*, Toledo 1914, III, 24f. (These are not included in Allison Peers' edition.—Translator.)
[2] *Ibid.*, 77, p. 25.   [3] *Ibid.*, 78.   [4] *Ibid.*, 80.   [5] *Ibid.*, 81.   [6] *Ibid.*, 83.
[7] *Ibid.*, 84.   [8] *Ibid.*, 87.   [9] *Ibid.*, 293, p. 49.
[10] *Other Counsels*, n. 7, *Ed. crit.*, III, 58 (not in Allison Peers).
[11] *Other Maxims of the Spiritual Life*, n. 1, *Ed. Crit.*, III, 67 (not in Allison Peers).

you and the other Sisters ought to treat him all the more kindly; thus you would be disciples of Christ. And he added: it is much easier to bear the small bitterness of such a circumstance than the double bitterness of indulging our will with such feelings for our neighbour."[1]

In a conversation with a religious he said emphatically: "If ever a person, and be he your superior, should want to persuade you to follow a teaching that counsels mitigation do not believe him nor accept it even if he should confirm it by miracles, but embrace penance and detachment from all things and do not seek Christ without the Cross; we Discalced Carmelites of the Blessed Virgin are called to follow Him and His Cross by renouncing all things, even ourselves, not by indulging our comfort and softness. See to it that you do not forget to preach this as often as there is an opportunity, for it is of such great importance for us."[2]

This exhortation truly shows his love of Christ that urges the disciple of the Cross to lead others in the way he has found himself. "Did you not know that I must be about my father's business?" (Luke 2. 49)—this first word of our Saviour that has come down to us was applied by John to the great life work of the Lord and his followers: "That which is the business of the Eternal Father can be understood only of the redemption of the world, above all of the salvation of souls for which Christ our Lord used the means that had been fore-ordained by the eternal Father. St Dionysius the Areopagite has confirmed this truth by the wonderful saying: 'The divinest of all divine works is to co-operate with God in the salvation of souls.'[3] This means: the highest perfection of every being in its rank and state is to rise and grow into the image of God according to its capacity and power; but the most marvellous and divine thing is to co-operate in the conversion and home-bringing of souls, for this reflects God's own work, and to imitate Him is the greatest glory. Therefore Christ our Lord called it the work of His Father and the concern of His Father. It is also an obvious truth that sympathy with one's neighbour grows in the measure that the soul is united to God by love. For the more it loves God, the more it desires that He should be loved and worshipped by all. And the more it desires this, the more will it work for it by prayer as well as by other practices necessary and profitable

---

[1] *Ibid.*, n. 2, p. 68.
[2] *Ibid.*, 5, p. 69. Almost literally identical with the fragmentary Letter 23 (Allison Peers, II, p. 297).
[3] *Heavenly Hierarchies*, 3. 3, Migne, *PG*, 3. 165. The citation is not quite literal.
9+s.c.

for this. And so great is the fire and strength of their love that those who possess God are not satisfied and content with their own gain; it seems too little to them to enter heaven alone, they strive with great longing and heavenly desires and extraordinary care to take many to heaven with them. This comes from their great love of God; it is the fruit and the inclination that spring from perfect prayer and contemplation." [1]

Here the zeal for souls is taken to be a fruit of union; on the other hand, love for our neighbour is an important means to this union: "Two things . . . serve the soul as wings to rise to union with God: sincere compassion with the death of Jesus and with its neighbour. And if the soul is seized by pity for the suffering and Cross of our Lord, it will also realize that He took all this upon Himself for our redemption." [2] This means, if a man in the state of loving recollection enters into the mind of our Lord on the Cross, i.e. into a love even to the utter surrender of oneself, he will by this very fact be united with the divine will; for the saving will of the Father is accomplished in the redeeming love and surrender of Jesus. Thus a man becomes one with the divine Being which is self-giving love: in the mutual surrender of the divine Persons in the inter-trinitarian life as well as in outward action. Thus the perfection of one's own being, union with God and work for the union of others with God and the perfection of their being are all inseparably united. The Cross gives access to all this, but the preaching of the Cross would be vain if it were not the expression of a life of union with Christ crucified.

"My Beloved, all for You and nothing for myself; nothing for You and all for myself. All that is hard and difficult I demand for myself and nothing for You.

"O how sweet to me is Your Presence, You who are the highest good. I will come to You in silence and seek to discover Your footsteps so that it may please You to unite me to Yourself in the union of marriage; and I shall not find rest until I am happy in Your arms; and now I beg You, Lord, let me never take myself back but give my whole soul to You." [3]

The whole life of St John of the Cross is reflected in this effusion of a loving heart. He has followed in the footsteps of his beloved Master who chose the Way of the Cross. For this reason he preferred a hard bed even as a child; for this reason he served the sick with

---

[1] *Maxims on the Spiritual Life*, 10, *Ed. Crit.*, III, 63f. (not in Allison Peers).
[2] *Ibid.*, 11.   [3] *Ed. Crit.*, III, 57.

unflagging devotion when he was a boy, a living image of the Saviour who allowed himself no respite when men crowded round him to seek his help in their sufferings. John retained this love of the sick, the suffering members of Jesus Christ, throughout his life. When he later came into a monastery as a superior and Visitor his first attention was given to the sick: he would prepare their food with his own hands, empty their slops, and did not allow them to be taken to hospital to save money; he also severely reproved any negligence.[1]

In the monastery of St Anne at Medina del Campo and at the College of St Andrew at Salamanca the young religious had shown his love of the Cross by such an austere life that, at the beginning of the reform, St Teresa said of him (in contrast to his much older companion Anthony of Heredia) that he "had no need to be tried; for though he had been living among the Calced, he had always led a life of high perfection and strict religious discipline".[2] At Salamanca he had scourged himself to blood every evening and spent a great part of the night in prayer; during his short period of rest he used a kind of trough for his bed. When St Teresa inspected the poverty-stricken house at Duruelo her companion said: "No one, however spiritual, could endure it here, were he ever so pious."[3] But for those two Fathers it was a paradise. We have already mentioned that it was adorned with crosses and skulls. "The choir was in the loft, the centre of which was a little higher so that they could say the Hours, but one had to stoop very low to enter to hear Mass. They had turned the two corners next to the chapel into two hermits' cells in which they could only sit or lie; they were filled with hay, as the place is very cold. The roof nearly touched their heads, two little windows overlooked the altar, two stones served as pillows." After Matins at midnight they remained in choir till Prime "so absorbed in prayer that sometimes, when they were about to say Prime, their habits would be covered with snow without their having noticed it".[4] To instruct the poor ignorant people of the neighbourhood "they went out to preach barefoot, despite the snow and the intense cold . . .; after they had preached and heard confessions they returned to their monastery very late, filled with an interior joy that made everything easy for them".[5] While John had his mother and brother with him at Duruelo the latter sometimes accompanied him on his pastoral expeditions. After the sermons they would quickly retire and refused invitations to dine in

[1] Bruno, *Vie d'Amour*, p. 218.   [2] *Foundations*, ch. 13.
[3] *Ibid.*   [4] *Ibid.*, 14.   [5] *Ibid.*

the presbyteries, but had bread and cheese, provided by Mother
Catalina somewhere by the roadside.[1] Thus the saint lived according
to the maxims he later wrote down for others: "Seek solely for the
love of Christ to attain to detachment, renunciation and poverty in
all things for this world",[2] and "the man poor in spirit is quite content
and happy in need; he who has set his heart on nothing will find all
peace."[3]

The austerity of the first two Discalced Carmelites was so great
that St Teresa asked them to moderate it a little. It had cost her "so
many tears and prayers" to find suitable religious for beginning the
reform, and now she feared the devil incited them to exaggerated zeal
in order to exhaust them before their time and thus to destroy the work
at the start. But the Fathers did not heed her words and continued
their austerities.

Some time later, when the two had already collected a small religious
family, Father John one day was feeling so weak and sick that he asked
his Prior, Father Anthony, for permission to have his collation a little
before the appointed time. But no sooner had he taken this small
refreshment than he was seized by bitter repentance. He hurried to
Father Anthony and asked to be allowed to accuse himself before the
Community. Then he heaped up stones and broken earthenware in
the refectory and knelt on them during the evening meal, scourging
his bared shoulders till blood began to flow and only interrupted the
severe discipline to accuse himself in a loud voice and touching words.
Then he continued to scourge himself cruelly until he broke down. The
horrified brethren looked at the spectacle with admiration. Eventually
Father Anthony told the innocent penitent to retire and pray that God
might pardon them all their miserable weakness.[4]

Even in later life John never spared himself. When he was superior
his cell was always the poorest in the house. In the summer of 1586,
sick and weak, he traversed Spain, covering four hundred miles in
the scorching heat, clothed in his heavy habit and woollen tunic which
he wore summer and winter. As Prior of Segovia he began the building
of a new monastery. He not only supervised the work but helped with
his own hands, fetching stones from the rocks all the year round, his
bare feet shod only with alpargatas.[5]

[1] Bruno, *Vie d'Amour*, p. 45.
[2] *Other Counsels and Maxims*, n. 355, *Ed. Crit.*, III, 56 (not in Allison Peers).
[3] *Ibid.*, 356.
[4] Bruno, *Saint Jean*, p. 92.
[5] Hemp sandals, part of the habit of Discalced Carmelites.

In the great conflict within the Order he took up an intermediate position between Nicholas Doria and Jerome Gratian. He saw the good as well as the mistakes on both sides and sought to mediate, but his words made no impression. Then he again took the discipline. Brother Martin, his travelling companion, could no longer listen to the cruel blows and came in with a burning candle. The saint told him he was old enough to look after himself. The same Brother Martin, while nursing him during a grave illness, took away the chain John had worn for seven years and which had grown into the flesh so that it could not be removed without drawing blood. He never gave it back. Father John the Evangelist, however, who travelled with him, tried in vain to make him take off another instrument of penance, a knotted garment which John wore on his legs under his habit. The Father told the saint that this was cruel, since he was so ill. "Be quiet, son," was the reply, "it is enough relief to ride. We must not be completely at peace."[1]

During St John's last illness Brother Peter of St Joseph had the idea to distract him a little from his atrocious pains and ordered the three best musicians of Ubeda to play to him. His biographer Jerome of St Joseph writes that John wanted to dismiss them after a few moments, since it was not fitting to mix earthly with heavenly enjoyment. But as he would not give pain to his brethren he let the artists continue. When asked how he had liked it he had to confess: "I did not hear the music; another one, a thousand times more beautiful, delighted me all the time."[2] We can well understand that Baruzi prefers the account of another witness, according to which the saint said to his nurse: "My son, give them a refreshment and thank them for the service they have done me and let them go. It is not reasonable for me to while away with music the time of pain that God has given me."[3] This is quite in the spirit of St John, to want to bear his Cross to the end without accepting relief. On the other hand, the second part of the first account has also points in its favour: the consideration for his brethren is quite in line with the delicate tact of the saint; nor need the heavenly music be rejected, since the great lover of the Cross had evidently been overwhelmed with all kinds of divine consolations

[1] Bruno, *Saint Jean*, pp. 312ff, statement of Father John the Evangelist, Obras, IV, 392.
[2] Jerome of St Joseph, *Life and Works of St. John of the Cross*, French ed. of the Carmelite nuns of Paris, p. 252.
[3] Baruzi, *Saint Jean*, p. 221. Many accounts of witnesses have been preserved of this incident. On that of Brother Peter cf. Bruno, *Saint Jean*, p. 358f: "If God has sent me these great pains . . . why should I want to assuage and weaken them by music? . . . I will suffer the beneficial gifts of God without any relief."

throughout his life. He was probably given so much sweetness precisely because he had sought nothing but bitterness.

However much John practised physical austerities, he never regarded them as an end; though they were an indispensable means for him. On the one hand they served to subject body and sensuality completely so that these would not hinder the much more important interior mortification; on the other hand the suffering of bodily pains united him to the suffering Saviour. But he attached far greater importance to interior mortification. This can be seen from the much greater place the latter is accorded in his writings, for generally there is a striking disregard of physical concerns as compared with those of the soul. It is true, he sometimes mentions reciprocal influences, especially of the body's share in the life of grace and glory, but to him man is above all a soul. In fact, he hardly ever speaks of men, sometimes of persons, but mostly of souls. He has himself stated quite clearly his view about the relation between external and interior mortification: "Subjection and obedience are a penance of the understanding and the judgement, therefore they are a more agreeable and pleasing sacrifice before God than all other, physical, works of penance."[1] Physical penance without obedience is very imperfect, because beginners are drawn to it only by their own desire and the pleasure they take in it: "And as they act only according to their own will, they will increase in faults rather than in virtues."[2] He disapproved even more of superiors who inflicted excessive austerities on their subjects; he himself always practised wise moderation in these matters and frequently corrected what others had spoilt by their excessive zeal. At the request of St Teresa he was sent to the novitiate at Pastrana in 1572, to put a stop to the exaggerations of the novice master Father Angelus. In the autumn of 1578, a few months after his escape from prison, he was sent as prior to the hermitage of Calvario; there, too, he found an unreasonably exaggerated asceticism and saw to it that it was mitigated. He recognized with great psychological insight that such violence was due to interior uncertainty. He predicted that Peter of the Angels, who could never have enough austerities, would go to Rome a Discalced and return a Calced Carmelite. In fact, the over-zealous ascetic succumbed to the soft Neapolitan court, whereas John never wavered.

In the relation between external and interior mortification, too, the

---

[1] *Other Maxims*, n. 286, *Ed. Crit.*, III, 48 (not in Allison Peers).
[2] *Ibid.*, n. 287.

decisive factor is not the doctrine but the life. From the lifelong austerities of the saint it might seem as if they could hardly be surpassed by the purely spiritual Cross. Indeed, in such a case it is impossible to make exact comparisons. There is no numerically definable standard for interior mortification since this is purely spiritual, even less can it be compared with external works. None the less, if we think of the maxims set out in the *Ascent*:[1] to enjoy nothing, to know nothing, to possess nothing, we may well say that this is the *non plus ultra* of detachment which can never be reached even by the maximum of external works. For these alone would rather increase one's self-esteem and certainly not lead to the "nought", the death of self.

But how can it be proved that John actually achieved himself the perfect spiritual detachment he demanded of others? For the inner life of this silent saint seems closed to us. Now it is true that we cannot read in it as we can read in the heart of St Teresa and of so many others who had to write down the history of their soul. Yet his heart betrays itself involuntarily in his writings, especially in his poems. There is also a large number of contemporary witnesses whose statements give a strong, consistent picture of his personality. Some of these are based on confidential communications of St John himself; for there were some people who were so closely united to him in God that he showed them something of the secrets of his heart, especially his brother Francis and some Carmelite nuns.[2]

The purest impression of his personality is probably to be gained from his poems. Here he speaks from his heart, and in some of them with unearthly purity. But only in some, not in all of them. The *Song of the Dark Night* breathes profound peace; in the blessed stillness of this night the noise and bustles of the day are completely hushed. In the *Living Flame of Love* the heart burns with the purest heavenly fire; the world has disappeared, the soul embraces God alone with all its powers. Only the wound still bears witness to the rift between heaven and earth.

The complete appeasement of the soul from which these canticles proceed shows itself not only in their content but also in their poetic form. Their stillness and simplicity are the natural expression of a heart that opens itself in these pure sounds quite unconstrained and

---

[1] *V. supra*, II, §1. 3b and 2. 1.

[2] P. Bruno and Baruzi have used these sources, Bruno especially the Roman acts of the process, Baruzi MS 12738 and others in the National Library of Madrid. Silverio has also included part of these depositions in his edition, vol. IV, appendix, pp. 354ff.

without conscious effort, as the nightingale sings or a flower opens. They are perfect works of art, because no art can be discerned in them.[1]

The same is probably true also of the *Shepherd's Song* (*Pastorcico*) and the *Song of the Triune Fountain*,[2] though they differ in form and content from the other two canticles as well as from each other. The *Shepherd's Song* does not directly express the movement of the soul. The poet has seen an image and given it an artistic form. He sees Christ crucified, he hears his lament for the souls that "proudly avoid His love". He fashions it into a pastoral song according to the taste of his time, as he had done in the grand manner in his *Canticle*. If this had been suggested by the Biblical book, the *Pastorcico* may surely have been inspired by the parable of the Good Shepherd who lays down his life for his sheep (John 10), and the shepherd's grief at the coldness of his shepherdess would echo the sorrowful words of the Saviour when he wept over Jerusalem (Mt. 23. 37). The fundamental mood is reflected in the refrain *El pecho del amor muy lastimado* (his breast burdened with the pain of love). It comes from a heart that has forgotten itself and entered into the heart of the Saviour. These verses express the pure suffering of a soul freed from itself and united with the crucified Lord. (Cf. the account according to which St John was unable to leave the house at Segovia in Holy Week because he was living so deeply in the Passion.)[3]

In the *Song of the Fountain* he again sings of something that moves him very deeply, as in the *Dark Night* and the *Living Flame*. But this is not, as in the other poems, the destiny of his own soul, but the inner life of the Godhead as it is revealed by faith: the ever flowing fountain from which all beings come and which gives them light and life; which of itself brings forth a river like unto itself and together with the second yet a third of equal abundance. The song that praises these truths is by no means didactic. It is really pure music. In it the doctrines of the faith have become stirring life: the silent waves of the eternal sea sing their Canticle in the soul, and whenever they touch the shore there is a dull echo: *Aunque es de noche* (Though it be night). The soul is finite, it cannot contain the infinite sea. Its spiritual eye is not adapted to the heavenly light which appears dark to it. And thus even when it is united to the Triune God and feeding on the Bread of Life

---

[1] This is not inconsistent with the fact that John was influenced in his forms by the poets of his time and even sometimes has verbal similarities. On the literary appreciation of the poems cf. Silverio's Introduction in vol. IV of the Works, LXXIX ff. and Baruzi, 10ff.

[2] Nos. 7 and 8 in Allison Peers, II, p. 453f.   [3] Bruno, *Saint Jean*, p. 239.

in which he communicates himself, it still lives a life of desire: *Porque es de noche* (because it is night). The essence of dark contemplation is expressed in these verses.

The poem *Vivo sin vivir en mí*[1] (I live without living in myself) expresses almost the same thought in its leitmotif: *Que muero porque no muero* (I die because I do not die). But here the leitmotif is not a melody, as in the *Fountain* and the *Shepherd* spontaneously ascending time and again from the depth of the heart. It is rather a theme deliberately treated in variations. The poet who constructs these elaborate verses is conscious of his own art. He plays with his subject: the agony of this life which is not the true life is not the living pain expressed in song, it is its reflexion in retrospect, reproduced by the author. His own faculties are still active. And because his soul is not yet united to God in utter surrender it still fears to lose God, mourning its sins which it feels to be strong fetters tying it to this life.

It is similar in the case of several other poems that have a leitmotif repeated as a refrain. It is impossible to discuss them all. But in this context we must once more return to the *Spiritual Canticle*. Father Silverio[2] calls it the first and also the most beautiful of his poems, and it is true that it contains verses of incomparable charm. We have also found that the wealth of images is held together by the unity of the dominating symbol of the bride and her Spouse.[3] But it cannot be asserted that all this image language arises from the depth of the soul without arbitrary creative action. Much is the work of the intellect and rather artificial, many comparisons are far-fetched. And this variety of images and ideas corresponds to the contents: they reflect the unrest of an agitated inner development. If we compare this song, both in content and form, with the four that have already been discussed, these five together answer the question in what way the saint may have practised interior mortification. His soul had, indeed, attained to perfect detachment, to simplicity and silence in union with God. But this was the fruit of an interior purification in which a richly gifted nature burdened itself with the Cross and surrendered itself to God to be crucified, a most powerful and lively spirit made himself a prisoner, an impassioned fiery heart found peace in radical resignation. The accounts of the witnesses confirm this result.

John did all things "with admirable calm and dignity", writes Father Elisaeus of the Martyrs.[4] "In his manner and conversation he

---

[1] N. 5 in Allison Peers.   [2] Obras, IV, LXXIX.   [3] *V. supra*, II, §3, 2 (c) and (d).
[4] Allison Peers, p. 308.

9*

was kind, very spiritual and of great profit for those who heard him and had to do with him. In this respect he was so unique and had such an influence that those who knew him left him spiritually enriched, full of devotion and enthusiasm for virtue. He had an intense grasp of prayer and communion with God and answered all questions that were put to him on these matters with such profound wisdom that all who asked his advice left him most satisfied and with great profit. He was fond of recollection and spoke little; he laughed rarely and with great moderation." "He persevered in prayer and in the presence of God, raising his mind to God and using ejaculatory prayers."[1] He never raised his voice nor made rude or silly remarks or gave nicknames to people. He treated all men with equal reverence; in his presence no one was allowed to speak about others except to praise them. Even at recreation he only spoke of spiritual things, and as long as he was speaking, no one else thought of saying anything. At the end of a meal, too, he would begin a spiritual conversation which held the attention of all to such an extent that they remained quite still without shifting their posture. In fact, his influence on others was remarkable. Even among the Calced Fathers his appearance would command silence. With one short sentence he could assuage fears and temptations for ever.[2] He was an expert in the discernment of spirits: he sometimes sent away postulants who asked to be received into the Order though they seemed very suitable to others, or received them when others had misgivings, because he saw clearly what was hidden from ordinary human judgement.[3] In confession he once reminded a Carmelite nun of a grave fault committed a long time ago, which she had never noticed and hence had not confessed.[4] In this context we would also mention the well-known story of St Teresa, whom he gave only half a Host when she made her Holy Communion in the Convent of the Incarnation, evidently to mortify her, because he knew her preference for large Hosts.[5] He was even more severe to Mother Catherine of St Albert at Beas. She had said she was sure to communicate on a certain day. When this day came, John passed her over; he did the same even when she returned a second and a third time. When he was asked the reason he replied: "The Sister thought this was certain; and I acted in this way to make her understand that what we imagine is by

---

[1] *Ibid.*, saying n. 3, p. 309.
[2] Cf. Baruzi, *loc. cit.*, p. 290ff, the evidence of Martin of St Joseph, Obras, IV, 377.
[3] Cf. the same witness.   [4] Baruzi, *loc. cit.*, p. 292.
[5] St Teresa, Spiritual Relations, 35, *ibid.*, p. 293.

no means certain."[1] In both cases the saint evidently knew what was necessary for souls to rid themselves of imperfections. This supernaturally enlightened insight was accompanied by an inflexible determination that cannot be considered a merely natural quality either. We know with what reverent love he regarded St Teresa—surely the humble young friar would not have dared thus to treat the aged Foundress unless the Holy Spirit had given him the fortitude to do so, nor would this kind and gentle saint have corrected someone in such humiliating manner as the nun at Beas. But his kindness and gentleness were no merely natural gifts either; we know from his sharp words about inexperienced and dictatorial spiritual directors in the *Living Flame of Love* and elsewhere that by nature John was by no means a gall-less dove. His descriptions of certain types of piety in the last chapters of the *Ascent* are of a sarcasm that might have been very offensive in personal intercourse. If he never gave way to it either as a superior in his relations with his subjects or at recreation this shows that he had completely mastered his nature. He faithfully practised what he taught. If we compare his sayings on virtues and gifts with the evidence of his own behaviour we find the most perfect agreement between the two.

He demanded a faith that kept solely to the doctrine of Christ and his Church without seeking support from extraordinary revelations. During a Chapter at Lisbon many Fathers, and very serious ones among them, went to visit a nun whose stigmata had caused great excitement. They preserved small pieces of linen with blood from her wounds as if they were relics. John cared nothing for these things and did not visit her. Later, at a recreation at Granada, he was asked if he had seen this nun. He answered: "I have not seen her and did not want to see her, for I should be very sorry if my faith would be increased even ever so little by seeing such things."[2] His faith gained "more from the wounds of Jesus Christ than from any created things" and needed no other stigmata.[3]

John wanted a hope that "is constantly directed towards God without turning to any other thing" and was convinced that such a soul "gains as much as it hopes".[4] Father John the Evangelist testifies that in the eight or nine years he lived with the saint he had always seen that he lived and was sustained entirely by hope. He could convince

---

[1] Baruzi, *loc. cit.*, p. 293.   [2] Cf. Martin of St Joseph, *Obras*, IV, 377f.
[3] Deposition of Father John the Evangelist, Allison Peers, III, p. 366f.
[4] Saying 110, *Ed. Crit.*, III, p. 29.

himself of this especially when he was procurator of the monastery of Granada while John was Prior. One day there was great need in the convent and he asked permission to go out to obtain what was wanting. He was told to trust in God, they would lack nothing. After some time he returned, maintaining that it was already late and he had sick persons to provide for. The saint sent him back to his cell to ask God for what he needed. He obeyed, but after a time he went once more to the Prior and told him: "Father, this would be tempting God. Give me leave to go . . . it is already very late." This time he received permission, but with these words: "Go, and you will see how God will put your lack of faith and hope to shame." In fact the necessary things were brought to the house just as he was on the point of going out. On other occasions he had had similar experiences.[1]

It is hardly necessary to speak of St John's charity: for his doctrine is full of it, instructing the soul how to be transformed into God who is love. All depends on love, for at the end of our life we shall be judged by it. The saint's whole life was a life of love: the most intimate relationship with his nearest and dearest in the love of God; self-sacrificing care for the sick, fatherly goodness towards his subjects, endless patience with penitents of all kinds, reverence for souls and a burning desire to detach them from all things and bring them to God. He was acutely aware of the different ways in which God leads souls, hence he could adapt himself perfectly to the most varied needs: he went with his novices into the country to let each choose a solitary place where he could weep, sing or pray as the Spirit led him.[2] Nor had he sharp words for his enemies, regarding all they did to him as the work of God. We shall return to this later. All these various forms of neighbourly love were rooted in his love of God and Christ crucified. For we have seen time and again that to him love is essentially "the practice of perfect detachment and suffering for the Beloved";[3] it will become even clearer in what follows how far he practised this in his own life.

We should show this agreement between doctrine and life only in one other, very important point. John has constantly stressed in his writings that souls must renounce not only natural knowledge and enjoyment, but also all supernatural favours such as visions, revelations and consolations to meet the incomprehensible God in dark faith alone,

---

[1] Deposition of Father John the Evangelist, Allison Peers, III, p. 367.
[2] Bruno, *Vie d'Amour*, pp. 218ff.
[3] Saying 123, *Ed. Crit.*, III, p. 30.

beyond all apprehensions. The depositions of witnesses referring to various periods of his life indicate that the saint had been overwhelmed with extraordinary graces; but they also show that he tried to resist them with all his strength. Often when going through the house at Segovia he would secretly bang his fist against the wall to guard against ecstasy even while talking to someone, so as not to lose the thread of the conversation.[1]

He confided to Mother Anne of St Albert: "My daughter, I always keep my soul in the interior of the Most Holy Trinity; my Lord Jesus Christ wants me to keep it there." Frequently he received such overwhelming graces that he thought his weak nature would succumb, and he did not dare to give himself up to complete recollection. It has been mentioned before that he would refrain from saying Mass for days, for fear that something extraordinary might happen.[2] He repeatedly complained of this "weak nature", which was too weak to bear the superabundance of grace, but strong enough to seek and desire the Cross in every form. The Lord did not fail him in that either.

The Cross laid upon a man by God, whether it be external or interior, is more effective than mortification practised from one's own choice. Like the way of the Saviour, that of his faithful servant was a way of the Cross from beginning to end: great want and poverty in his childhood, unsuccessful attempts to assist his mother in her hard struggle for existence, then work demanding great physical and spiritual effort as well as constant self-conquest: these were the beginnings of the school of the Cross. They were followed by disappointments caused by the spirit of the Order to which God had called him, certainly doubts and interior struggles when faced with the question whether to become a Carthusian, and after the happy beginnings of the Reform at Duruelo a series of heavy trials and sufferings in the struggle for his ideal.

In our Lord's life the happiest hours were surely those spent in solitary converse with the Father in the silence of the night. But they were only breathing spaces after an activity in the midst of the crowds that offered him daily and hourly the mixture of human weakness, meanness and wickedness, like a drink of vinegar and gall. John, too, knew the bliss of the quiet hours of the night, the dialogue with God in nature. While he was rector of the College of Baëza he acquired a piece of land near the river, where he spent days together with John

[1] Bruno, Vie d'Amour, p. 327.
[2] Ibid., p. 225, and deposition of Anne of St Albert, Allison Peers, III, p. 371ff.

of St Anne. There he would stay alone at night, absorbed in prayer, or sometimes fetch his companion to walk with him along the river and speak of the beauty of the sky, the moon and the stars.[1] While he was Prior at Segovia, too, he had such an oasis, a hermitage high up on a hill that afforded a fine view. There he retired as often as affairs would allow.[2] To live in silent, solitary prayer had been his desire from his youth to the end of his life. But he, too, was burdened for the greater part of his time with the duties of office. And as he had followed the Saviour in his loving care of the sick (he also had the gift of healing), so he imitated him in his self-sacrificing pastoral work for souls. While he was rector of Baëza confessions were heard there from morning to night. He was at everyone's disposal. Once the porter, Brother Martin, asked him for a "peaceable confessor" for a relative of his, a reckless colonel. John went himself and converted this man of the world so thoroughly that he now went to the monastery "day and night" to take part in the spiritual exercises.[3] He had an inexhaustible patience with scrupulous persons whose confessions no one else was prepared to hear. It was the greatest grief to his loving heart to see souls tyrannized and led astray by ignorant or brutal directors. For these the otherwise so gentle and kind saint had as hard words as our Lord for the Pharisees. In the *Living Flame of Love* he interrupts his description of the unctions of the Spirit given as a proximate preparation for union with God by a long discussion of spiritual directors. "So great is the pity and sorrow of my heart when I see so many souls sinking back again from their height that I cannot find rest." The spiritual guide "must be wise and prudent as well as experienced . . . ; if he is lacking experience in purely spiritual things he will not be able to cope with the direction of a soul that is thus gifted by God. . . . In this way many spiritual guides do many souls great harm. . . . Since their knowledge does not go beyond the elements—and would to God they knew *them* properly—they will not permit a soul whom God wants to raise to higher things to relinquish the meditations of beginners."[4] "If a coarse and inexperienced hand daubed bad and unsuitable colours on an extremely beautiful painting this would be a greater and more important damage than if many other, mediocre pictures were spoilt. Now the Holy Spirit, too, has painted with a delicate hand, and His work has been spoilt by a crude hand. Who shall be able to undo this damage? . . . How often does not God

---

[1] Obras, I, 105.   [2] Bruno, *loc. cit.*, p. 325f.
[3] *Ibid.*, p. 228.   [4] *Living Flame of Love*, 3. 31.

anoint the contemplative soul with a most delicate unction, a loving, quiet, peaceful, quite unique knowledge transcending all thought and consideration . . . : and then there comes a spiritual director who, like a blacksmith, can do nothing but hammer and pound with the faculties of the soul . . . and at once commands the soul: Away with all these things, they are only sloth and loss of time." [1] If these directors lack the necessary knowledge "they ought not to dare put their coarse hands to a work they do not understand, but to leave it to another who has the necessary knowledge. For it is no small responsibility and no slight wrong to be guilty of a soul losing inestimable blessings and even sometimes missing its goal altogether because of rash counsels. If a director therefore errs by his presumption . . . he will be punished according to the harm he has done. For the affairs of God must be treated with great care and circumspection, especially those that concern so important matters and such an exalted office as the direction of souls, where the right treatment may bring infinite gain, but mistakes may result in immense loss." [2] There is no excuse whatever if a director "never allows a soul to go out of his jurisdiction . . . for vain considerations and intentions", though it needs a more advanced direction than his. "Not everyone capable of hewing a block of wood is able to carve an image; nor is everyone who can carve it able to perfect and polish it. Nor is everyone that can polish it able to paint it, nor can he that is able to paint it give it the final touches. . . . If you are no more than a crude workman who can lead a soul only to the contempt of the world, the mortification of its passions and affections, or if you were a good carver of images who could instruct it in holy meditations, and if you did not understand more—how could you give the soul its last perfection . . . which . . . consists in the work of God? . . . God leads souls in different ways. . . . Where can be found the man who, like St Paul, makes himself all things for all men so as to gain all? (1 Cor. 9. 22). In this way you tyrannize souls and deprive them of their liberty." [3] Thus when John himself was superior, gaining all hearts by his self-sacrificing goodness and reproaching his subjects only with fatherly gentleness and love, he definitely rejected brutal government: "If . . . in an Order Christian and monastic courtesy . . . has vanished and if, instead, the superiors behave savagely and brutally . . . the Order should be mourned as lost." [4]

Such words were inspired by the saint's anxious care for souls.

[1] *Ibid.*, 3. 42f.   [2] *Ibid.*, 3. 56.   [3] *Ibid.*, 3. 57–59.
[4] *Spiritual Sayings*, 11 (Allison Peers, III, p. 314).

Christ had bought them with his Passion and death, each one of them was infinitely dear to him and to his faithful disciple. It was the aim of his reform to provide conditions in which chosen souls could quietly be fashioned by the hand of God without any disturbance. We know what sufferings John joyfully endured when this work of God was threatened by external enemies. Perhaps his soul suffered even more when a spirit that threatened God's work in souls gained the upper hand within the reformed Order itself. The danger came from opposite directions, represented by Father Jerome Gratian and Nicholas Doria. The former urged external missionary activity. Now John was certainly not without interest in the apostolate in pagan countries. It had made him very sad that "our true God and Lord" should still be unknown in almost all parts of the world and known only in such a small section of it.[1] But he did not want an external activity that would harm recollection. Nicholas Doria represented the other extreme: he wanted solitude and austerity, but he intended to cast this ideal in a hard and fast form, and this was quite contrary to the spirit of St Teresa and her first companion, indeed, it is opposed to the Spirit of God himself that blows where it lists. Teresa herself had suffered much from inexperienced confessors lacking understanding, in her Constitutions she therefore ensured freedom for her daughters to consult the spiritual directors they trusted. Nicholas Doria wanted to take this freedom away from them. In 1585 he had become Provincial with far-reaching powers accorded by Rome. As such he introduced a centralized government under a General Council that had to nominate priors, preachers and confessors. Together with St Teresa's great daughters, Anne of Jesus and Mary of St Joseph, and with the old friends of the Reform, Luis de Leon and Dominic Bañez, John fought for the heritage of the holy foundress. For these were also his own daughters whose interior life was at stake. Under the loving care of his firm but gentle guidance many souls had blossomed forth in a splendour such as he had described in his *Spiritual Canticle*. Must he not have felt as if his life's work had been spoilt when the hailstorm of persecution now broke upon these spiritual gardens?

At the Chapter at Madrid he opposed the Provincial with great determination, according to his own principle: "If no one dares to warn the superior nor to oppose them when they go astray . . . if those who have influence and are obliged to it by the law of charity

---

[1] Bruno, *loc. cit.*, p. 300.

and justice do not dare to . . . raise objections . . . the Order should
be accounted as lost." For this reason he was deprived of all offices
and thus of any power to give external help. His enemies attempted to
cast aspersions on his personal honour so as to have a pretext for expel-
ling him from the Order. He preserved perfect peace of mind. Now
he proved that he meant his words when he asked to be allowed to
suffer and be accounted for nothing for the sake of the Lord, and when
he wrote that Christ had done the greatest work when he was hanging
on the Cross.[1] Father Elisaeus of the Martyrs writes that St John,
when commenting on St Paul's saying "The signs of my apostleship
have been wrought on you, in all patience, in signs and wonders and
mighty deeds" (2 Cor. 12. 12), had once remarked that the apostle
mentioned patience before miracles. "By this he meant to say that
patience is a much surer sign of the apostolic man than the raising of
the dead to life. And I can testify that, as regards this virtue, John of
the Cross was indeed an apostolic man; for he bore the trials that came
to him with incomparable patience and resignation, though they were
so severe that they could have brought down the cedars of Lebanon."[2]

His letters from the Chapter of Madrid give a clear insight into the
saint's state of mind after he had been passed over in all elections.
On 6 July 1591, he wrote to Anne of Jesus:[3] "Even though matters
have not turned out as you desired you must yet be comforted and
thank God with all your heart. For His Majesty has so arranged it, and
therefore it is what is best for all of us. We must only submit our will
to Him, then it will appear to us as it really is: the unpleasant things
seem bad and obnoxious to us, even though they may actually be good
and advantageous; and this thing is evidently not bad, neither for me
nor for anyone else. For as regards myself it is very profitable: freed
from the care of souls I can, if I so wish, by the grace of God enjoy
peace, solitude, and the precious fruit of forgetting myself and all
things. It is good also for others . . . for thus they will remain free
from faults which they would have committed because of my
unworthiness."[4]

At the same time he made this request to Mary of the Incarnation,
the daughter of Mother Anne, who was then Prioress at Segovia:
"For my sake, my daughter, you ought not to be sorry, for I, too, am

---

[1] *Ascent*, 2. 7. 11.   [2] *Spiritual Sayings*, 9, Allison Peers, III, p. 313.
[3] This is not the famous collaborator of St Teresa, but the foundress of the Carmel
of Segovia.
[4] Letter 21.

not sorry. What pains me much is that one should attribute blame to someone who has none. For these things come not from men but from God, who knows what is good for us and ordains them for our good. Think only that God has ordained it all. Where there is no love, put love and you will find love." [1]

He who could speak thus had inwardly become like Christ crucified. It was time that he should also become so outwardly and be allowed to suffer love's death on the Cross. Now his last wishes were to be fulfilled:

"I desire only that death should find me in a distant place, far from all converse with men, without friars I would have to direct, without joy to comfort me, visited by all pains and sufferings. I would that God should test me as His servant after He has so often tested my perseverance in my work. I would that He should visit me in sickness as He has tempted me by health and strength; I would that He should lead me into temptation through shame, as He has exposed me to it by the good name I had even with my enemies. Lord, deign to place the crown of martyrdom on the head of Your unworthy servant." [2]

At the Chapter of Madrid the hermitage of La Peñuela was assigned to him as his residence. This was no punishment for him; for there he hoped to find the solitude he desired. Nevertheless, we ought not to imagine that the discussions and decisions of Madrid had not moved and hurt him in his inmost being. On his way from Madrid to La Peñuela he arrived one morning at four o'clock with Father Elias of St Martin at Toledo. Both said Mass and then locked themselves in together. Without eating anything they remained thus till late at night. Then John declared before all that he departed much consoled and prepared to bear any suffering God might send him by virtue of the grace he had given him that day. [3] Was this not a night of Gethsemani, when the Lord sent him an angel to comfort him? All the severe penances of his life, all the persecutions, even the imprisonment at Toledo and the hostile treatment by the Prior of Ubeda, all this, thinks Father Silverio, [4] are scarcely more than shadows of afflictions compared with the sufferings caused him by the institution of the famous *consulta*. Seen from the human point of view, his life work lay in ruins when he made his way to La Peñuela, as in the case of the Saviour, when he let himself be bound and be led from the Mount of Olives to Jerusalem.

[1] Letter 22.
[2] J. Brouwer, *De Achtergrond der Spaansche Mystiek*, Zutphen 1935, p. 217.
[3] Bruno, *Vie d'Amour*, p. 243f.   [4] Obras, I, 113 (Preliminares).

The mountain solitude of La Peñuela was still a breathing-space of silent prayer before the ascent of Cavalry.[1] It is true, he was not entirely left to himself even there. The friars were happy to have the Father of the Reform among them. The Prior asked him to become the spiritual director of them all, and he was with them at recreation. But they realized that till the hour of recreation he had been in constant prayer. Before daybreak he would go into the garden, kneel among the willows by the brook and remain in prayer till the warm sunshine reminded him that it was time for Mass. After he had celebrated he retired to his cell and there devoted himself completely to prayer unless community duties interrupted him. Sometimes he also went to a hermitage and there remained utterly absorbed in God. The same witness mentions that he sometimes also occupied himself with writing spiritual books. (We do not know what this refers to. The extant great treatises had been written before this time.) The rocks were his favourite companions. "Be not surprised if I like their company" he would say, "I have then less to confess than when I converse with men."[2] The news that came to him from the world outside was well suited to disturb his recollection and peace of mind. Father John the Evangelist wrote to him how Father Diego Evangelista interfered with the Carmelite convents of Andalusia to extract from the sisters incriminating evidence against the saint. "At that time Sister Augustine of St Joseph at Granada had to burn a large collection of his letters which the Sisters valued as highly as the Epistles of St Paul and notes of his spiritual conferences and conversations, so that they should not fall into Diego's hands." In answer to the complaints made to him Nicholas Doria declared that the Visitor had had no authority to do these things, but he did not punish him; Diego was and remained Doria's close friend. John had once sharply reprimanded this Diego because he had remained outside his monastery for months in order to preach. Now he wanted to profit from his opportunity to take revenge. Several months later, after the death of the saint, he declared: "If he had not died his habit would have been taken away from him and he would have been expelled from the Order." Some faithful sons of the Father of the Reform had feared this, and John of St Anne had written to him about it. He received this reply: "My Son, be not troubled about this; the habit can be taken away only if a person refuses

---

[1] Cf. Bruno, *Saint Jean*, p. 343ff and *Obras*, V, 112ff (deposition of Father Francis of St Hilarion).
[2] Bruno, *loc. cit.*, p. 344.

to be corrected or to obey; I for my part am perfectly prepared to correct all my faults and to obey whatever penance they may impose on me." And he wrote to Father John the Evangelist: "My soul is far from suffering because of all this; on the contrary, it takes it as an instruction in the love of God and one's neighbour."[1]

Thus he preserved the peace of his heart undisturbed "in this holy solitude"; and when the fever forced him to leave it he did so "with the intention of shortly returning here".[2] As before his removal to La Peñuela he had not chosen where he would stay but went where obedience bade him go, so now again he let others decide the place where to seek a cure. He was given the choice between Baëza and Ubeda. Baëza was the college he had founded, whose first rector he had been. The Prior Angelus of the Presentation was one of his faithful sons ready to receive him lovingly. Ubeda, on the other hand, was a new foundation governed by Father Francis Chrysostom who had become his enemy for the same reason as Father Diego Evangelista. Thus John had no hesitation; he chose Ubeda because the house had not been established for long and was poor, and because he was unknown in that town, so he hoped "there to endure the pains of sickness with great profit and merit".[3] Thus, on 22 September 1591, he mounted the small mule placed at his disposal by a friend to begin the last journey of his life. It was a veritable way of the Cross. For several days he had been unable to eat anything and could hardly keep himself in the saddle for weakness, while his sick leg was aching as if it were being cut off. For there was the seat of the disease: it had first swollen up, then five festering wounds had appeared one after the other. They caused the saint to pray: "I greatly thank You, my Lord Jesus Christ, that Your Majesty was pleased to give me in this foot alone the five wounds that Your Majesty had in Your feet, hands and side: How have I deserved so great a grace?"[4] In this state he now had to ride seven miles on mountainous paths. It was a very slow journey. When they had covered three miles his companion suggested a rest by the banks of the Guadalimar: "In the shade of this bridge Your Reverence could rest a little; the joy of seeing the water might give you an appetite for some food." "I will gladly rest a little; but I cannot eat, for of all that God has created I would only like asparagus, and

---

[1] Bruno, *loc. cit.*, p. 347f.
[2] Letter 25, to Doña Ana de Peñalosa of 21 September 1591.
[3] Deposition of Father Peter of St Joseph, Obras, V, 99.
[4] Deposition of Diego of the Conception, Allison Peers, III, p. 335.

they are not in season." The brother helped him to dismount and sit down. Then they noticed on a stone a bundle of asparagus bound as for the market with willow bark. The Brother believed this to be a miracle. But John would not hear of it, and told him to look for the owner. When no one was to be discovered he had to place a *cuarto* on the stone by way of payment.[1]

After another few hours they reached their destination. The Prior received the mortally sick man and gave him the poorest and smallest cell. The doctor, Ambrose de Villareal, examined his wounds. He diagnosed erysipelas and discovered much pus that necessitated a very painful operation. Wanting to find the origin of the disease, the surgeon laid bare bone and nerves from the heel to the middle of the calf. Feeling an intense pain the saint asked: "What have you done, sir?" Then, looking at the wound he exclaimed: "Jesus, that's what you have done!" Later the surgeon said to Father John the Evangelist: "He bore the most incredible pains with incomparable patience." To others, too, he expressed his astonishment that his patient suffered with such tranquillity and serenity; he declared John of the Cross must be a great saint, for it seemed impossible to him to suffer so great and constant pains without complaint unless one were very holy, had a great love of God and were supported by heaven.[2] This was also the impression he made on his entourage. The religious considered it a grace to have such an example in their midst. Only the Prior remained a long time bitterly resentful. Whenever he visited the sick man he would remind him that he, John, had reproved him when he had been Vicar Provincial of Andalusia. He could not endure that friars and people from outside should vie with each other to relieve the saint's torments. (In this respect John's precaution of choosing an unknown place had been in vain: sanctity remains nowhere so hidden as not to find some admirers.) Once, at the foundation of La Mancha, Don Fernando Diaz of Ubeda had heard John sing the Gospel; this had sufficed to inspire his confidence. As soon as he heard of the arrival of the patient he visited him and since then came every day, sometimes even three or four times, to look after him. Once he met the Prior, when he was just taking away linen and bandages to be washed. Some pious women considered themselves happy to be allowed to do John this service; they were rewarded by marvellous perfume that emanated

[1] Cf. Bruno, *loc. cit.*, p. 352, deposition by Bartholomew of St Basil, Allison Peers, III, p. 369, and Francis of St Hilarion, Obras, V, 114.
[2] Deposition of Father Ferdinand of the Mother of God, Obras, V, 331.

from this linen saturated with pus. Now the Prior forbade Don Fernando to do this, saying he would take care of it himself. He was often heard to complain about the money spent on the food for the patient. Thereupon Diego of the Conception, the Prior of La Peñuela, sent six bushels of wheat for the community and six chickens for the saint. Father Bernard of the Virgin, who nursed him, had daily evidence of the Prior's ill-feeling. He gave orders that no one was to visit the patient without his special permission and finally even forbade Father Bernard to assist him because he thought he was doing too much. The infirmarian at once informed the Provincial of Andalusia, the aged Anthony of Jesus, John's old companion at Duruelo.[1] He hurried to Ubeda to put matters right and stayed four or six days. He sharply reprimanded the Prior and ordered all the others to visit and assist the patient as much as they possibly could. Father Bernard was given back his office with the order to perform it with the greatest possible charity; if the Prior should refuse him anything necessary he should at once address himself to the Provincial and borrow money in the meantime. During all these events no word of complaint against the hostile Prior came from John's lips, he bore it all "with the patience of a saint".[2]

Father Anthony was present at the first operation. When he wanted to encourage him John apologized for being unable to answer, he was consumed with pain. However, the physical pains were not yet at their worst. New abscesses formed on the loins and shoulders. Before a second operation the doctor apologized. "This does not matter, if it has to be done" said this new Job. He urged the physician to begin at once. All pains and sufferings were to him "beneficent thoughts of God". The letters he wrote from his sickbed have not been preserved; we only know from the accounts of witnesses that they spoke of the joy to be allowed to suffer for our Lord. The physical torments did not prevent him from being absorbed in prayer. He sometimes asked his young nurse, Luke of the Holy Spirit, to leave him alone—"not", adds the witness, "because he wanted to sleep, but in order to devote himself the more fervently to the contemplation of heavenly things". After the infirmarian had realized this he did not only become himself more discreet but sometimes also sent the visitors away. Even the

---

[1] Father Anthony, who had once so generously placed himself at the disposal of the Reformers, received the great grace to assist at the deathbeds of both St Teresa and St John.

[2] Bruno, *loc. cit.*, p. 353ff.

doctor understood this. "We will let the saint pray" he would say. "When he . . . regains consciousness we will nurse him."

This doctor had "become a different person" at the bed of his patient. The saint gave him a copy of the *Living Flame of Love* which he had written himself,[1] in which he later often read for his consolation. The veil that separated John's soul from the glory of heaven became ever more transparent. When the doctor told the patient of his approaching death he was full of joy: "*Laetatus sum in his quae dicta sunt mihi: in domum Domini ibimus*" (Ps. 121. 1). His brethren offered John the viaticum, but he told them he would inform them when it was time. Since the Vigil of the Immaculate Conception he had known the day and hour of his death. He betrayed it with the words: "Praised be the Lady who wants that I should depart from this life this Saturday." Then follows the exact announcement: "I know that God our Lord will grant me the mercy and grace to enter heaven to say Matins."

Two days before his death he burned all his letters (a great number) in the flame of a candle, because "it was a sin to be his friend". In the evening of this Thursday he asked for and received the Last Sacraments. All those who asked him for a souvenir he referred to his superior: he himself was poor and owned nothing. He also called for the Prior, Francis Chrysostom, asked his pardon for all faults and added the request: "My Father, the Habit of the Holy Virgin that I have worn and used—I am a poor beggar and have nothing to be buried in—I beg Your Reverence for the love of God to give it me for charity's sake." The Prior blessed him and left the cell. It seems that even at this moment his inner resistance had not yet been broken. But finally, a contrite sinner, he knelt weeping at the feet of the dying saint and asked his pardon because "the poor monastery" could not offer him more to relieve his illness. John replied: "Father Prior, I am very content; I have more than I deserve. Trust in our Lord; the time will come when this house will have all it needs."

In the morning of 13 December he asked what day it was, and on being told Friday, he asked several times what hour; for he was waiting to say Matins in heaven. On this last day of his life he was even more silent and recollected than before. His eyes were mostly closed. When he opened them, he would look lovingly at a copper Cross.

Towards three o'clock he asked that before his death Father

---

[1] Bruno, *ibid.*, p. 359.

Sebastian of St Hilary should once more be taken to him. This was a young Father to whom he had given the habit at Baëza. Now he was lying sick with fever a few cells away from the saint. He was fetched and remained for about half an hour. John had to tell him something important. "Father Sebastian, you will be made Prior Provincial of the Order. Listen attentively to what I have to tell you and try to communicate it to the superiors; tell them that I told you these things immediately before my death." It concerned something of importance for the development of the Province. At five o'clock the saint uttered a cry of joy: "I am happy, for tonight I shall be in heaven without having deserved it." Shortly afterwards he addressed the Prior and Fernando Diaz: "Father, please let Your Paternity send a message to the house of Señor Fernando they should not wait for him, he must stay here tonight." Then he asked for Extreme Unction which he received with great devotion, answering the prayers of the priest. At his urgent request the Blessed Sacrament was once more taken to him for his adoration. He spoke tenderly to the hidden God, saying in the end: "Lord, now I shall no more see you with the eyes of the flesh."

Anthony of Jesus and several other older Fathers wanted to watch by his bed, but he did not allow it. He would send for them when it was time.

When it struck nine he said longingly: "I still have three hours' time; *incolatus meus prolongatus est*" (Ps. 119. 5). Father Sebastian also heard him say that for his consolation God had granted him three requests: to die not as a superior, in a place where he was unknown, and after much suffering. Then he lay so still, peacefully absorbed in prayer, that he was already thought to be dead. But he awoke again and kissed the feet of his Christ. At ten o'clock a bell was heard to ring. He asked why that was. He was told it was the religious going to Matins. "And I" he replied, "shall by the mercy of God say it in heaven together with the Blessed Virgin, Our Lady." At about half past eleven he had the Fathers called. About fourteen or fifteen friars came in, they were just going to say Matins. They hung up their lamps on the wall and asked the saint how he was. He seized the rope that hung from the ceiling and sat up. "Fathers, shall we not say the *De profundis?* I am very well." Saying this he looked "very quiet, beautiful and happy" said the Superior, Ferdinand of the Mother of God. He himself intoned the Psalm, the others responded. According to Francis Garcia they said "I don't know how many psalms" in this way. These were the penitential Psalms preceding the *recommendatio animae*. There are different accounts as to whether this immediately followed the Psalms and when John interrupted the prayers. For he had grown tired and had to lie back. He had one more wish, that somebody might read to him from the Canticle. The Prior did that. "What precious stones" exclaimed the dying man.[1] For it was the canticle of love that had accompanied him all his life.

He again asked what time it was. It had not yet struck midnight. "At that hour I shall stand before God to recite Matins." Father Anthony reminded him of what he had done for the Reform both in its beginnings and later as Superior. The saint replied: "God knows what has been done." But he would not trust in this. "Pater Noster,[2] this is not the right moment for that. I hope to be saved through the merits of the Blood of our Lord Jesus Christ." His brethren asked for his blessing, which he gave at the order of the Provincial. He exhorted them to be truly obedient and perfect religious.

Shortly before midnight he passed his "Holy Christ" to one of those around him, probably Francis Diaz. He wanted to have both his hands free to arrange his body for the final departure. But he soon took the image back and took leave of the Crucifix as he had done before from the Eucharistic Saviour.

Then it struck twelve from the belfry. The dying man said: "Brother Diego, give the sign to ring for Matins, for it is time." Francis Garcia, the bell ringer of the week, went out. John heard the sound of the bell and said, the Cross in his hands: "*In manus tuas, Domine, commendo spiritum meum.*" A farewell glance at those present, a last kiss for the Crucifix, then he was before the throne of God to sing Matins with the heavenly choirs.

Is there not in this dying something of the divine freedom with which Jesus Christ bowed his Head on the Cross? And as on that first Good Friday signs and wonders proclaimed that he who had died on the Cross was truly the Son of God, so now, too, heaven testified that a good and faithful servant had entered into the joy of his Lord.

Between nine and ten o'clock at night, when most of the religious had obeyed the saint's wish and retired to bed, Brother Francis Garcia had gone to the head of the bed and settled down between the bed and the wall to say his rosary. Then the idea came to him that he might

---

[1] Bruno, *Vie d'Amour*, p. 364.   [2] Form of address for the Carmelite Provincial.

perhaps have the joy to see something of what the saint saw. During the psalmody of the Fathers he suddenly saw a ball of light shining between the ceiling of the cell and the foot of the bed. It shone so brightly that it darkened the fourteen or fifteen lamps of the friars and the five candles on the altar. When the saint passed away without anyone noticing it, Brother Diego held him in his arms. Suddenly he saw a bright light round the bed. "It shone like the sun and the moon, the lights of the altar and the two candles that were in the cell seemed as if surrounded by a cloud, without giving any more light." Only then did Diego realize that the saint in his arms was without life. "Our Father has gone to heaven in this light" he said to those present. Later, when he laid out the sacred remains with Father Francis and Brother Matthew, a sweet scent went out from them.[1]

[1] The whole account of the death of the saint has been given according to Bruno, *Saint Jean*, pp. 361ff. The annotations contain partly verbatim accounts of the depositions of witnesses.

INDEX

Alcala, Carmelite College at, 15
Ambrose Marianus, Father, 16
Andalusia, Carmelites in, 17, 233, 235, 236
Angelus, Father, 220
Angelus of the Presentation, Prior, 234
Anne of Jesus, Prioress of Segovia, 231–232
Anne of Jesus, Ven., 131n., 176n., 212n., 230, 231n.
Anne of St Albert, Ven., 17n., 227n.
Anne Mary of Jesus, Sister, 13
Anthony of Heredia, Father, 217–218
Anthony of Jesus, Father Provincial, 236, 238–239
Ascent of Mount Carmel, 19–20, 22–24, 30, 31n., 33n., 39–81, 86, 88, 89, 114, 116, 125n., 127, 130, 131, 165, 176, 178, 221, 235
Augustine of St Joseph, Sister, 233
Augustine, St, 83–84, 133
Avila, Carmelite Convent at, 13, 15, 18, 131

Baëza, Carmelite College at, 12, 17n., 210, 227–228, 234, 238
Bañez, Dominic, 230
Bartholomew of St Basil, Father, 235n.
Baruzi, J., 5n., 130n., 219, 221n., 222n., 224n., 225n.
Beas, Carmelite Convent at, 210, 212, 224–225
Bernard, St, 106
Bernard of the Virgin, Father, 236
Bridget, St, 3
Brouwer, J., 176n., 232n.
Bruno de Jesu Maria, Father, cited in footnotes on pp. 5, 6, 12, 13, 15, 16, 17, 19, 209, 217, 218, 219, 221, 222, 226, 227, 228, 230, 232, 233, 234, 235, 236, 237, 239, 240

Calvario, Carmelite house at, 210, 220
Campbell, Roy, cited in footnotes on pp. 8, 18, 26, 28
Caravaca, 12
Carmelites of the Mitigated Observance (Calced), 6, 8, 13, 16, 217, 220, 224
Carmelites of the Teresian Reform (Discalced), *passim*
Castile, St John's affection for, 17
Catherine of Jesus, Sister, 17n.
Catherine of St Albert, Sister, 224–225

Contemplation, St John's teaching on:
  Dark Night of the Soul: night of the senses, 30–48, 58, 83, 89–90, 92; night of the spirit, 36–48, 58–90, 91, 92–114; (detachment and mortification, 31–34, 41–48, 52–58, 64–81, 90–91, 96, 99–102, 127–128; memory, stripping of, 42, 45, 48, 58–64, 90–91; understanding, natural and supernatural, powers of, 42, 44–45, 48, 50, 52–57, 87–88, 90–91, 96, 99–102, 127–128; will, purification of, 41–45, 48, 58, 64–80, 90, 96, 99–102)
  Dark Night of the Soul, Canticle of, *see below*
  faith and union with God, 39–57, 60–61, 66, 82, 86–91, 99–100
  indwelling of God by grace, 125–136, 176
  joy, 31–34, 65–81 (*see also* Dark Night of the Soul, detachment and mortification)
  knowledge, supernatural, dangers of, 61–62
  meditation and contemplation, 47, 48, 85, 87, 228–229
  soul, structure of, 115–121
  spirit, natural activity of, 82–84
  sufferings, 31–38, 92–103, 105–106, 195, 201
  union with God, through faith, 39–57, 60–61, 66, 82, 86–91, 99–100; through love, 97–108, 113–114, 122, 125–127, 129–207; through mystical marriage, 113–114, 122, 125, 130–136, 144–145, 157, 177, 180–183, 185–207
  visions and spiritual communications, 12, 22, 46, 49–57, 60–61, 88, 90, 110
  way of the Cross, 1, 6, 9–21, 24–44, 57, 194–207
Cordova, Carmelite Convent at, 210

Dali, Salvador, "Christ of St John of the Cross", 13n.
Dark Night of the Soul, Canticle of, 18–24, 28–30, 39, 80, 90, 98, 105, 114, 131, 165, 175, 176, 221, 222; St John's teaching on, *see under* Contemplation
De Trinitate, 83
Diaz, Don Fernando, 235–236, 238–239
Diego, Brother, 239–240
Diego Evangelista, Father, 233–234
Diego of the Conception, Prior, 234, 236